UNStudio

UN Studio

Design models
Architecture
Urbanism
Infrastructure
Ben van Berkel
Caroline Bos

RIZZOLI
NEW YORK

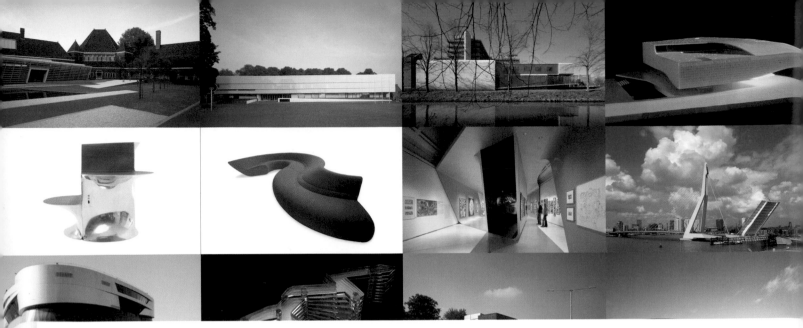

Contents

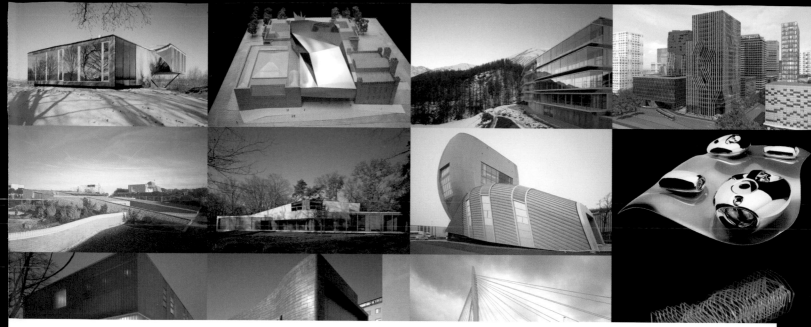

Contents

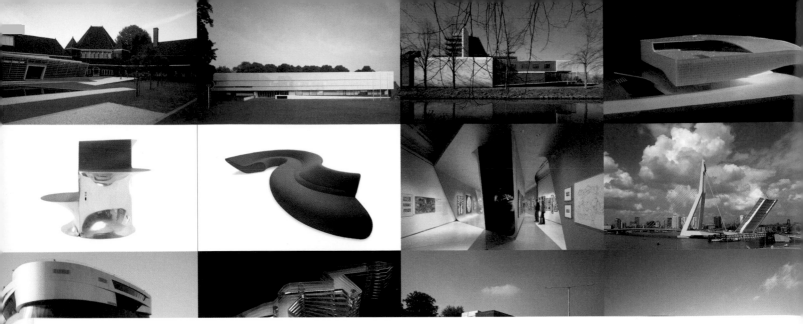

Contents

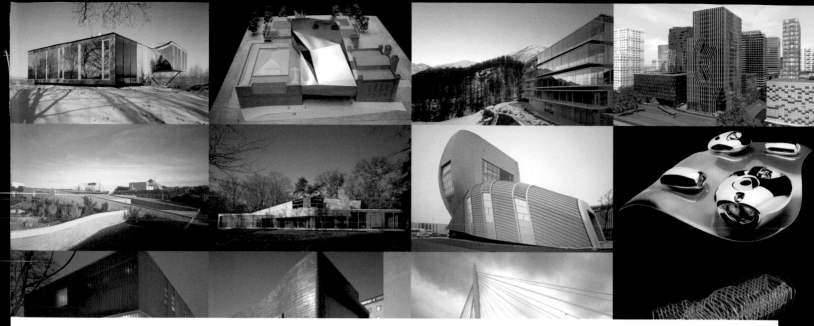

Contents

370 # After image

Introduction

At the heart of this book are two long-standing ambitions: to collect in one volume the bulk of our realized projects, together with the most important unrealized ones, and to offer an insight into the thoughts and techniques that went into the process of designing them.

Having been in practice since 1988, first as Van Berkel & Bos and later as UN Studio, we have completed over thirty projects in seven different countries, and have designed many more. As the follow-up to *Move* (1999), we want the concept of this book to reflect both our layered and relational approach to architecture, and our predilection for the projective and the speculative. And as we look back, we aim to give thought to the future. The two ideas that define this project, the design model and the after image, have evolved gradually over the last five or six years from a combination of practising and teaching, evaluating our various experiences and anticipating the future.

The two essays, as well as the project descriptions they bookend, spring from our consistently architecture-orientated approach to the field. Our outlook has always been focused firmly, and optimistically, on developing the discipline of architecture itself, and all of our efforts in writing, realizing buildings, and developing new design methods have taken place within the confines of that specific ambition.

In our opening essay, 'Design Models', we address the question of how to eliminate design from the practice of architecture, suggesting that architects, rather than designing project after project, moving from contingency to contingency, learn instead to produce work on the basis of longer-lasting design models. Taking our own practice as an example, we consider some of the implications of this new way of designing, such as the treatment of construction. The design model proposes a new approach to the subject of research, which today saturates architecture both in practice and in academies.

In the concluding essay, 'After Image', we question how the design model can affect the manifestation of architecture. In a sense, just as we propose the abolition of design, we seek to do away with the dominance of the planned, heavily published architectural image, and replace it with the more mobile, transient and unexpected images that the audience retains, long after it has left the building.

Design models

Why do we need design models?

The goal of this essay is to explain how architects can approach architecture in a new way – by no longer viewing design in terms of individual projects or buildings, and instead seeing it in relation to models that can be transferred from one project to another – and why we feel this method is necessary today.

The problem is the following: the digital revolution has profoundly affected architecture at all stages; the use of automated techniques impacts on conventions and processes leading to the design and execution of buildings, requiring new skills and new ways of imagining and realizing constructions.

Our critique is that while architecture is subject to many constraints, today's techniques do not acknowledge most of these limitations, but instead present an idea of design as the semi-automatic result of the interplay of an arbitrary selection of (not always appropriate) parameters, often leading to amorphous, academic results that do not translate into feasible constructions.

The solution presented here is based on our experiences, as architects of both failed and realized projects and as educators, which have convinced us that architects can train themselves to generate their own touchstones, or 'design models', that summarize a set of principles to help them select and implement the right parameters and remain true to their own vision. Using design models can contribute to acquiring a new form of control in digital design practices, such as parametric design.

Why don't we design buildings any more?

We like to be light-hearted, but can't always evade northern heavy-handedness; we like to think that we navigate a smooth space, but can't help sensing that we are actually swerving from near-collision to near-collision, with the occasional total wreck thrown in. But isn't this what it really means to believe in the experimental? What we don't like is risk-free architecture. In the long run, it makes no difference if that 'safe' architecture is of the commercial variety or disguised as 'critical' architecture, its criticality amounting to a recitation of the received opinions that have been echoing for thirty years. The meaninglessness of architecture that avoids risk is most eloquently expressed by the fact that it has recently noiselessly converted from a once staunchly defended modernist formal appearance, to a once vehemently opposed expressionist, or organic, formal appearance. Although we, and some of our contemporaries, have occasionally been labelled pragmatists, insinuating that what we really are is a bunch of morally lax, uncritical opportunists, it seems to us that only those who continually practice an experimental approach – concentrating all our efforts in a completely unknown outcome – are the ones who can truly be said to be the idealists of this world. Consequently, those of us who embrace this uncertainty must address the complex nature of the real.

And so we find ourselves plotting a trajectory of linear progress and fluidity, punctuated by brutal impacts. We must somehow merge together an often frantic, and sometimes downright dubious, series of projects that provide the opportunity to test out premises, with a more long-term, consistent vision. From the beginning, this is how we defined what we did: architecture as an art of the combinatorial, acknowledging that we will never, unlike the risk-free architect, enjoy the feeling of being absolutely in the right, nor accomplish as much as the successful pragmatist.

With our book *Mobile Forces* (1995), we took the initiative to articulate architecture as a material practice, after the field had for some decades been dominated by a conceptual, linguistic approach. Five years later, *Move* continued this theme, central to which was the intention to connect architecture to contemporary phenomena and to find significance in the global issues that affect our discipline. Architecture, with its strong roots in antiquity, had no means to address most of these issues, which could be as trivial as celebrity plastic surgery, as ubiquitous as the market economy, or as arcane as space travel. Yet our premise throughout remained the experiment. Our desire to bring contemporary themes into the architectural discourse was fundamentally different from an ambition to turn architecture into a critical medium, like literature or cinema, even though the proposition of a critical architecture draws upon much of the same socio-economic material that we used. Our more optimistic goal was to enrich architecture by expanding and updating our grasp of the sources it can draw upon. In an a-modern way, we adhere to the specific perspective of the architect because our contribution ultimately takes the shape of architecture. The only substantial achievement we can make is to bring some form of innovation or insightfulness to our own field. To us, the architect is not a power player, but rather a kind of artist, with a large and complex production process and audience.

Our decision to no longer design buildings emerged from the changes confronting our experiment-driven, material practice over seventeen years. Architecture became increasingly transnational in the 1990s and we covered more terrain and clocked up ever more frequent-flyer miles. Teaching became part of our practice. And a new question came to dominate our thoughts: what is it really all about?

The cycle of theory and practice, learning and teaching

From Gaudí's suspended constructions to Le Corbusier's five points of 'a new architecture', practising architects have long sought to formulate new models that encapsulate in one bold statement different aspects of construction, occupation and context. It is much harder for academics to come up with new models, just as it is difficult for an educational institute to be a laboratory for cultural experiment in the way that Andy Warhol's Factory was. Research and experimentation have to be based on real needs and real questions.

Yet the academization of architecture has become relentless, with ever more students prolonging their studies, more universities offering more and higher degree courses, and increasing numbers of practising architects supplementing their incomes and raising their profiles by teaching design. The question of *how* to teach has thus gained new relevance.

Since the architectural practice has transformed rapidly and profoundly due to digitalization and globalization, architectural teaching has necessarily changed, too. In the offices, the drawing tables have gone out and the staff has become international; in the universities and academies, the same shift has occurred. The architectural project has changed, often now consisting of a multi-functional, public-private hybrid of urbanism and infrastructure, and this, therefore, is what we teach. Architects have become hyper-conscious of the economic ramifications of their work. Rising ground values, commercial potential, investment values – these are phenomena that were meaningless until the client, in collusion with the economic news media, enforced a new awareness of their importance. In response, architects have begun to try to incorporate economic principles into their design approach. Students, having grown up in a world saturated by the media, have been quick to respond.

Preparing students for the new architectural practice has necessitated a heavy emphasis upon instruction in computational design methods, which, despite the differences in techniques and applications used, are increasingly gathered under the umbrella label of parametric design, referring to the practice of describing the various elements of architectural design as sets of parameters, which are themselves expressed as numeric and geometric relationships. The problem with parametric design, however, is that it requires rigorous pre-planning. Themes must be collected and parameters selected, and somehow you must devise some kind of tool that enables you to edit your own design as you go along. This is not yet taught to students, just as it is not practised widely.

In *Move*, we wrote that 'architectural constructions that were pure fantasy a few years ago can now be built, thanks to new design and construction techniques'. Now, however, we question if the cross-fertilization of a particular fantasy with computational design and construction techniques has really been that successful. The extreme focus on acquiring and perfecting design techniques has not been complemented by an equal development of the fantasy, the ideal image of what the product of those techniques would be and do. On the contrary, we seem to have arrived at a point where the fantasy has become repetitive, and thus the technique is becoming a pointless ritual. A small industry linked to conferences, exhibitions and lost competition entries offers desultory attempts at continuing to present parametric design as exciting and avant-garde, but even its obscuring rhetoric cannot conceal its stagnant state.

Digital design labs all over the world spew out an interminable stream of inchoate compositions in the form of hectically curvy spaghetti, impenetrable blobs and, as a last resort, dune-like shapes that result from morphing those blobs back into spaghetti. It makes no difference if the subject of the parametric design study is a museum, a school, a railway station, or a private residence, nor if the project is supposed to be situated on a beach, in a city, or in a postindustrial periphery. The same textureless wavy strands and prodigious lumps keep recurring. This is the Beaux Arts all over again; architecture has once again become restrictively academic. But how could this have happened? There is nothing intrinsically sterile to this technique. The only reason for the lack of evolution of computational design techniques is that they are taught and exercised in a hermetic way that is impossible to sustain in actual practice. It simply is not possible to foresee and to register in your computer all of the parameters that you will be working with as you engage in the long and complex process of architecture, beginning with an early vision, whether that of the architect or the client, and ending with a ruin in progress.

The conclusion? There is nothing like teaching to open your eyes to the pitfalls of design. Seeing twenty to thirty projects unfold similarly ineffectually every few months must be one of the most efficient forms of an early warning system. It tells you that no further time must be wasted. Architects must learn to apply more intelligence and more strategic planning to design.

Back to practice: from diagram to design model

Long before we employed parametric methods, we were teaching and practising the diagrammatic technique to establish a direction for a design in development. Before aspects relating to use, construction, form, or even location were fixed, we would have selected or made an organizational diagram that would serve as an abstract, yet firm mould for subsequent analyses. The emphasis of this technique, which is process-orientated and conceptual, has always been on the instrumentalization of the diagram, rather than its selection. It is what you find in the diagram and what you do with it that matters most.

Originally, from the early to the mid-1990s, we thought of the diagram primarily as a form of mediator; an external, 'found' element, between the object and the subject, which could be used to introduce other themes into a project. The role of the diagram was to generate ideas and to find inspiration in something that was purely organizational, rather than iconographic or metaphorical, and represented a strong, though not yet fully rationalized, conceptual potential. As far as we could see, the principal requirement was to escape from pre-existing typologies, not because of the need to be 'original', but because we felt that such typologies no longer provided adequate solutions to contemporary demands and situations.

Diagrams typically condense information, and when appropriate pre-existing diagrams were not readily found, we had to learn to produce our own. Thus we began to construct diagrams that (re)defined urban structures as sites of mobility and programmes as places of popular access. Those specific diagrams were intended to show what is actually happening on a location, uncluttered by presumptions about issues as high-minded as ideological representation, or as banal as square footage and building typologies.

Developing your own diagram, we found, begins with defining its parameters. Defining user categories, for example, in relation to territorial and time-based parameters, we managed to construct hard parameters, real, workable architectural ingredients, out of the soft notion of flow. The diagrams we made tended to accentuate the effects of the interaction between different actors. This relational approach to diagramming generated new insights into the developmental potential of locations in an integral manner.

Then, after several years of seeking out answers to questions about what, and especially when, is a diagram, something happened in the way we applied and conceptualized diagrams. We began to repeat ourselves. This repetition of specific diagrams incurred a greater, albeit more precise and focused, level of inventiveness. We had long been interested in seriality, admiring certain artists for their ability to view and plan their work as 'film stills', repeating and altering, copying and moving on, doing the same thing again, but differently. Artistic repetition endows themes with a longevity that enables a thorough exploration of premises, something that is indispensable in developing the long-term, consistent vision that we are after. Yet repetition is ideologically inseparable from the modernist principle of standardization, in which architecture is built up from mass-produced elements. Repetition in architecture is a matter of economic expediency, and is associated more with production processes than with those of design. Now, however, we had begun to discover a way to use repetition in architectural design in a meaningful and abstracted manner. During the last three years we have used and re-used a number of diagrams, and found that certain diagrams can be manipulated and applied in different ways. Thus the Möbius strip, its three-dimensional variant the Klein bottle, and the trefoil are variations of the same mathematical model, used in different ways in different projects.

An interest in the infrastructure of architecture, the way in which a building can be constructed according to how you move through it, first directed us to these mathematical diagrams, which belong to the field of knot theory. The fact that these diagrams possess topological qualities, and that through them run the themes of the combinatorial and the serial, makes their relation to architecture evident. Aspects intrinsic to structure, such as movement, orientation and direction, can be articulated with special clarity with the help of such mathematical diagrams. There need not always be such a pronounced overlap in the thinking systems of architecture and the field in which it looks for inspiration for its models; another example of a diagram that has become meaningful beyond the original project is an animated matrix diagram, which illustrates the patterns of usage of a location throughout the days of the week.

The recurrence of these diagrams in increasingly spatialized versions has caused us to think of them in a new way; repetition was instrumental in opening up an entirely new potential. The one-off diagram was increasingly exposed as a basic design model that worked for different projects in different ways. Using the same design model would never result in identical projects. Diagram-turned-design-models are profoundly abstracted, yet fully formed design concepts that are developed further by working out a catalogue of options and transformations, culminating in distinctive projects.

What are design models?

To scientists, a thesis is not complete if it is not wrapped up in a model. From the elegant mathematical compactness of the Standard Model of the 1970s to last year's humorous High Heels Formula, the language of models penetrates a wide range of discursive layers. Condensing the results of multiple investigations in a model with clearly defined, universal parameters is vital to the scientific process of verification and communication. It is much more effective than communicating individual cases, as architecture does when it proceeds from project to project.

The formulas and models of science may not be right for us, but what about design models? Design models are well known in the fields of computer programming and engineering. In these contexts, their meanings consist of a document containing a set of requirements and goals, formulated with the aim of reducing the range of options for implementation. These design models often take the form of a manual, illustrated by organograms and containing checklists that enable the designer to structure his process; if a suspicious number of questions elicits a negative response, the designer becomes aware that there is a high risk that the model will not adequately serve its purpose and should be adapted. Doubtless this carefully planned approach to design can be interpreted as part of the institutionalization of risk. It has been argued that a systematic way of managing risk is an intrinsic part of modernity, so it is hardly surprising that risk assessment should find its way into the design processes of disciplines that themselves have developed with the advance of modernity. In these fields, the numbers are high and mistakes are expensive.

Just as Le Corbusier observed ocean liners, we, too, observe the achievements of our age, which are increasingly the virtual and organizational techniques of the knowledge industry. Even though our own profession does not cultivate a preoccupation with caution or efficiency, our close working relationships with the disciplines that do ensure that most, if not all, architectural practices are continuously confronted with contemporary performance principles. It takes the smallest leap of imagination to recognize the potential of this rationalized application of prescience to one's own design processes.

How does it work? Let's imagine that you don't use a design model, but instead work according to a more familiar linear process, beginning with a concept sketch. You will soon find your process interrupted, as design often goes in repeating cycles or iterations. These interruptions are experienced as setbacks; the architect must choose between heroic failure and unfulfilled compromise. There is no way to value the alterations of the repetitive design process, because the designer has not articulated preformed objectives, but only has his original concept sketch to fall back on. How can the potential danger or benefit of any proposed changes be evaluated on the basis of this vision? What you need is a reality check! We see design models as packages of organizational or compositional principles, supplemented by constructional parameters. The design model does not include site-specific information; it exists at a more abstract level and may be implemented in various situations and projects. It is formulated in such a way that it becomes an internal point of reference that can be used for the duration of the process to help check if the design is progressing according to your principles and purposes. The design model is never constrictive. It is conceived as a form of 'translation model', and contributes to the project by becoming more and more real as it affects and interconnects with other forms of structures and organizations.

We see the design model as an introduction to any design technique, but especially to the contemporary, process-orientated parametric design technique. Even the simplest design model describes designing as a movement among the three activities of analysis, synthesis and evaluation, and thus enables a cyclical procession and evaluation of new input, helping you to evolve and edit your design.

In architecture, we strive to keep the textual part of the design model minimal and to develop an image-based model, which dictates that the instructions that usually form the body of the design model are implicit, rather than explicit. Despite this, it is not always possible for a design model to be compressed into one formula, or one image, as a diagram is, although one key image may be chosen to represent the design model approach. Often the design model includes organizational schemes, or matrixes, with lists of parameters showing the possible interactions between various elements.

Design models as thematized constructions

We often bring design models into a project as a means of elaborating on the constructional aspects of architecture. In our experience, this topic, though vital to architectural thinking, is difficult, even among experts, to address. Many disciplines that have both a scientific and an artistic face will be in this position; discursively, the technological aspects are marginalized. In the study of architecture, the tendency to view construction as an unyielding and inflexible topic is ubiquitous. We have taught at some of the most highly regarded architectural schools, and have visited many more, and find that very few students are willing pick this subject up, partly perhaps because the metaphorical potential of construction is narrow, which limits its communicative qualities. For years, even when we explicitly challenged students to think about and experiment with unusual constructions, we would be ignored. Each time we set a project we would encounter the same reluctance to invest creative effort in anything related to constructional issues. We wondered if the disinterest in something so intrinsic to our field was perhaps symptomatic of our age. Would the interest in structural techniques disappear with the flowering of the concept-fixated and 'critical' architect, who would persist in seeing architecture and construction as two different systems? And would, on the other hand, the rare works of architecture that feature constructional aspects be of the 'heroic' variety, like the celebrations of power from the 1950s and 1960s? Either position pertains to an extreme, and thus falls short of the balanced and integral vision of architecture that we pursue.

What is far more interesting to us is to isolate a constructional idea, and to then work with it in a similar manner to how we imagine an artist would manipulate a compositional theme; to turn it around, elaborate on it, manipulate it, stretch it out in all dimensions, to *name* it, to contextualize it socially and economically, and almost forget all about it, until the constructional idea transcends itself and, when finally realized, is encountered everywhere and nowhere in your architecture.

Why no design, why no projects?

01 Here is the first trap, the one you might enter as a student. Parametric design techniques have resulted in an extreme focus on technique and an accompanying loss of perspective on the desired result, leading to a deadly homogeneity of 'avant-garde design'.

02 Then comes the second trap, the one the cool guys have fallen into. Critical, conceptual architecture also cannot progress; the futility of 'being against' is transformed into outright hypocrisy when related to architecture. Look at the examples of using the pretence of criticality to sniff out a new market.

03 Finally, for the lucky ones, the third trap lies in wait; this is the situation the stars are now in. Design has become overorganized and, in some ways, prepackaged, market-oriented and trend- and fashion-driven.

04 Sophisticated, thought-through experimentation entails a balance between a process-oriented approach, with its unknown outcome, and an enduring professional vision that requires the articulation of a long-term ambition.

05 Formulating this driving ambition in architectural terms necessitates the formulation of concepts that mix verbally expressed ideas with constructional, compositional and organizational paradigms.

06 Today there is no aesthetic discourse, and little ethical discourse. The design model is an attempt to try to circumvent prejudices and chewed-up arguments by formulating 'dry' concepts, still free from the manipulations to which our profession is horribly prone.

07 We need an editing tool; design is boundless. The design model is a calibrating instrument that helps you determine where you succeed and where you go wrong.

08 The design model integrates several elements, rather than providing the designer with one important paradigm. It does not simply state 'surface' or 'fold', but instrumentalizes such concepts to incorporate the real ingredients of a realized work of architecture.

09 The design model is prototypical, and can evolve and be implemented in various situations and projects.

10 The design model condenses complexity, incorporating routing, construction, budget, programme and direction, as well as its own driving principle.

Conclusion

Design models represent a new approach to architecture. Buildings and projects no longer matter. Rather, our focus is on models that are able to generate whole series of projects, models that are designed to be instrumentalized directly as they contain in their very cores the enduring ingredients of architecture.

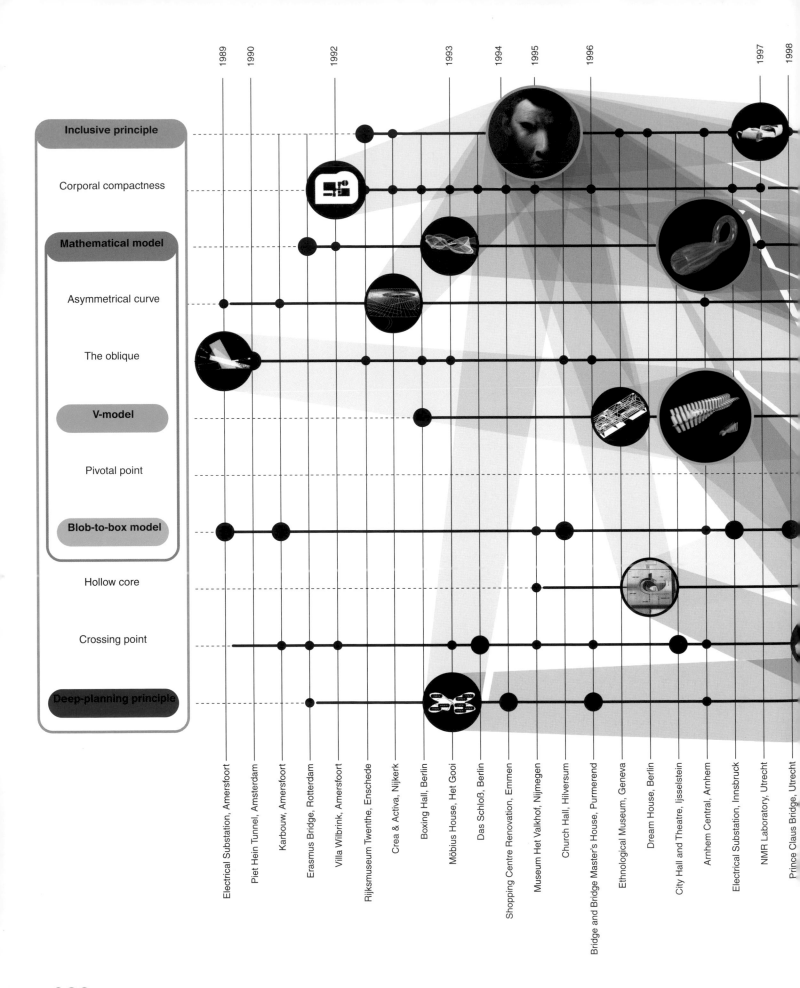

1989 **1990** **1992** **1993** **1994** **1995** **1996** **1997** **1998**

Inclusive principle

Corporal compactness

Mathematical model

Asymmetrical curve

The oblique

V-model

Pivotal point

Blob-to-box model

Hollow core

Crossing point

Deep-planning principle

Electrical Substation, Amersfoort
Piet Hein Tunnel, Amsterdam
Karbouw, Amersfoort
Erasmus Bridge, Rotterdam
Villa Wilbrink, Amersfoort
Rijksmuseum Twenthe, Enschede
Crea & Activa, Nijkerk
Boxing Hall, Berlin
Möbius House, Het Gooi
Das Schloß, Berlin
Shopping Centre Renovation, Emmen
Museum Het Valkhof, Nijmegen
Church Hall, Hilversum
Bridge and Bridge Master's House, Purmerend
Ethnological Museum, Geneva
Dream House, Berlin
City Hall and Theatre, IJsselstein
Arnhem Central, Arnhem
Electrical Substation, Innsbruck
NMR Laboratory, Utrecht
Prince Claus Bridge, Utrecht

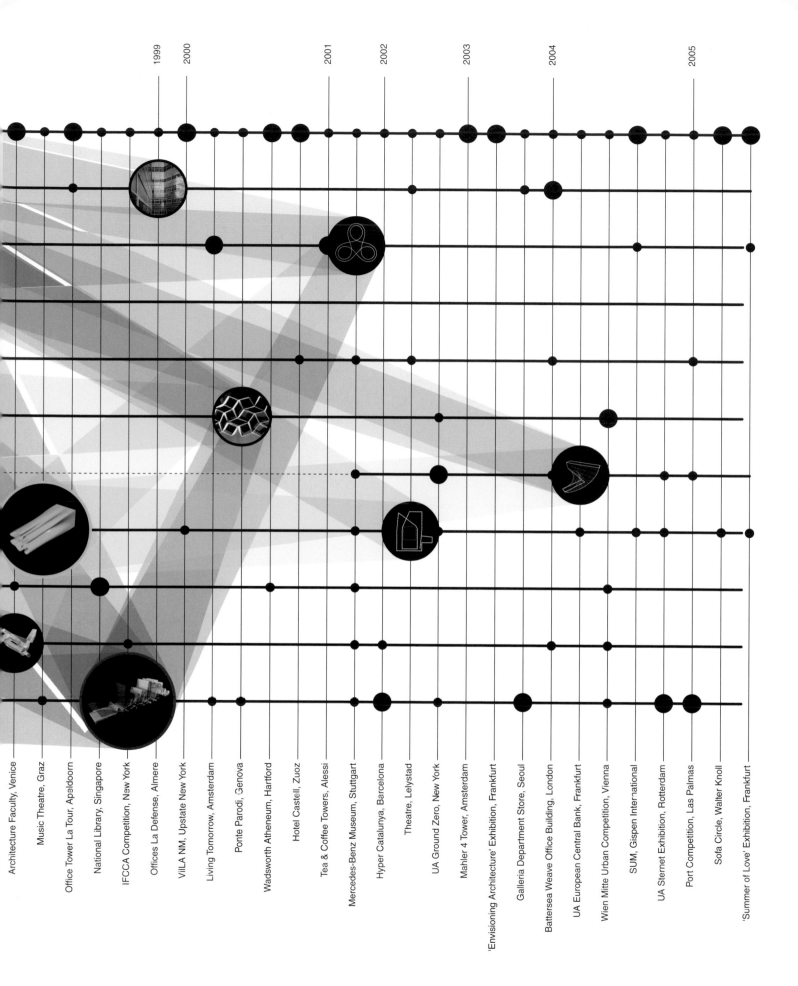

1999 2000 2001 2002 2003 2004 2005

Architecture Faculty, Venice
Music Theatre, Graz
Office Tower La Tour, Apeldoorn
National Library, Singapore
IFCCA Competition, New York
Offices La Defense, Almere
VilLA NM, Upstate New York
Living Tomorrow, Amsterdam
Ponte Parodi, Genova
Wadsworth Atheneum, Hartford
Hotel Castell, Zuoz
Tea & Coffee Towers, Alessi
Mercedes-Benz Museum, Stuttgart
Hyper Catalunya, Barcelona
Theatre, Lelystad
UA Ground Zero, New York
Mahler 4 Tower, Amsterdam
'Envisioning Architecture' Exhibition, Frankfurt
Galleria Department Store, Seoul
Battersea Weave Office Building, London
UA European Central Bank, Frankfurt
Wien Mitte Urban Competition, Vienna
SUM, Gispen International
UA Sternet Exhibition, Rotterdam
Port Competition, Las Palmas
Sofa Circle, Walter Knoll
'Summer of Love' Exhibition, Frankfurt

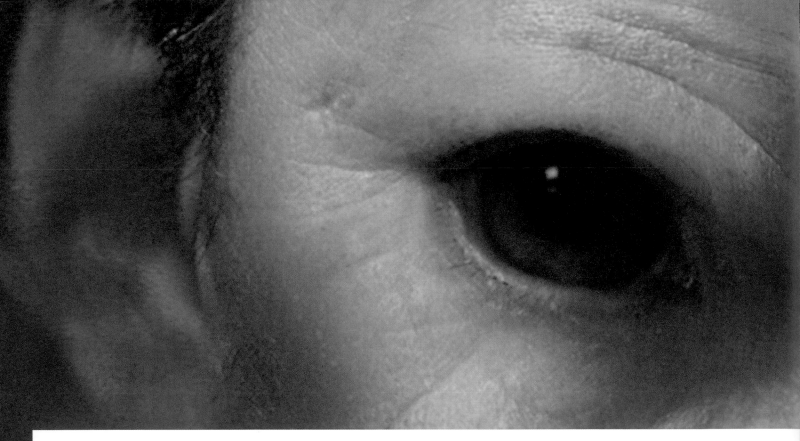

Inclusive principle

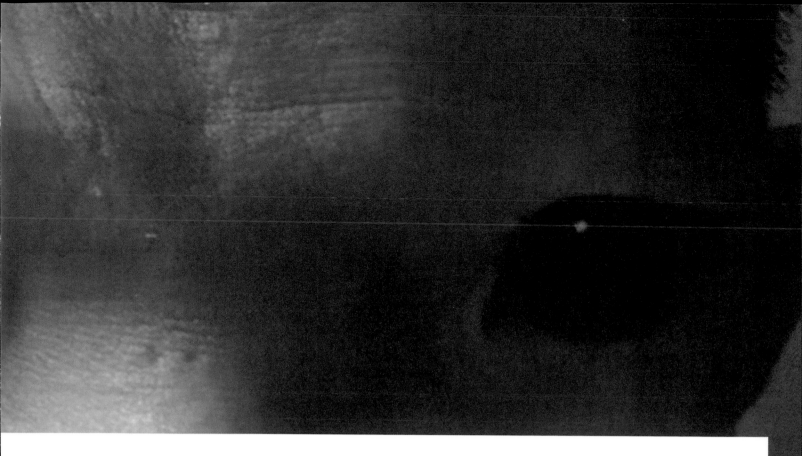

Inclusive principle

At the heart of the design models developed by our practice over the years is our long-term desire to see the systems that inform a work of architecture as one. We have consistently argued against postmodernist fragmentation and the 'collage' approach, both of which we see as remnants of the industrial ideology of early modernism. Achieving both an integral, relational treatment of the elements of a building and a tightly woven, efficient organization in which those elements exist in mutually profitable, multiple-use constellations, is the overriding principle behind all of our design models. In *Move* (1999), we explained how this approach, which builds on the contemporary imagination,

engenders rich effects. The design models presented here spring from this thought, which also embraces an expanded concept of utility. Departing from the narrow interpretation of a Fordist, economy-driven functionality, we find new ways in which architecture can and must be useful. The design model is used as a vehicle with which to attach to architectural prototypes a wide variation of thoughts, from efficiency and wastefulness, to time in relation to planning, to the 'black holes' of our society, the energy-devouring places of unprecedented flux like airports, and the general increase of an infrastructural, movement-driven occupation of space.

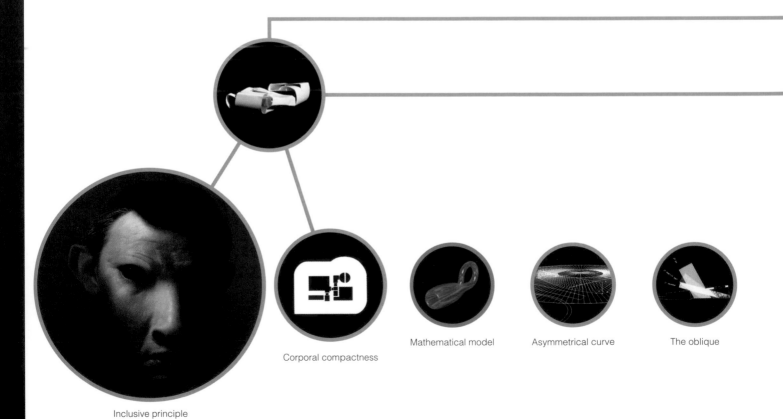

Corporal compactness

Mathematical model

Asymmetrical curve

The oblique

Inclusive principle

Fragmented organization
of disconnected parts

Displaced organization
of connected parts

Seamless organization
of disconnected parts

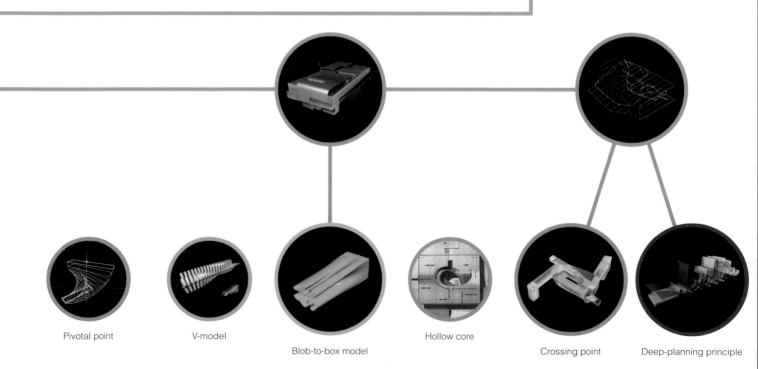

Pivotal point

V-model

Blob-to-box model

Hollow core

Crossing point

Deep-planning principle

Rijksmuseum Twenthe, Enschede
Early flow-based restructuring
1992–1996

This dark brick, cloister-like building was purpose-built as a museum by a private collector in 1928, and divided internally into a series of cramped and stuffy rooms.

The renovation of the museum structure entailed the introduction of extensive climate and technical installations, and thus provided our first opportunity to experiment with an integrated approach to architecture and construction, including machinery. The resulting improved flow of both air and visitors formed the basis for the design. In keeping with the inclusive methodology, the oblique principle was employed as the mathematical model that governed the project's design decisions, as illustrated by the pavilion façade.

Roofing over one of the two courtyards created a large, new space for temporary exhibitions, whereas the second courtyard remained open, and was landscaped by Lodewijk Baljon. The multifunctional pavilion directly opposite the entrance was added to the existing structure, improving the routing system throughout the museum by lining up the openings to the different rooms and increasing the incidence of light.

Museum Het Valkhof, Nijmegen

Against fragmentation

1995–1998

It is a building that is more like a gallery or loft than a traditional museum; a light, plain space that can and does incorporate the most diverse of art objects. Three elements – the massive column of the branching staircases, the wave-like ceiling, and the corridors, or 'streets', of the museum floor – together form the organization of the building, with each element combining various utilities.

The slatted ceiling, therefore, functions as an orientational device, softening the box and containing the installations. The stairwell is both the main construction and the vertical lobby, connecting the square, entrance and museum floor above, and the museum shop, archaeological patio, café and sculpture garden below in one uninterrupted oblique cut that slices through the entire building. The five parallel corridors, which run at right angles to the three different collections, provide a range of spaces for displaying both ancient and contemporary artefacts, while allowing the visitor freedom to move around in diverse ways.

The inclusive model of capturing the functions of architecture in just a few components generates a corporal compactness, wrapped up in a tight package. Ideologically, inclusiveness seeks to reverse the fragmentation of postmodernism by positioning an approach diametrically opposed to the strategy of breaking up systems, seeking instead a new coherence by combining hard and soft architectural parameters.

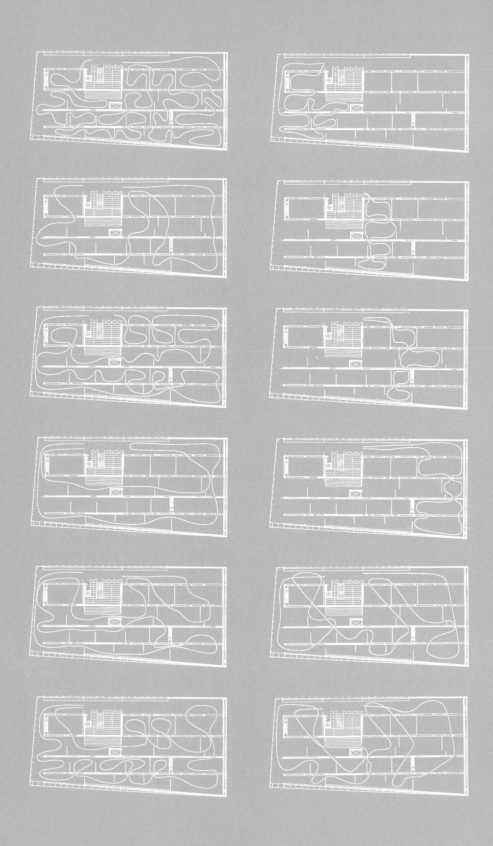

The diagonally placed openings in the five museum 'streets' allow limitless
circulatory patterns.

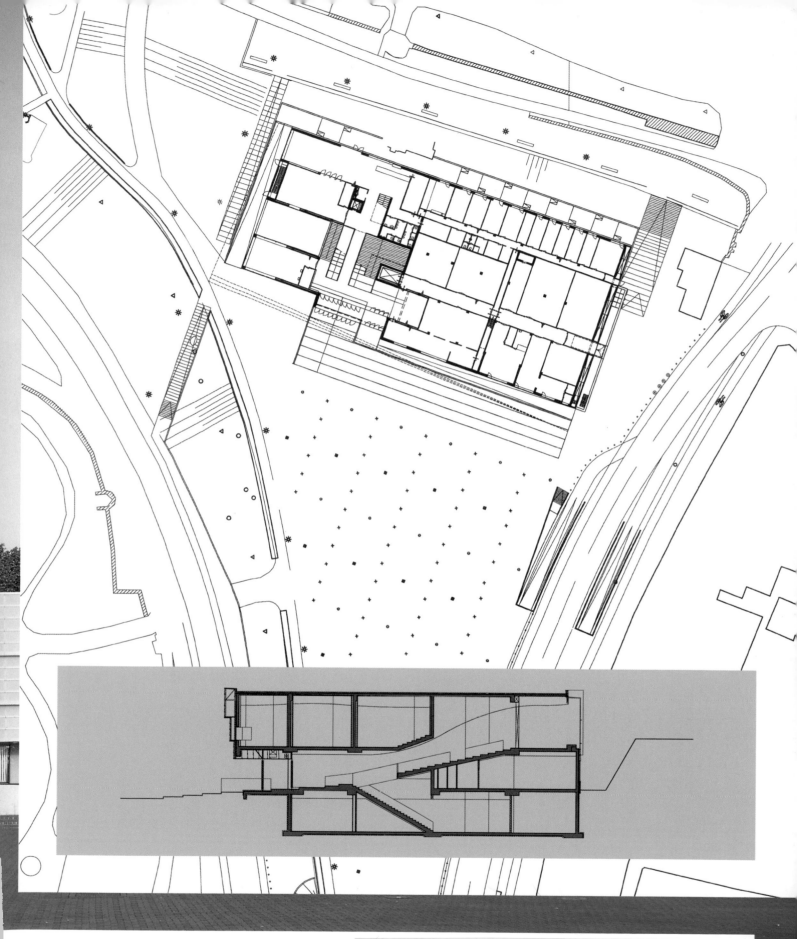

The drawings illustrate the museum's integration of topographical height differences.

The different shades of blue are caused by the deceptive unity of the glass box:
there are in fact two façade systems. The front façade is mostly closed and made of
glass over blue-coloured plates.

The back façade is primarily transparent. The glass box is opaque in those places in which no daylight must penetrate, and transparent in others to allow views to the outside.

First-floor balcony zone, with its framed images of the surrounding natural landscape and light.

The double-curved, undulating ceiling softens the box and subtly orients the visitor.

The ceiling also houses the technical installations – light fittings, acoustic panels, heating and air conditioning – behind aluminium louvres.

Branching from the front entrance, the staircases form the structural and
infrastructural core of the museum. They scissor through the three vertical layers of
the building, connecting its parts and forming a social crossing point.

042   **Museum Het Valkhof, Nijmegen**

NMR Laboratory, Utrecht

More than
a single surface

1997–2001

The specific research technique to which the laboratory is dedicated has inspired its design. 'NMR', or 'neutron magnetic resonance', analyzes molecular structure and the behaviour of proteins with the aid of high-frequency magnetic pulses.

The two floors of the building are designed around eight spectrometers and ancillary equipment. These powerful magnets radiate force fields that cannot be disturbed, thus determining the various dimensions of the rooms that house them. Another important constraint was caused by the impossibility of installing a lift, as the electrical currents would interfere with the magnetic resonance. For this reason an outside ramp has been added to the circulation system, enabling access to all parts of the laboratory.

The laboratory itself is much smaller than the surrounding facilities, yet engages the same architectural issue that was current at the time of its inception, namely that of the 'single surface', the smooth continuation of the floor plane into wall and ceiling. Partly because of the building's small size, but mostly because of our long-standing interest in an integral approach to construction, circulation and programme, the laboratory takes up this issue in an advanced form. The flipped-over surfaces are constructive, and thus are not traversed by a secondary support structure of columns, as is the case with other buildings that feature this element.

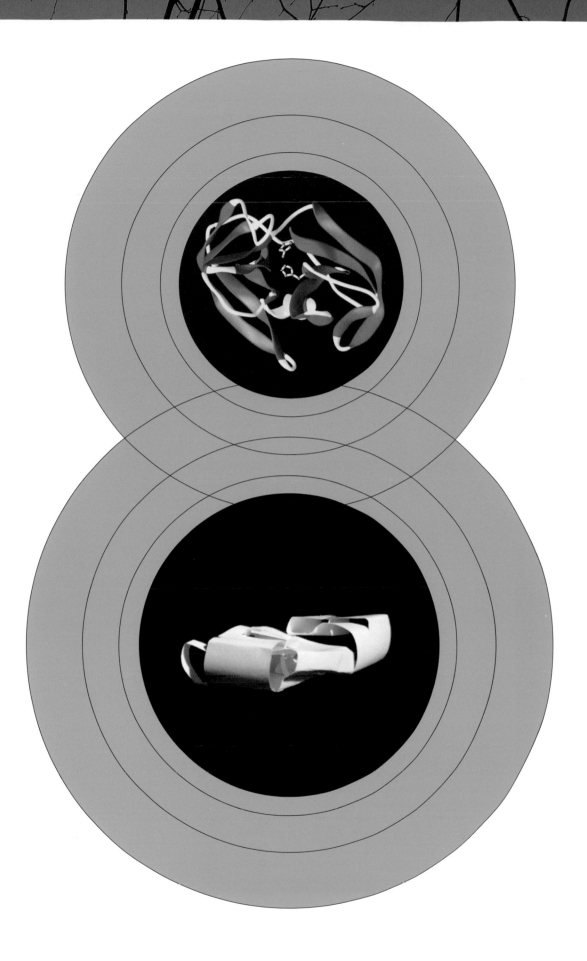

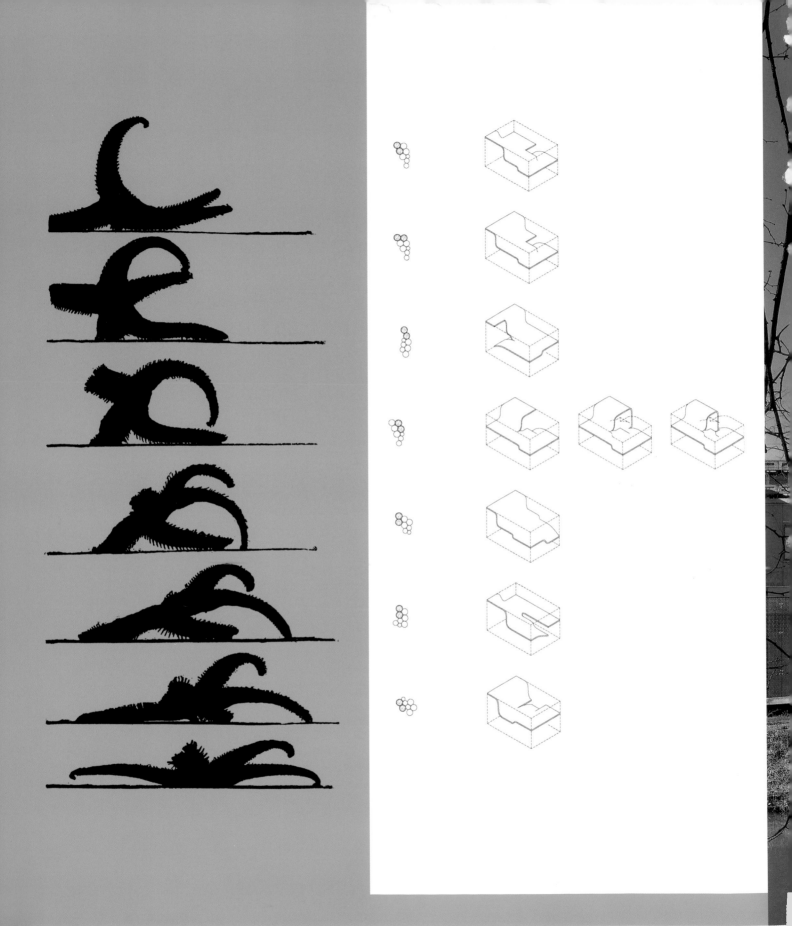

Conceptual diagrams show the concrete folding around the spectrometers and ancillary equipment.

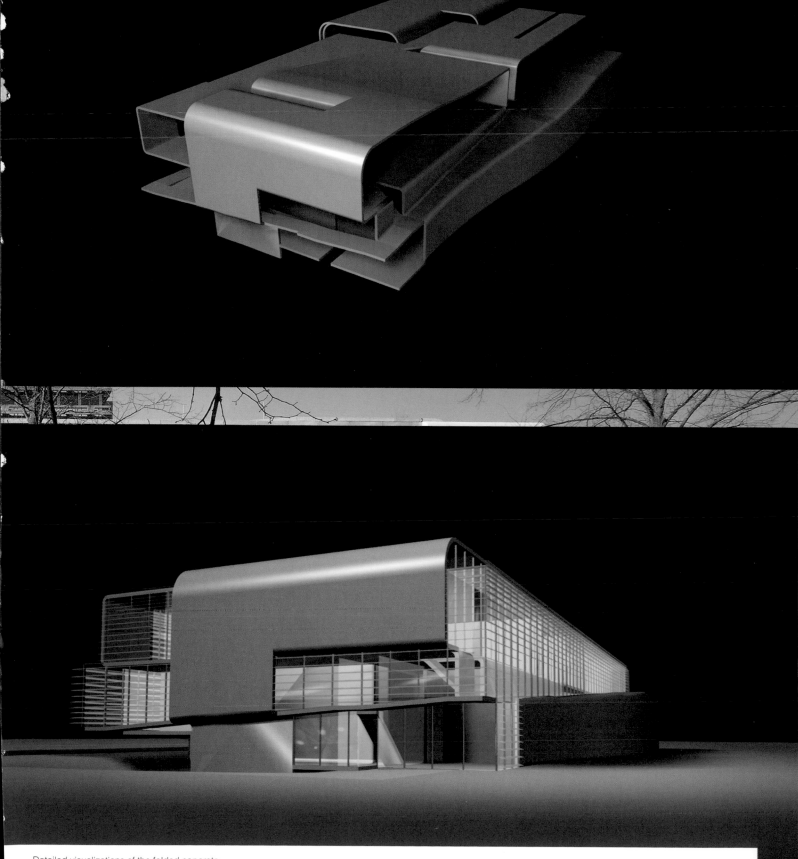

Detailed visualizations of the folded concrete.

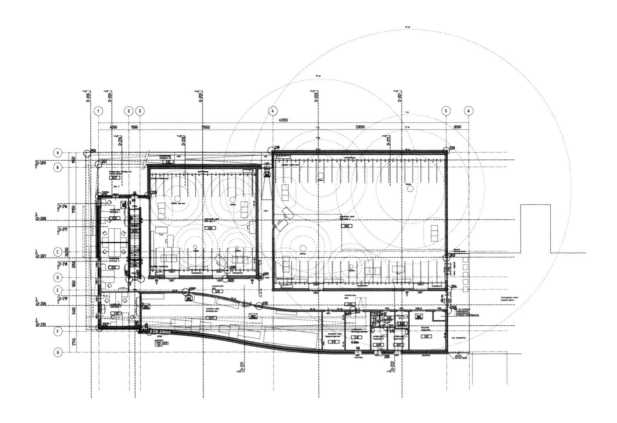

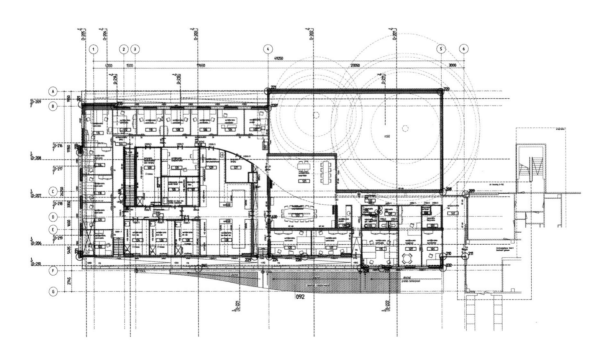

The circles in the plans illustrate the spectrometers' force fields.

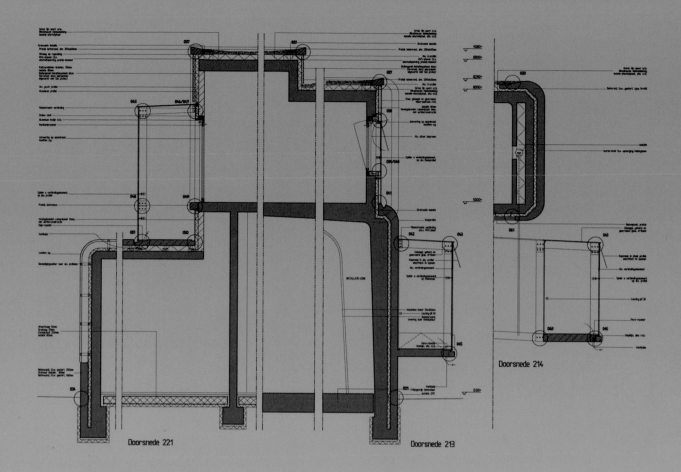

Doorsnede 221

Doorsnede 213

Doorsnede 214

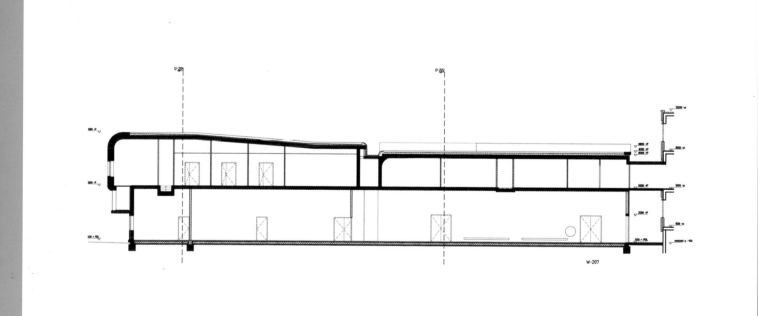

Sections show the concrete floor of the main laboratory room, separated from the
construction to ensure a resonance-free environment.

Access to the first floor from the ground is provided by a ramp, rather than a lift.

The facility does not have a public front entrance; the laboratory is accessed via the science faculty next door.

054 NMR Laboratory, Utrecht

Because the laboratory is subject to frequent technical rearrangements, the technical installations have been left uncovered and freestanding.

Positive note 1 It's not that we particularly enjoy flying, but isn't it great to cross cultures and build a fantastical hybrid **retail-museum-office-living-space** on the other side of the world? UN Studio was founded specifically to accommodate the apparently **insatiable** and **transnational** desire for public buildings of this kind. Reformulating the architectural project as a seamless constellation of infrastructure, urban planning and public policy was an ideological choice that was confirmed by emerging tendencies in the contemporary geo-political field. We come across **postindustrial, densely urban** sites that warrant the **multifaceted approach** of deep planning in Europe, the US, South East Asia, literally everywhere. With UN Studio, we have learnt to see projects as public constructions and have organized ourselves as a flexible platform organization, in which the **architect**, as the **coordinating and networking** expert of the public realm, has replaced the **Baumeister**. An intimate understanding of the potential and problems of these urbanized sites is as important as local knowledge.

Architecture Faculty, Venice
Hollow core
1998

This competition entry is one in a long line of experiments with a centrifugal distribution of forces and programmes around a middle void. The spatial distribution model was still in its infancy at this point, but soon germinated into a strong organizational tool in later projects, most notably the Wadsworth Atheneum, in Hartford, Connecticut (see p. 86), and the Mahler 4 Tower, in Amsterdam (see p. 112).

Conceived as a continuation of the embankment along which the building is situated, the quay is folded inward and twisted upward. The resulting void is a development of the idea of the 'crossing point', in which the building is a knot in a radiating network of routes. The elliptical void is framed by four propeller-like tubes that function both as corridors, along which the classrooms are situated, and as the support structure for the entire building.

While few of the hollow-core projects have been realized in their entirety, some aspects of this design model have since been applied in other buildings. But it is the façade principle of the Venice project, with its theme of the hollow core, which has elicited the most response. The system of layered panels in different materials, with larger or smaller perforations to let in more or less light, has generated subsequent designs in which standardized, repetitive components contribute to a non-standard, variegated surface organization.

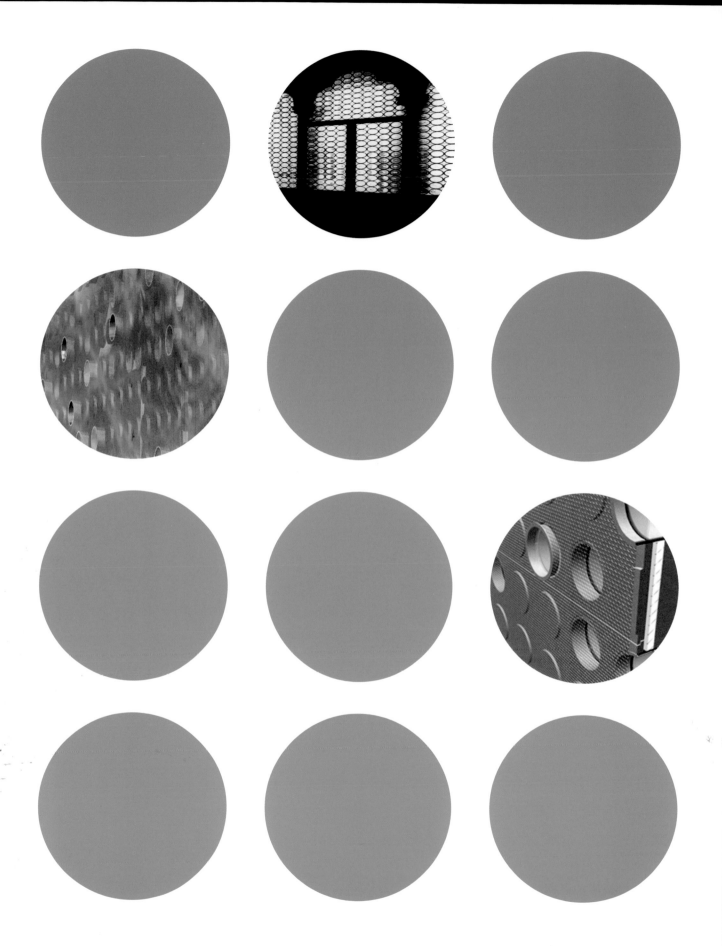

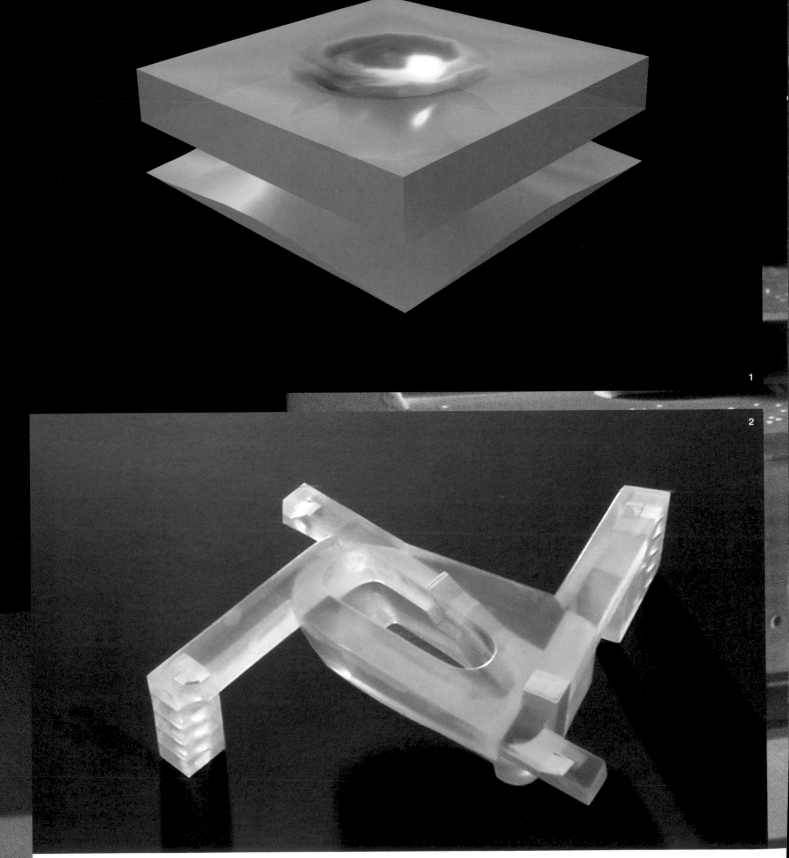

1 Volumetric diagram of elevated structure with central hollow core.

2 Infrastructural model of the core and circulation areas.

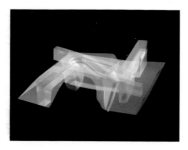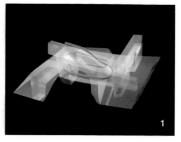

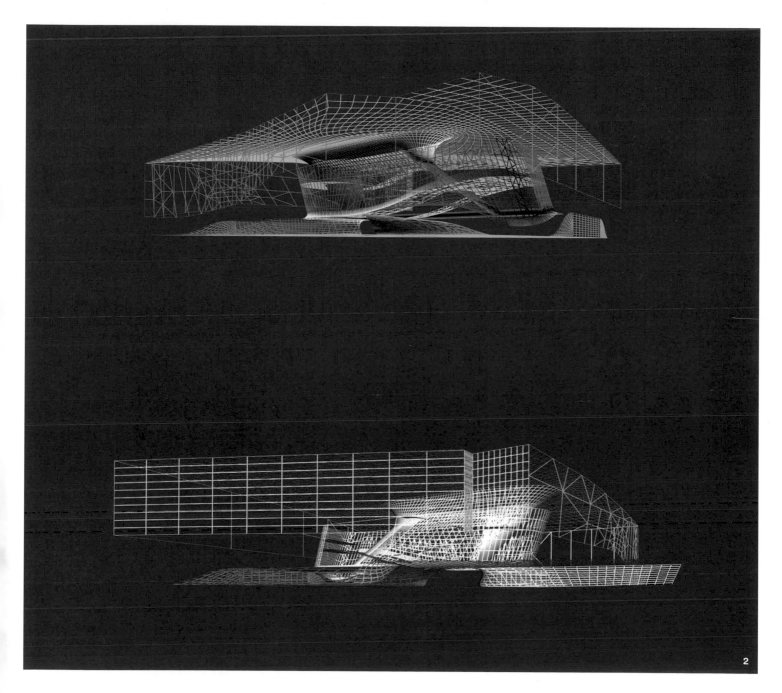

1 Diagrams of circulation systems for different user groups.

2 Wire-frame diagrams show how the quay is continued in the core, and then folds over to form elevations and roof.

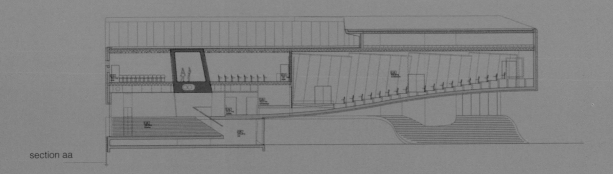

section aa

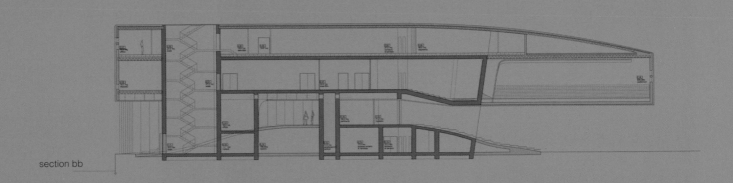

section bb

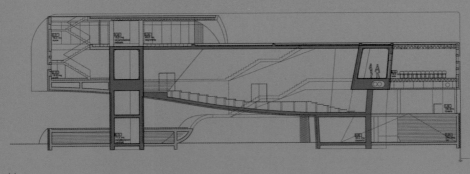

section dd

Section aa: the auditorium.
Section bb: the circulation areas.

Section dd: the staircase at the periphery of the hollow core, together with a public space underneath the building.

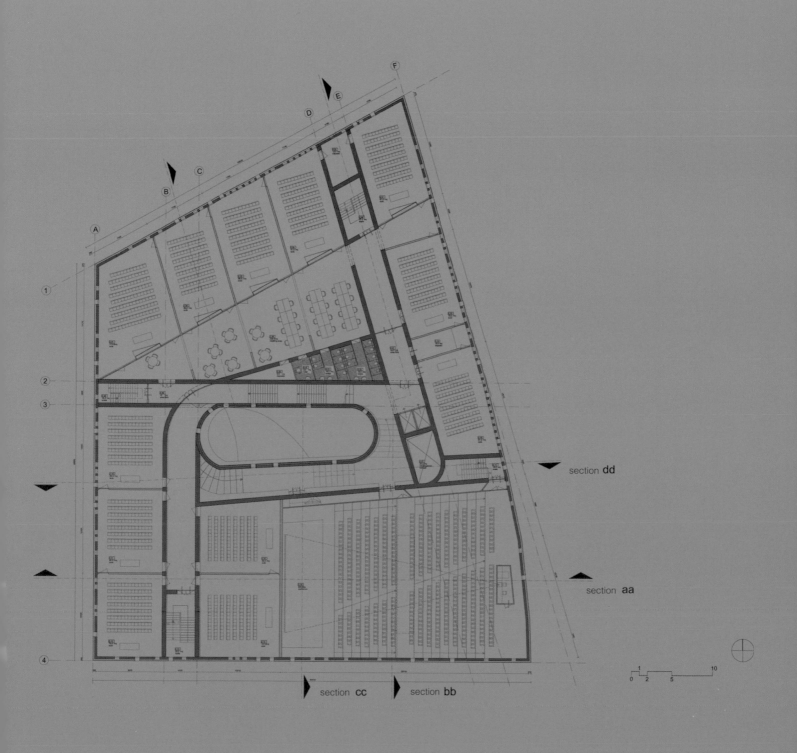

Plan showing the hollow core and circulation spaces, with their connecting
programme.

section dd

section aa

section cc   section bb

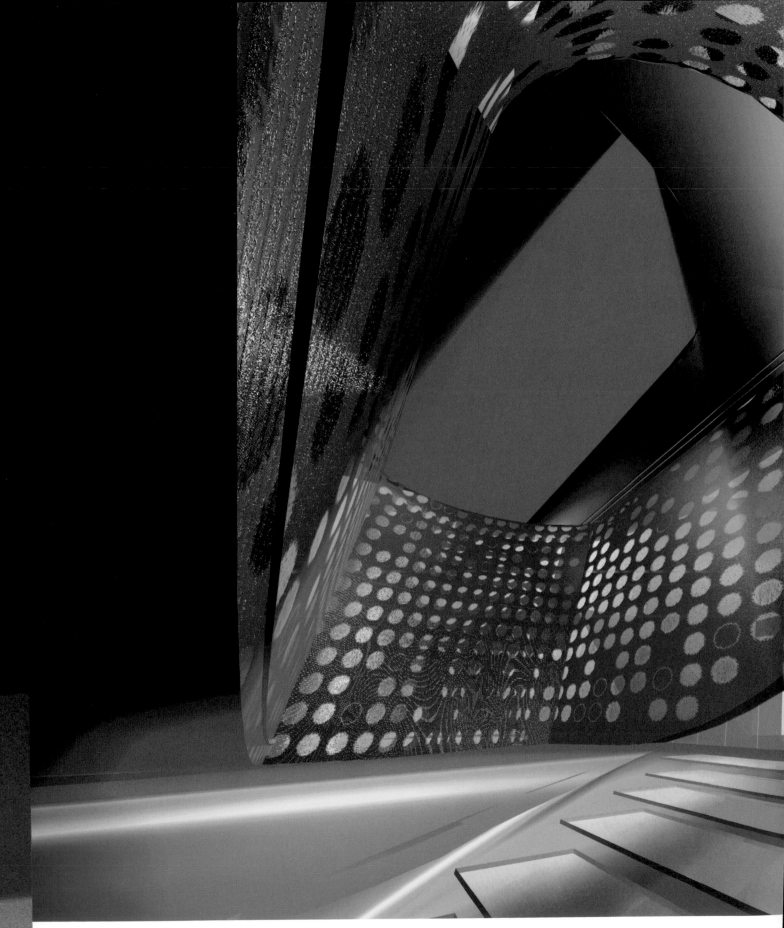

There is a minimum of difference between the materialization of the inner and outer surfaces as the external façade is pulled through the hollow core.

Model illustrating the continuity of the roof into the floating front elevation.

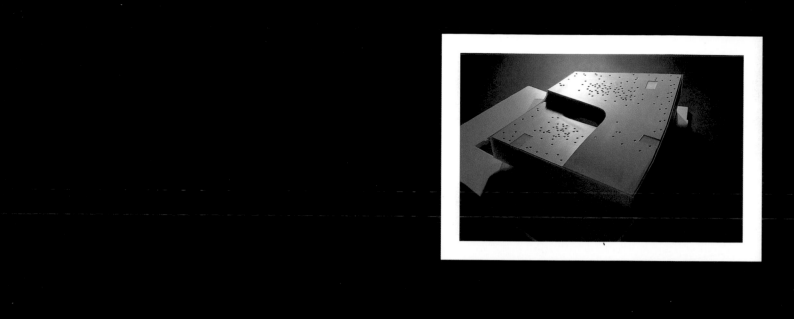

The layered façades are designed to pick up colours of the city, and to reflect the
Venetian character.

VilLA NM, Upstate New York
Viewfinder dacha
2000–2005

The design model for this summerhouse is a box with a blob-like moment in the middle, a twist in both plan and section that causes a simple shoebox shape to bifurcate into two separate volumes, one clinging to the northern slope, the other detaching itself from the ground to leave room underneath for a covered parking space.

The resulting internal split-level organization generates its own brand of view-orientated efficiency. The kitchen and dining area on the ground floor are connected by a ramp to the living space above, the 1.5-metre (5-ft) difference in height allowing for a sweeping outlook over the surrounding woodland and meadows. A similar ramp connects the living area to the master suite and the children's bedrooms on the second floor. The bathroom, kitchen and fireplace are clustered in the vertical axis of the house, leaving the outer walls free. Large, glazed windows feature in all but the most private rooms.

As can be seen most clearly in the construction photos, in which the house is shown in its skeletal incarnation, the volumetric transition is generated by a set of five parallel walls that rotate along a horizontal axis. The walls become floor, and vice versa. The ruled surface maintaining this transition is repeated five times in the building. Standardizing and prefabricating this structural element lowered building costs without reducing the spatial quality of the interior.

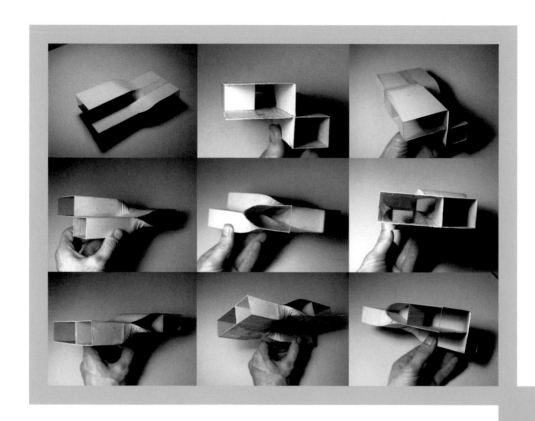

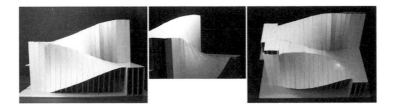

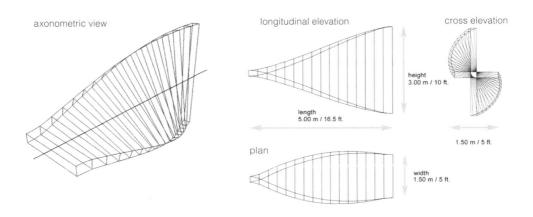

axonometric view

longitudinal elevation

cross elevation

height
3.00 m / 10 ft.

length
5.00 m / 16.5 ft.

1.50 m / 5 ft.

plan

width
1.50 m / 5 ft.

Materializing the surface

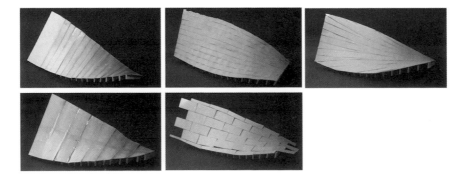

Diagrams and models using ruled surface geometry to describe the twisted
elements.

structure of volume

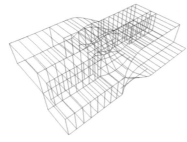

diagrammatic section

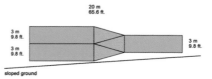

20 m
65.6 ft.

3 m
9.8 ft.

3 m
9.8 ft.

3 m
9.8 ft.

sloped ground

planar volumes

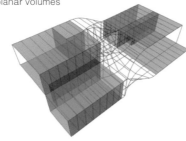

diagrammatic plan

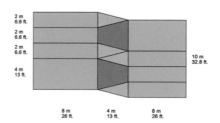

2 m
6.6 ft.

2 m
6.6 ft.

2 m
6.6 ft.

4 m
13 ft.

10 m
32.8 ft.

8 m
26 ft.

4 m
13 ft.

8 m
26 ft.

twisted surfaces

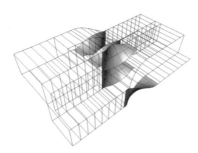

glass walls

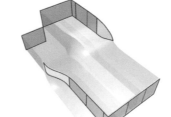

single-curved surfaces

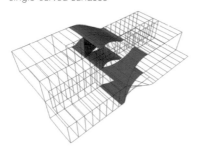

structural support and
two additional walls

Volumetric and surface-study diagrams.

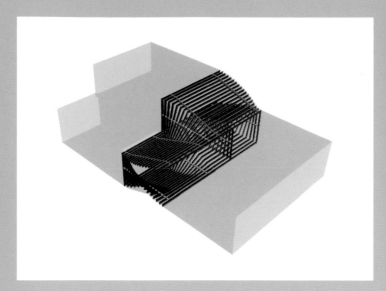

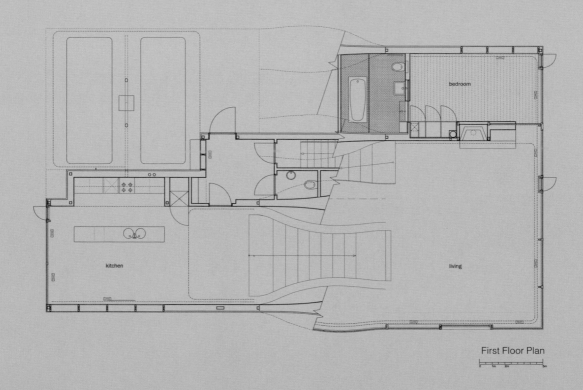

First Floor Plan

0   1m   2m   5m

The twisting surfaces are intentionally positioned to allow the building to take
advantage of the site's topography.

080 VilLA NM, Upstate New York

In-situ construction: standardized design proved impossible in the local situation.

Wadsworth Atheneum, Hartford

Hollow core as multi-level connector

2000

The Wadsworth Atheneum, the USA's oldest public museum, has slowly grown over time into a maze of small, unconnected rooms. These labyrinthine logistics, in our view, contributed to the museum's élitist positioning within the Hartford community. Visitors had to be intimate with the museum's layout, ideally as a member of staff or a well-heeled volunteer, to find their way around the rambling collection. This, along with the shortage of gallery space, was the main issue we sought to address. Unfortunately, our attempts to persuade the museum to become more inclusive, including the introduction of access via the more European system of public transport, proved ultimately to be unacceptable.

For two years we worked on a design that would increase gallery space and improve traffic flow. The blob-to-box organizational principle was used where the rigid grids of the existing buildings were interwoven with a fluid circulation system, revolving around the central hollow core. Our proposal consisted of replacing the 1969 addition with a central distributor space, thus giving access to the separate buildings whilst accommodating the varying floor heights, and creating a transparent and more welcoming entrance that would increase gallery space by a third. At the new entrance, an enclosed glass-walled concourse would have spanned the entire museum, and a cone-shaped opening, woven in fine metal mesh, would have descended from the rooftop to allow for increased light.

Although initially the proposal elicited favourable reactions, the project collapsed before advancing beyond the pre-schematic design stage.

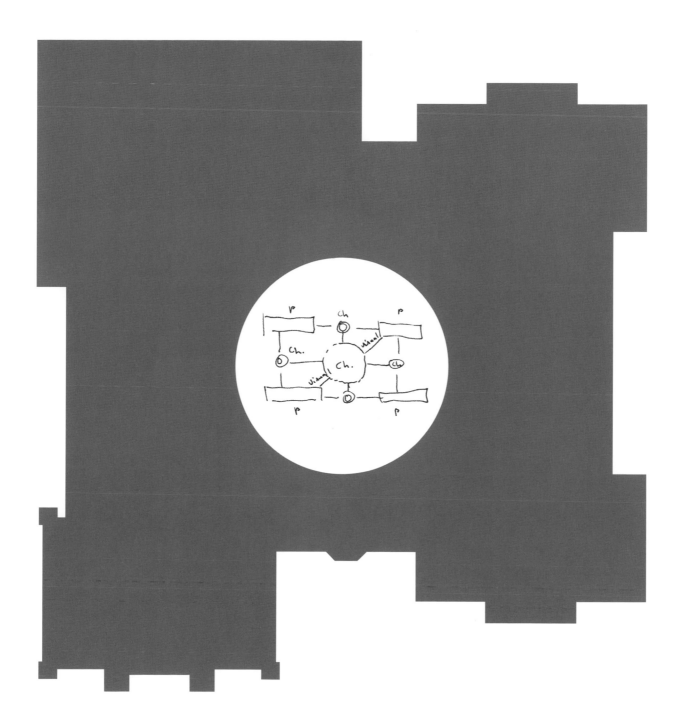

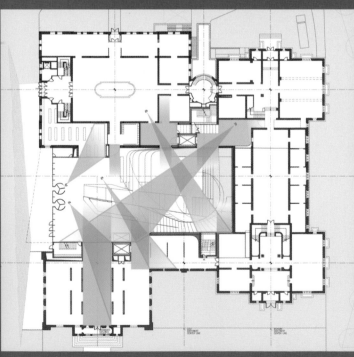

Above Ben's initial sketch shows a floating structure that is vertically connected to a spiralling public pathway.

Below Plans of the public concourse and view corridors at entrance level.

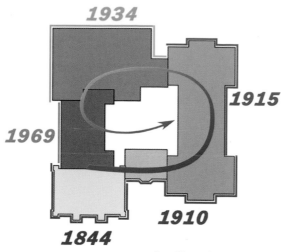

1934

1969

1915

1844

1910

five different façades

1934

1915

1969

1910

1985

three types of construction

Façades

Construction

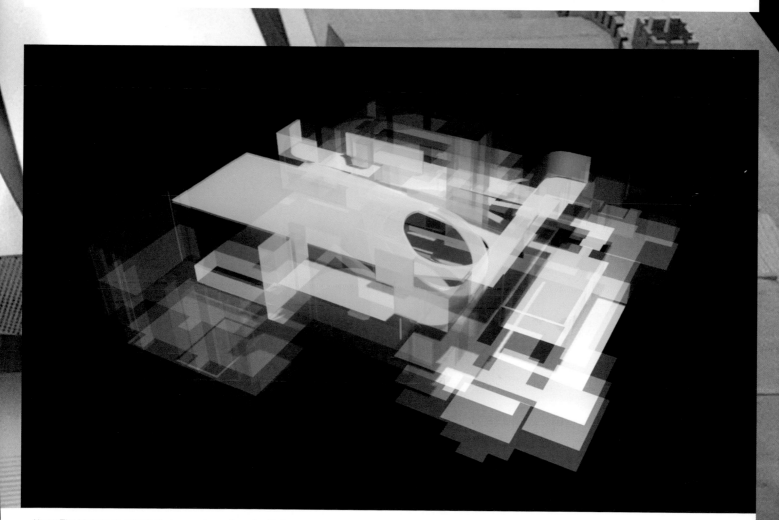

Above The historic counterclockwise amalgamation of galleries.

Below Diagram of the double-helix connector, linking the different height levels of the various galleries.

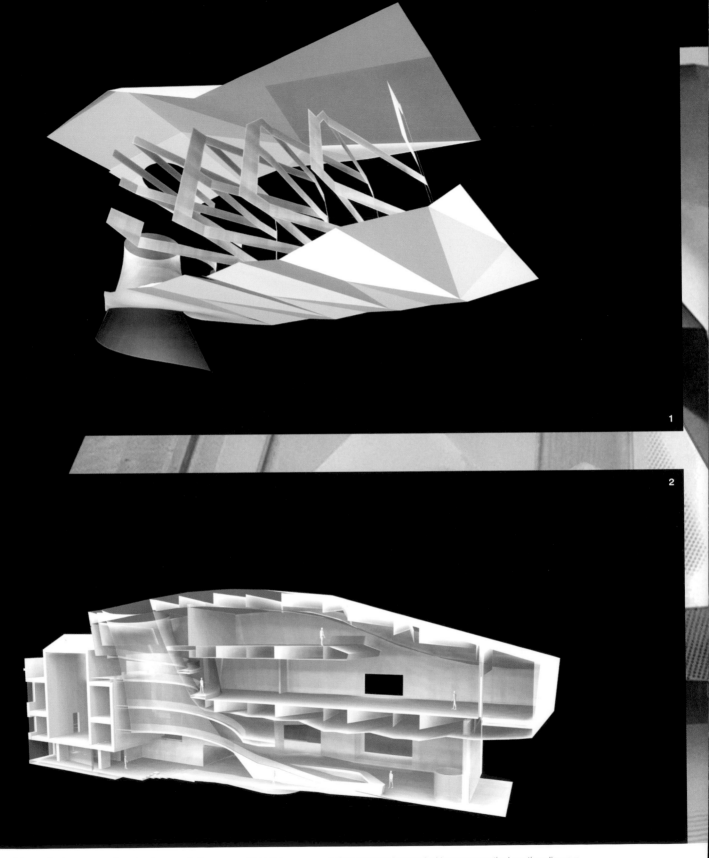

1 Diagram of the roof, whose concertina structure results from connecting the presence of existing bearing points.

2 Construction is revealed in a perspectival section diagram.

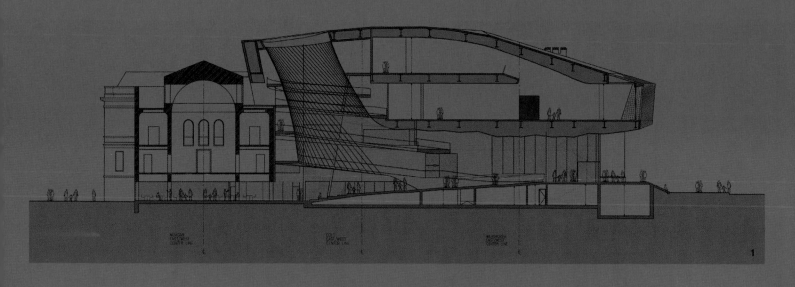

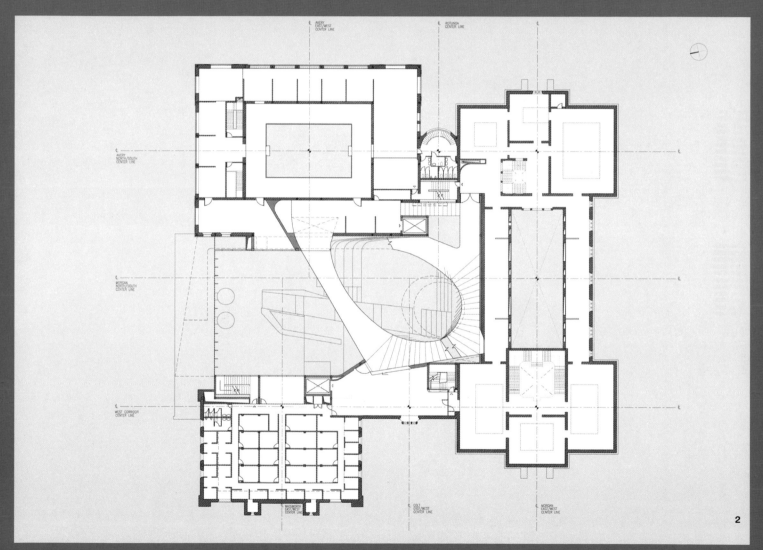

1 This section shows the continuous public access zone through the site at ground level, the flexible exhibition spaces at the higher levels, and the light cone with its double-helix.

2 The second floor's access points are generated by the double-helix, which connects to existing exhibition areas.

Museum
Shop

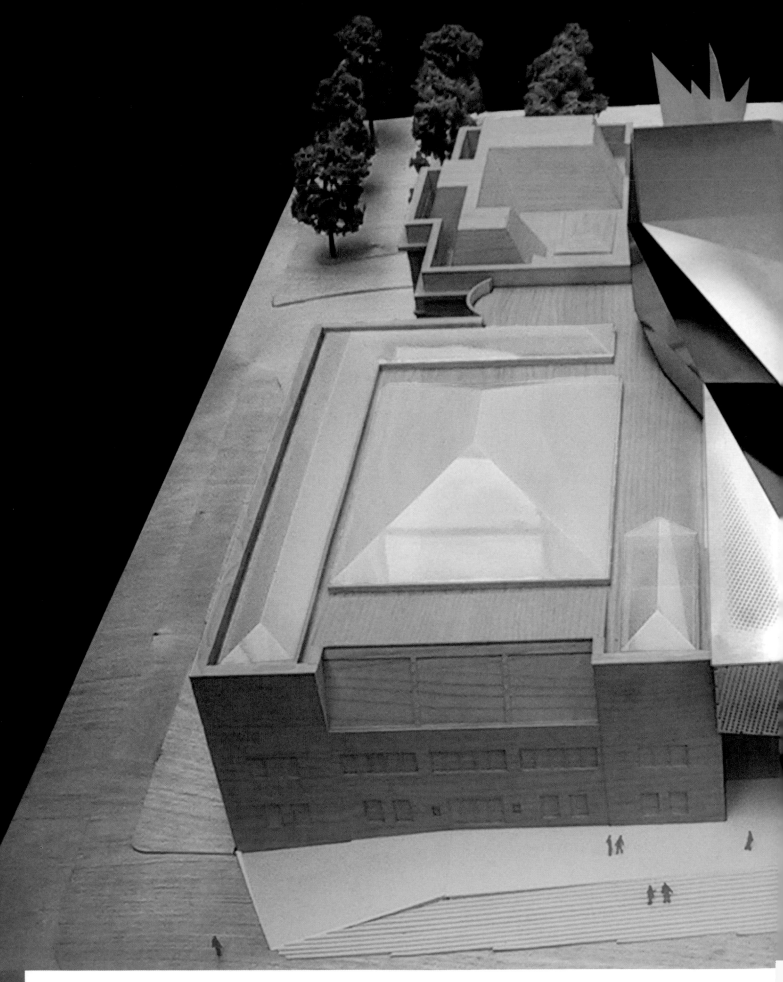

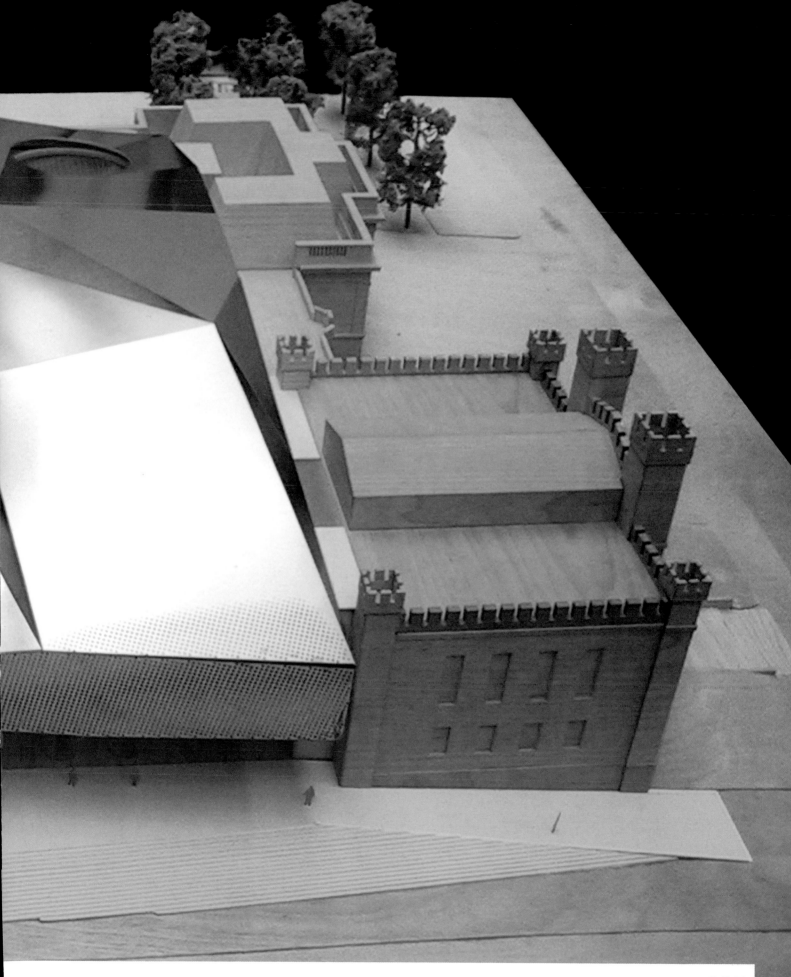

Positive note 2 You can always renew, reinvent and rediscover things about buildings. New production techniques and materials are constantly evolving and leading to design innovations. But we also find inspiration in new uses, effects and concepts. Throughout the 1990s architecture was in the grip of a renewed fascination with science, inspired to a large extent by Gilles Deleuze and his most prominent interpreters in our field. Among the Deleuzian models that architects have attempted to signify spatially, structurally and organizationally are the smooth and the striated, becoming animal, the diagram and the fold. At the same time, new insights into complex geometries have become more accessible. Architects, having tended to follow engineers with their cautious and applicability-oriented handling of science, have begun to believe that they are justified in searching for more **expansive concepts**; the rigid dogmas of Modernism and standardization have been **fundamentally challenged.** We can go to the core of our understanding of time and space, and discover processes that themselves **discover proliferation** instead of **atrophy** as a paradigm for architecture. Both the theoretical understanding and the production processes of architecture have benefited from this **expanded understanding** of structures, forces and organizations that have been brought to the fore in different ways.

Hotel Castell, Zuoz
Intertwining landscapes revisited
2000–2004

Situated at an altitude of 1,900 metres (6,234 ft), with panoramic views over the Engadin valley towards nearby St Moritz, the original 1913 building has been renovated and extended under the ownership of Swiss artist and collector Ruedi Bechtler into a contemporary wellness centre and art hotel.

A building with fourteen large, open-plan apartments has been added to finance further conversions to the hotel. Consisting of two different interlocking volumes, the structure offers two types of apartment: the glass-fronted half contains conservatories, and the other half open balconies. This intertwining of different volumes continues a theme that has been present in our work from the beginning. The sculpted obliquity of the building's mass complements both site and structure. While corresponding to the volume inflection of the existing hotel, the angular glass-and-metal façade also responds to the Alpine topography with its shift between open and enclosed balconies, structuring the southern front as a tectonic formation of shifting horizontal strata.

The basement in the east wing now houses the first hammam to exist in the Swiss mountains. The typology of the traditional hammam, consisting of a central space with secondary spaces grouped around it and skylit by a dome, has been reinterpreted to contain five cones and cylinders, which allow streams of light to pour into a sunken plaza. These oversized, hollow columns veil the existing structure with their colourful, incandescent glass skin, and articulate different areas for activity and tranquillity, collectivity and intimacy.

Finally, the hotel's sixty rooms have been enlarged and improved, to combine simplicity with clarity of spatial organization, and to strive for a light synthesis with the hotel's permanent art collection and temporary exhibitions.

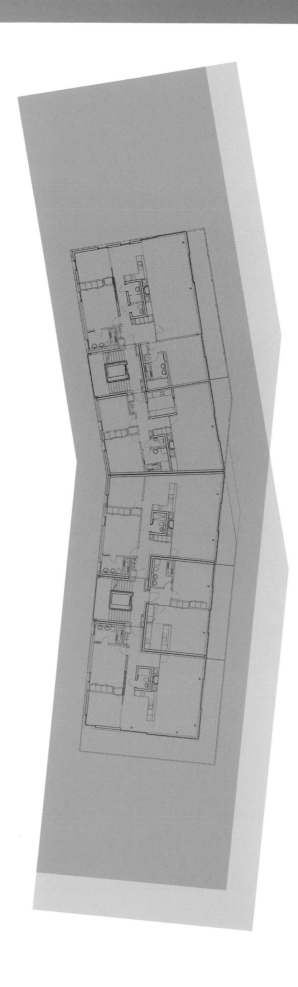

Plan and elevation showing the relationship between the new and existing building.

View of the interlocking façade elevation.

Interior view of a renovated room in the original building.

The integrated surfaces of the floor and bench, along with the column, are covered
with a continuous layer of tile in this intimate bathing space.

The colours of the walls in the steam rooms are programmed to reflect duration.

Hotel Castell, Zuoz **111**

Mahler 4 Tower, Amsterdam
A tower for work or living
2003–2006

The Mahler 4 area is situated on Amsterdam's South Axis, connecting Schiphol Airport to the business districts of the southeastern part of the city. The development of the neighbourhood, intended ultimately to provide a lively mix of working, living and commercial developments, at first advanced rapidly during the 1990s, but has since slowed down somewhat.

Our tower is one of six, each designed by a different architect. With heights ranging from 85 metres (279 ft) to 100 metres (328 ft), the six towers are arranged in a checkerboard pattern. According to the master plan, the plinths are reserved for public facilities, and the higher floors for housing or offices.

The 23-storey tower has a footprint of 40 by 40 metres (131 by 131 ft) and was originally designed for office use. With the current market surplus of office space, an additional housing variant has been designed, making use of the same column grid. The function of the space, therefore, can be determined later in the day, or even changed after construction.

In order to meet light requirements and aid building efficiency, a series of voids was designed to ensure a maximum of daylight at the working units. A hollow core runs through the centre of the building's mass, branching out horizontally towards the façades at different intervals and orientations. The positioning of the various voids results in flexible floor plans, offering future users multiple ways of organizing their working and living spaces.

The voids engage with the different façades of the building, causing diverse atmospheres, whilst their orientation permits views overlooking the old city centre, airport and neighbouring park. The vertical strips on the façades bifurcate at points were a void has been designed, giving an optical illusion of depth.

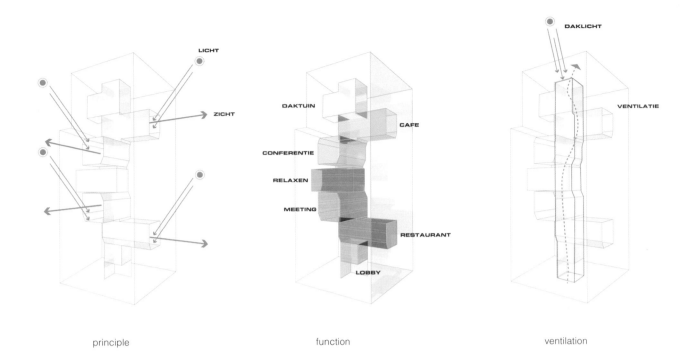

principle   function   ventilation

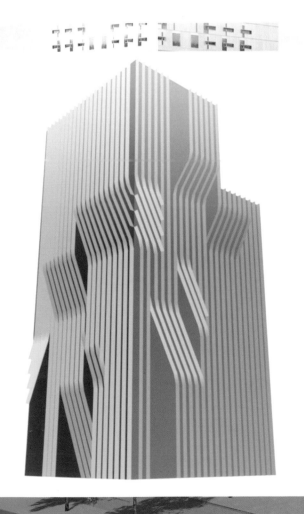

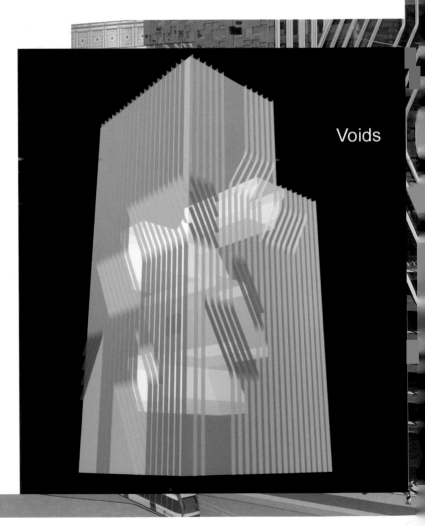

Voids

Diagrams show (above) the internal voids branching out towards the façades, and
(below) the vertical fins shifting at points where the voids touch the façades.

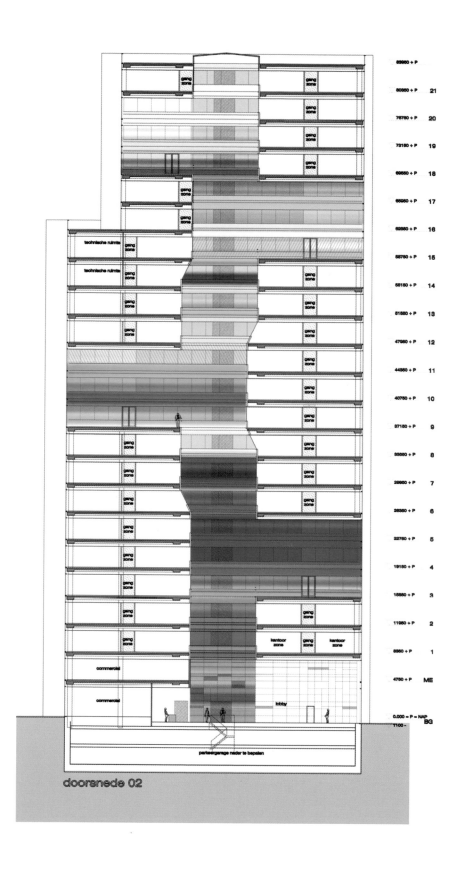

doorsnede 02

Voids are oriented in three different directions: towards the city centre, airport and park.

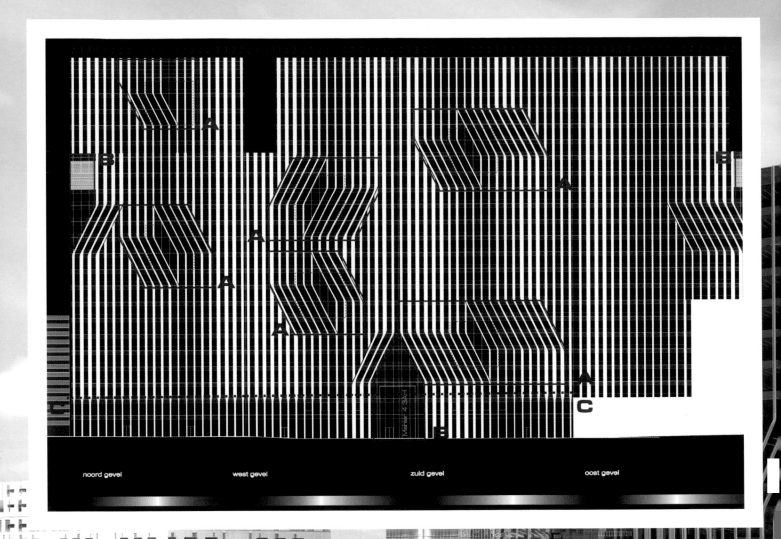

noord gevel west gevel zuld gevel oost gevel

1. VINNEN

1.1 BASIS ELEMENTEN

1 2 3

1.2 BASIS RITME

2 3 3 3 2 2 2 1 1 1 1 1 1 1 2 2 3 3 3 2

83950 + P	
80350 + P	21
76750 + P	20
73150 + P	19
69550 + P	18

The unfolding building elevation depicts (in red) the rhythm of the perforations emanating from the bifurcation of fins.

The composition optically breaks up the building's volume; the fins are thicker and denser at the corners, gradually thinning towards the centre of the elevation.

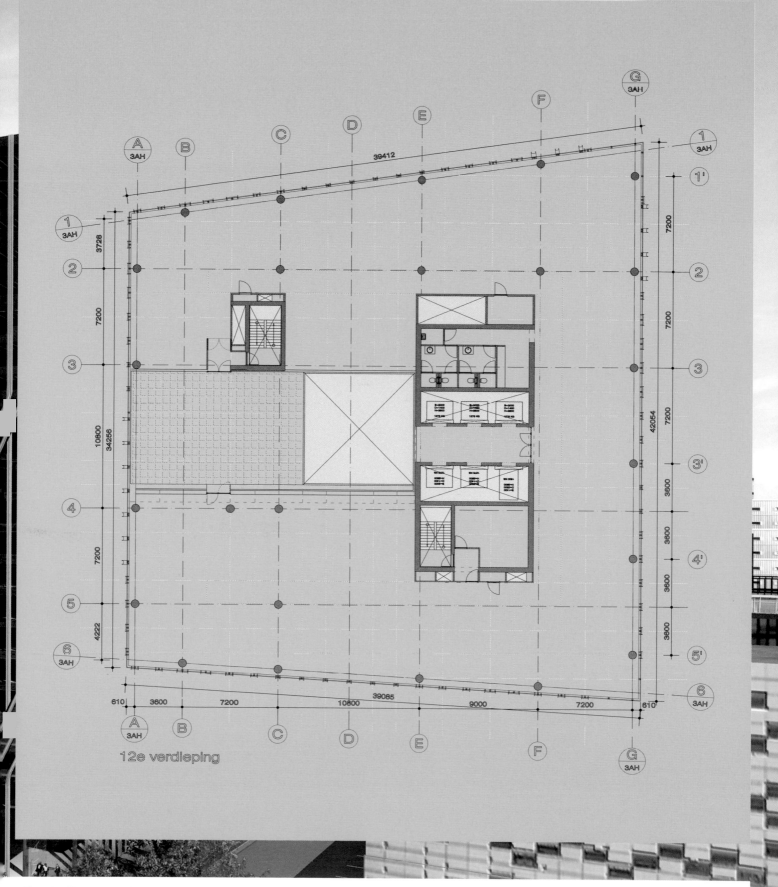

Floor plan illustrating the façade rhythm.

The fins pull back like curtains, opening up the corner of the building to indicate the entrance location.

Mahler 4 Tower, Amsterdam

Vertical fins are narrower at ground floor level, creating a light and transparent
ground floor.

Sum, Gispen International BV
The cubicle explodes
2004

Dutch design firm Gispen is well known for its early twentieth-century tubular steel furniture, but today its primary concern is to produce and sell contemporary designs for the office. By commissioning a future-orientated workplace from UN Studio, the company is bridging the gap between its two identities.

The Gispen Sum workstation embodies flexibility in a new, user-generated way. The three semicircular blades, positioned at different heights, stimulate the user to work in different positions; standing, sitting at normal desk-height, and hunkering down informally. The curved forms also encourage conferring on equal terms. The object as a whole invites the user to occupy the space around the unit by moving and changing working positions frequently during the day. The passive comfort and spatial restriction of traditional office furniture, therefore, is replaced by active comfort and increased spatial freedom.

The unit is executed in cast aluminium with wood-veneer table blades, and can be used either as a stand-alone piece, or linked with others to form a group. The prototype was exhibited at Living Tomorrow (see p. 164), in Amsterdam.

Positive note 3 Innovation exists! You just have to accept that today innovation is impossible on your own. Real, significant innovation occurs when several people **simultaneously** have the same idea and move in the same direction, following **subliminally emitted** and **received signals**. The contemporary inclination to see innovation as an inherently collaborative effort, a communal **growing** and **groping** towards the new, appears to find confirmation throughout history, from the Renaissance, to **Picasso** and Braque, to the radical architecture groups of the 1960s and 1970s. So we experiment by working with others, including other architects. What do we have to lose? Instead of being afraid of **losing our identity**, perhaps we should be glad. Let's liberate ourselves from our brands.

Positive note 4 Architects age really well. There is no need to get bored. Once you have **articulated what fascinates you**, the years fly by, expanding upon a theme. Like philosophers, some of whose best friends have been **dead for over 2,000 years**, architects feel at home in history.

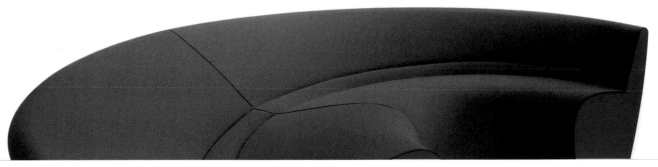

Sofa Circle, Walter Knoll
Posture perfect
2005

This seating system-in-the-round consists of up to four sections, which, when slotted together, form a circle. While the height of the backrest is constant, the width of the seat shifts between that of a chaise-longue to a conventional chair. As a result, different kinds of sitting positions are possible, from a relaxed slouch to a more formal posture.

The sections can be arranged in various ways, generating an extensive range of spatial, seating and orientation options. The circular arrangement, a contemporary variant of the 1970s conversation pit, creates a closed space for intimate communication or concentration.

Sofa Circle was designed in collaboration with Stichting Zetel and German furniture brand Walter Knoll, with the lobby of the Mercedes-Benz Museum (see p. 184) in mind. It was first exhibited at the Salone Internazionale del Mobile 2005, in Milan.

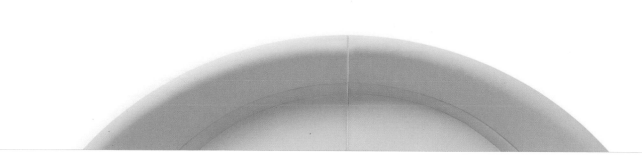

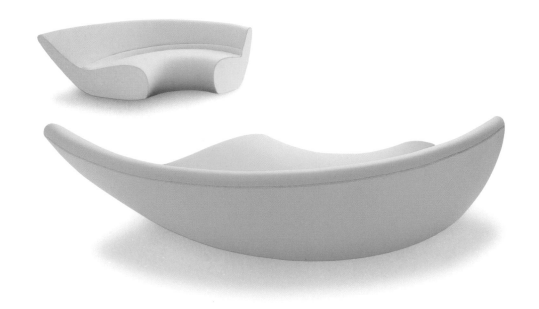

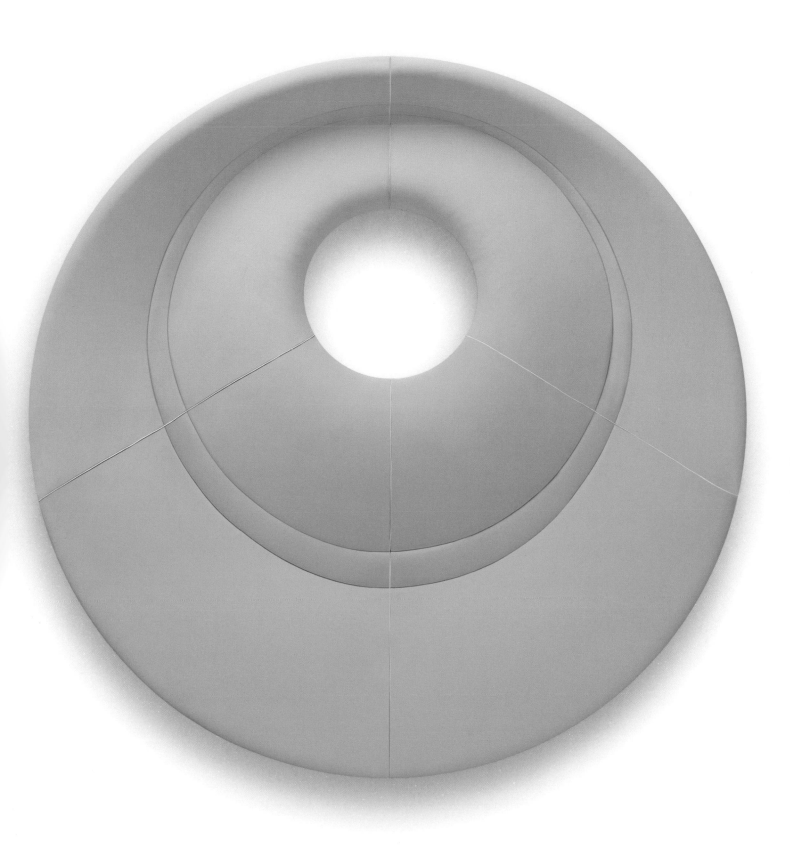

Schirn Kunsthalle, Frankfurt
Summer of love
2005

The Schirn Kunsthalle poses a special challenge to the exhibition designer, being 70 metres (230 ft) long and 10 metres (33 ft) wide, with a circular atrium at the end. Thinking up ways to break up the linearity of the space has resulted in two very different exhibition layouts. An earlier design, consisting of a suspended construction in purple for the architectural show 'Visions and Utopias', darkened the space to focus attention on the finely detailed work, whereas 'Summer of Love' (shown here) achieves the opposite effect.

The exhibition of psychedelic art from the 1960s and 1970s, consisting of 350 widely differing items from the fields of painting, sculpture, photography, film, environment, architecture, graphic design and fashion, capitalizes on the strong visual impact of the works. Two abstracted and stretched-out spirals intertwine, generating interstitial spaces into which installations and larger-sized works are placed. The entire construction has been painted silver as an homage to the spirit of the time.

Mathematical model

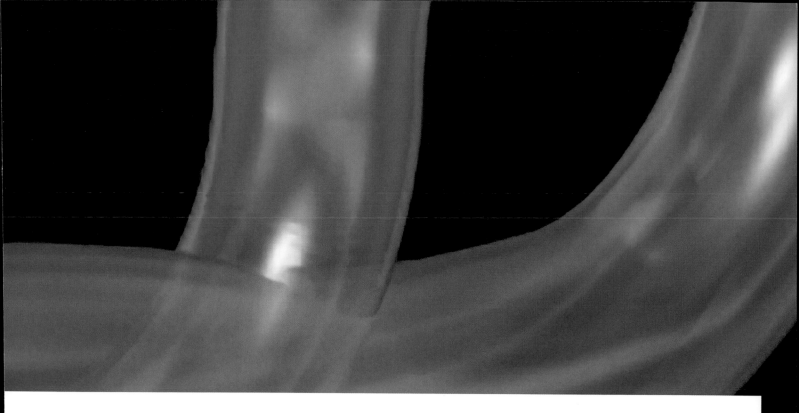

Mathematical model

The introduction of the mathematical figure as a diagram, like the other design models, has a long history; design models evolve by working in series. The Möbius House (see p. 150) was based on a transformative interpretation of the Möbius strip. The Klein bottle, its three-dimensional variant, later became an important model that helped us to implement organizations dealing with large influxes of people moving around a system (Arnhem Central; see p. 272). The most recent evolution in this series is the design model of the double-helix that forms the basis of the Mercedes-Benz Museum (see p. 184).

But, in fact, an earlier history can be found, going as far back as our first realized works, or even to student projects, in which the interplay between lines or between line and curve, has set in motion a development that continues to this day. This development takes a geometric figure, and, in opposition to the modernist equation of mathematics and structure, reads and translates the mathematical model in different dimensions and directions; as construction, landscape, detail, routing, light, material, spatiality and atmosphere.

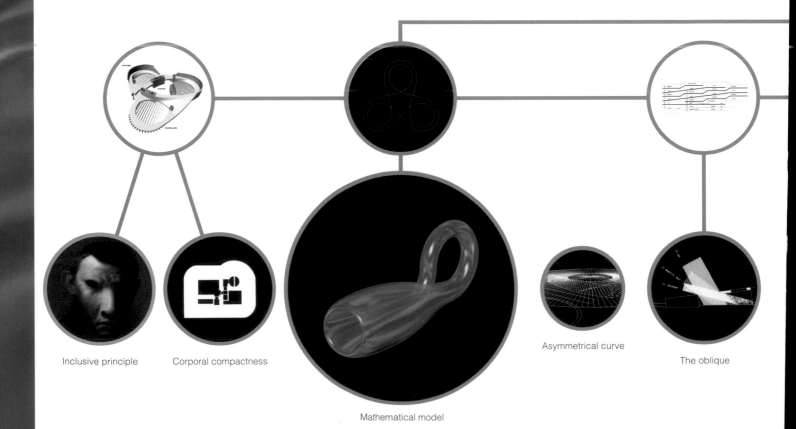

Inclusive principle

Corporal compactness

Asymmetrical curve

The oblique

Mathematical model

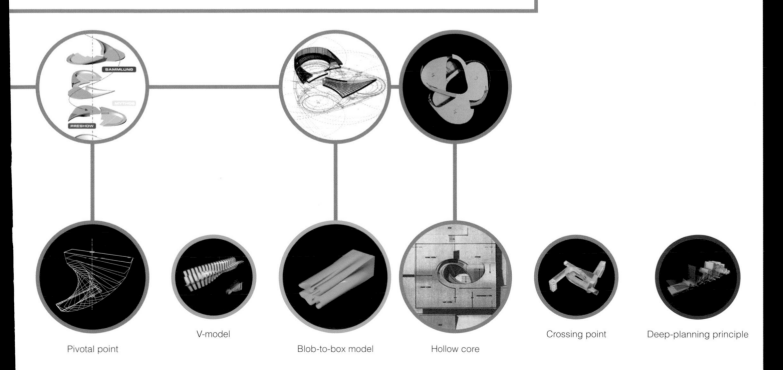

Unit-based additive grid

Linear disconnected element

Endless loop

Geometry-based continuity

Pivotal point

V-model

Blob-to-box model

Hollow core

Crossing point

Deep-planning principle

Erasmus Bridge, Rotterdam
Enigmatic signifier
1990–1996

The bridge is the product of an integrated design approach, as well as a lot of struggle and strife. Construction, urbanism, infrastructure and public functions are given shape in one comprehensive, albeit complex, gesture. The local and national success of the bridge derives, we believe, from its quality as an unknowable emblem. During the preliminary stages, the design was continuously refined, although its main outline and features remained constant. The railings, landings, maintenance equipment, and five differently shaped concrete piers, as well as details of the fixtures and joints, were all integrally designed.

Rising to a height of 139 metres (465 ft), and extending to a breadth of 800 metres (2,625 ft), the bridge over the River Maas forms an orientation point within the city. The asymmetric pylon, with its bracket construction in sky-coloured steel, can appear as thin as a needle or as 'wide as a harp', a phrase which became one of the bridge's nicknames. The long diagonal cables link Rotterdam South, both physically and metaphorically, to the city centre. Thirty-two stays attached to the top of the pylon and eight backstays keep the construction in balance. The five piers carry the steel deck, which is divided into different traffic lanes: two footpaths, two cycle tracks, tram rails, and two carriageways for cars.

Sweeping concrete staircases lead up from the parking garage on the north side, both extending the curve of the landing to pedestrian level and contributing to the appearance of the bridge as a square in the sky. At night, when the bridge is reduced to a silhouette, a special light project emphasizes the interior of the bridge, with its bundled cables rising high above the water as a dematerialized reflection of its daytime identity.

Erasmus Bridge, Rotterdam **141**

Villa Wilbrink, Amersfoort
An almost holiday home
1992–1994

It is all about the light; light in this case that enters the middle of the house from the hidden patio, both because the owners require lots of it and because they prefer the privacy and tranquillity of a courtyard.

The house is extremely private; there are no façades and no gardens (although the neighbours have crept in, planting conifers next to the grey railway gravel covering the leftover space at the back of the house). It is located in a suburb where the streets bear the names of famous Modernist architects, but our choice to make the frontage disappear was not inspired by irony. Would you make clients live with your sense of humour?

The features that dictated the design and that now distinguish the appearance of this unassuming family house are the diagonal lines that make the building invisible from the street, the glued bricks that render the walls as smooth as concrete, and the light-filled interior patio that gives the house a year-round, holiday home feeling.

Positive note 5a

Thank God that architecture is not art. Do architects kill themselves, cut off body parts, and imbibe dramatic quantities of dangerous substances? On the whole not (see positive note 4). Architects suffer less from self-imposed restrictions and instructions than artists. Of course architects labour under the same yoke as anyone else; they, too, must seek to produce work that is innovative, reflective and relevant to all that seems to be innovative, reflective and relevant in the present time, but that continuous mirror does not have the same crushing effect that it has on art. Because outside the frame of the artistic looking glass, the architect faces the client and engages with questions of utility, economy and construction. The fact that the architectural search for form is invested with so many questions and demands makes it easy. Architecture today is the 'lighter' art; fine art has become a bit heavy since it has been pronounced dead so often.

Positive note 5b

Thank God that architecture is art. Or is at least halfway art, located between art and airports. The airport, or network of airports, is the most extreme example of architecture as the accumulation of capitalist logistics. It is a portal, a business, a science-fiction fantasy, an escalation of short-lived consumption, a unique system that has some of the characteristics of a city, but which is also a high-risk disaster site, a place where incredible densities of people collect and where we experience strong emotions of fear, loss and elation. The relationship between architecture and the airport is obvious. But what about art? Today, poetic notions of the ideal city are useless in view of the highly specific systems that work within a global economy. Taking a new look at the convergence of spatial and socio-economic structures raises specific questions. What are the spatial and structural characteristics of our intensified systems of production and consumption? How can we envisage these systems to change the living and working environment? We need to develop a specifically architectural perspective on these new urban conditions, using information from sociological, economic and geographical sources, as well as ways of seeing inherent in the architectural discipline itself. But even as we collect, manipulate and present information, we realize the insufficiency of our diligent, and hopefully imaginative, tracing of movement patterns and user groups, and the various virtual and infrastructural ways in which we distribute ourselves across the globe. For what does it all mean? These numbers tell us too little about the motives triggering these patterns, or about the effects of these structures and constellations. We end up sculpting the statistics, painting with information in bold, brutal brushstrokes or refined minimalist gestures, just like any old artist.

Möbius House, Het Gooi
Living as continuous difference
1993–1998

The Möbius house integrates programme, circulation and structure seamlessly. The house, a private commission, interweaves different activities into one building; work, social life, family life and individual time all find their place in the loop composition. Movement through this loop follows the pattern of an active day. The Möbius strip is not used with mathematical rigour, but is instead interpreted as a diagram upon which such architectural ingredients as light, space, materials, time and movement find an organizational structure.

The diagram of the double-locked torus conveys the arrangement of two intertwining pathways, which trace the progress of two people living together yet apart, meeting at certain points that become shared spaces. Formally, the spatial interplay of the interior creates a virtual cross, dividing the house into four loosely defined quadrants. This cross generates a balanced composition that is further enhanced by the placement of programmatic elements. The upper and lower studies, for example, are complemented by the upper and lower bedrooms.

The idea of two entities running along their own trajectories, but sharing certain moments, is extended to include the materialization of the building and its construction. The structure of movement is transposed to the organization of the two main materials used in the house's construction, glass and concrete; concrete construction becomes furniture, and glass façades turn into partition walls. Taking full advantage of its location, the house unfolds horizontally, allowing the occupants to take in the surroundings during their daily activities.

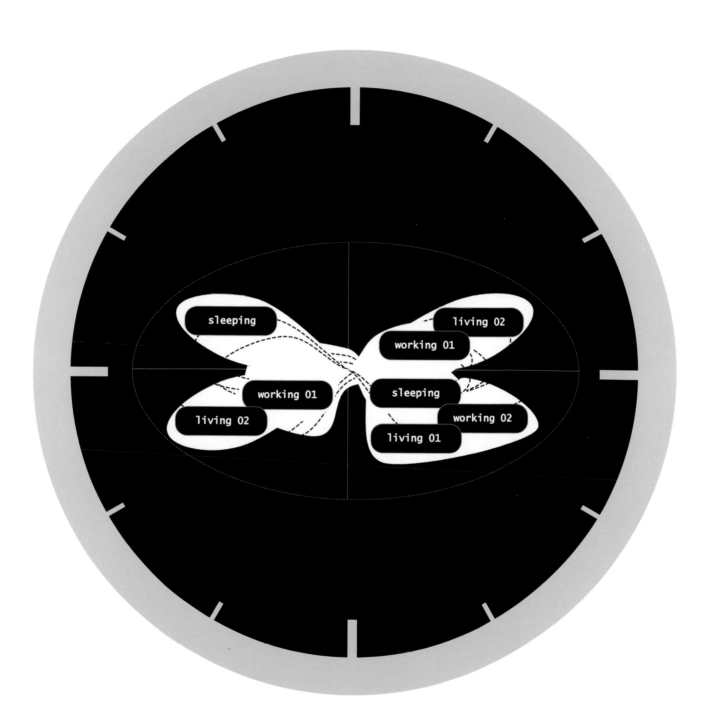

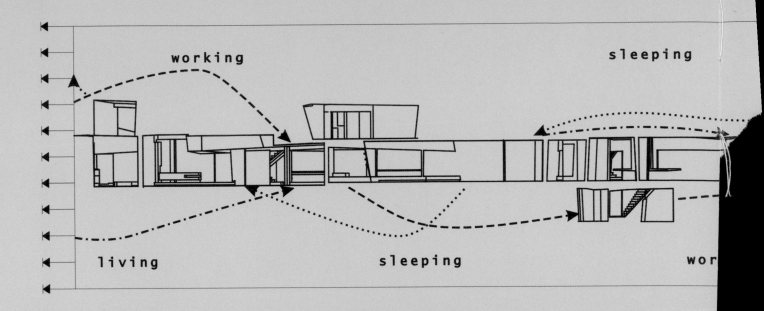

working

sleeping

living

sleeping

wor

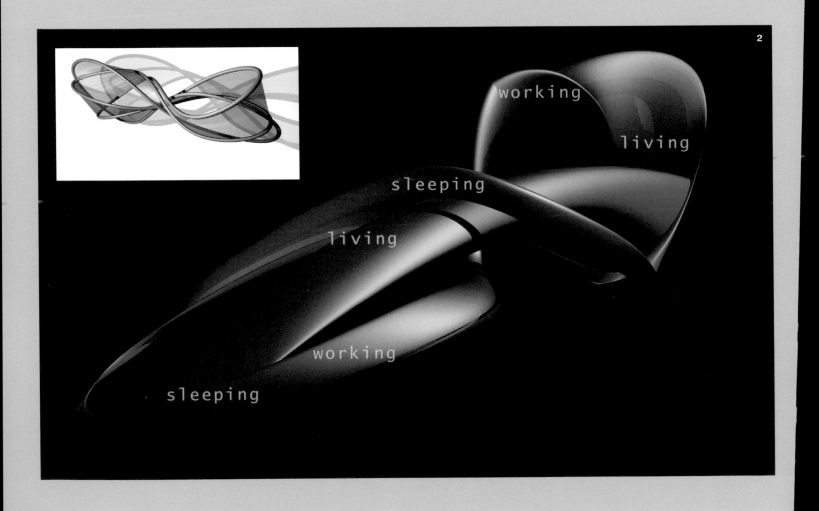

working

living

sleeping

living

working

sleeping

1 The unfolded drawing describes the various living patterns within the loop-like structure of the house.

2 A virtual cross divides the house into four loosely defined quadrants.

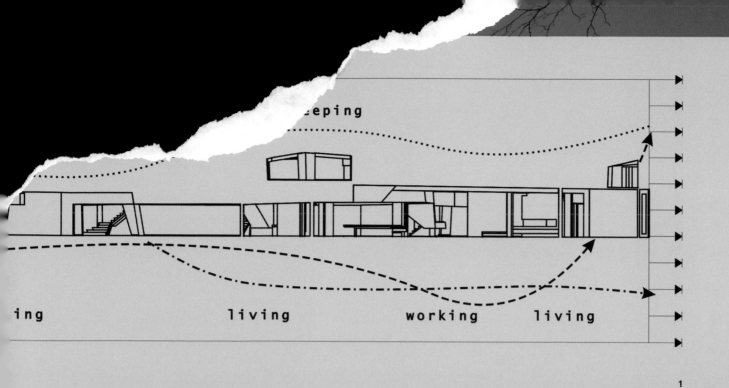

eeping

living   working   living

ing

1

3

3 The model explores the interplay between the two primary materials, glass and concrete.

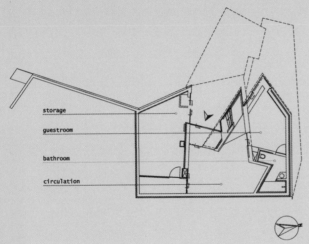

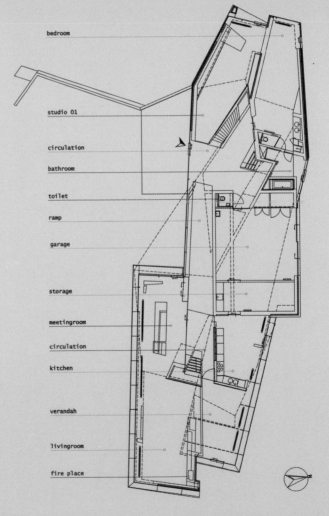

storage
guestroom
bathroom
circulation

bedroom

studio 01

circulation

bathroom

toilet

ramp

garage

storage

meetingroom

circulation

kitchen

verandah

livingroom

fire place

Inclusiveness: the concrete table and fireplace are part of the construction,
whereas the floor plans express the interlocking of spaces and surfaces.

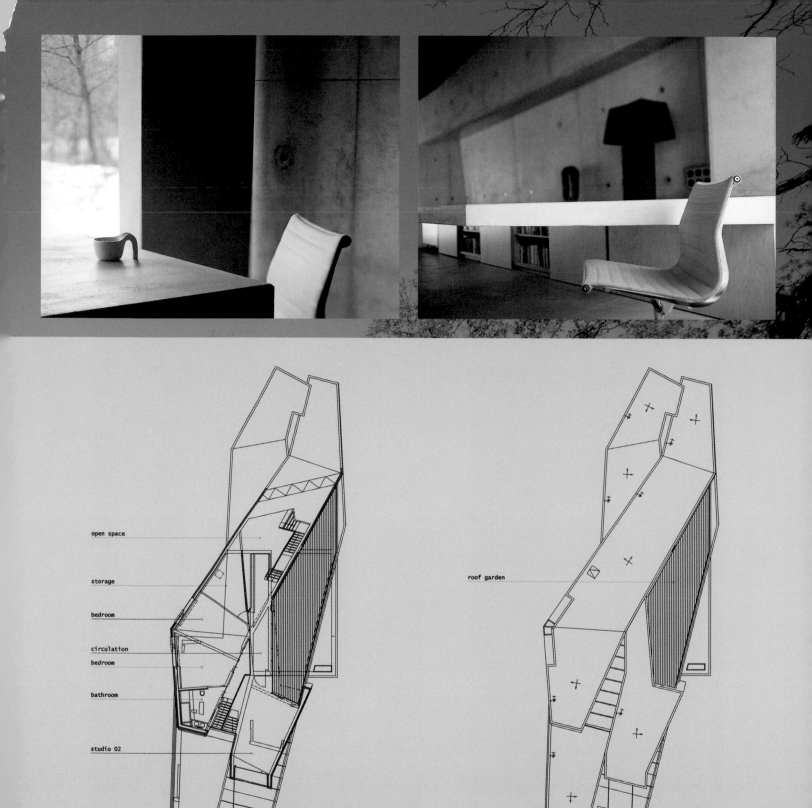

open space

storage

bedroom

circulation
bedroom

bathroom

studio 02

roof garden

After image: views of the surroundings and movement through the space generate
perceptual mobility.

Kaleidoscopic effects of the interior: transformative geometry has allowed
construction, routing and programme to come together to create different
focal points and multiple perspectives.

The dune landscape with its mature trees creates natural variations in height.

Living Tomorrow, Amsterdam
Klein bottle from horizontal to vertical
2000–2003

'Living Tomorrow' is a temporary pavilion, with an intended life span of five years, that was created to showcase concepts for the House – and Office – of the Future. Crouched between giant corporate headquarters, the pavilion resembles a toy robot executed in lilac metal.

The Klein-bottle model was the crux of the design. The fluidity of the volumes can be directly attributed to this design concept, which sinuously stitches the inside and outside spaces together by folding surfaces back upon themselves. The inclusive principle lends itself well to the internal spatial planning, connecting skylight to atrium, and atrium to entrance lobby, in which the transmutation of the internal walls into external skin completes the circuit. Within the volume, visitor circulation patterns were carefully orchestrated, both in relation to the performance envelope and to allow for simultaneous permutation of the various user groups without causing congestion.

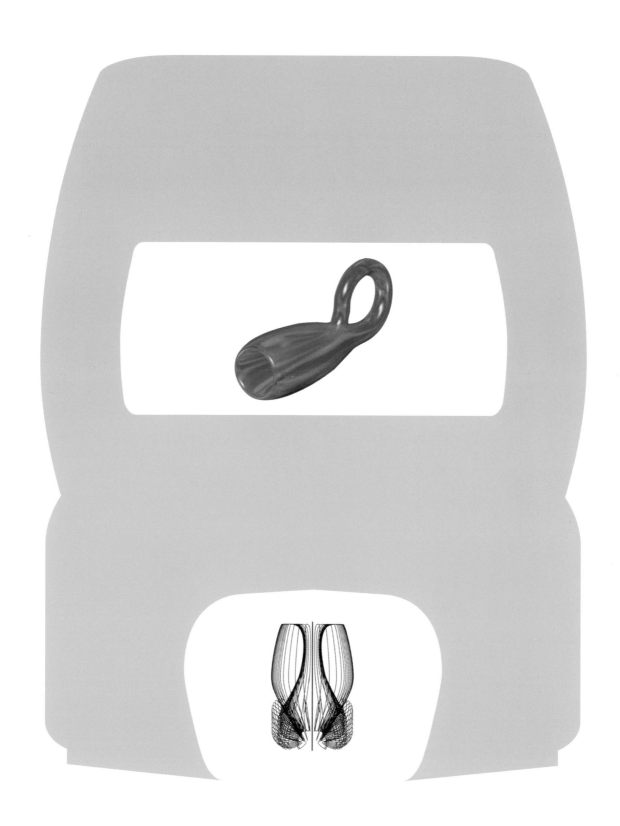

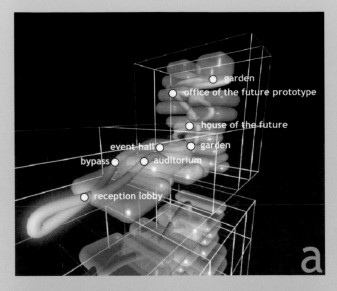

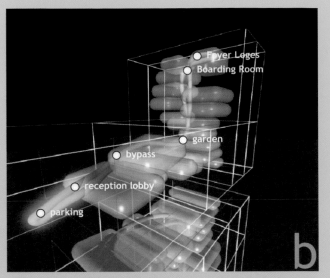

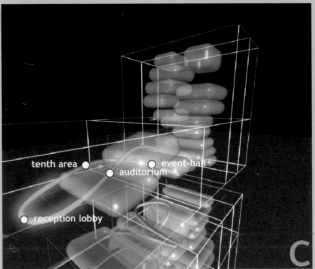

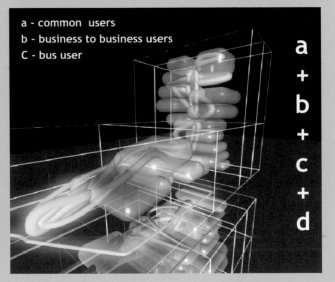

a - common users
b - business to business users
C - bus user

1

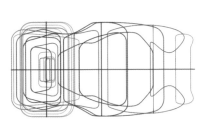

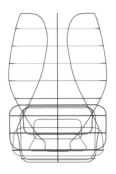

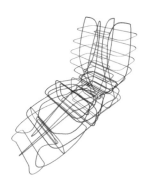

2

1 Different user groups are dispersed across the building through a variety of circulatory patterns.

2 Wire-frame diagrams of the building surfaces.

01 vertical in

02 horizontal in

03 horizontal out

04 vertical in

1

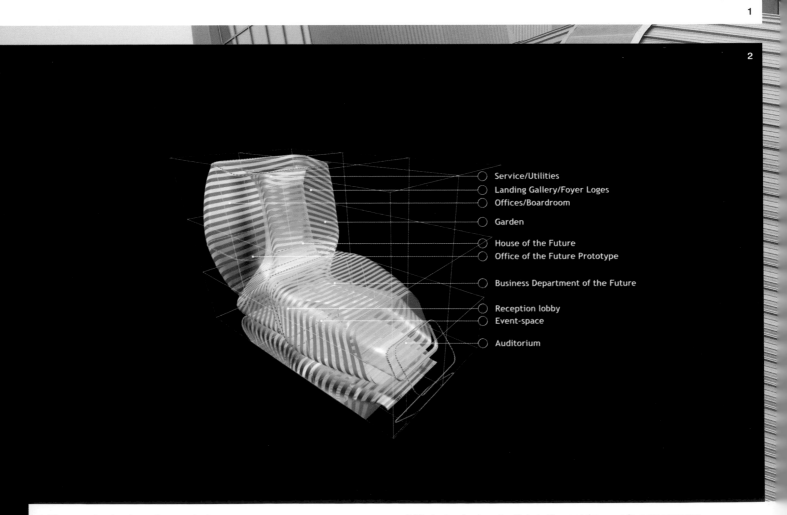

2

- Service/Utilities
- Landing Gallery/Foyer Loges
- Offices/Boardroom
- Garden
- House of the Future
- Office of the Future Prototype
- Business Department of the Future
- Reception lobby
- Event-space
- Auditorium

1 Diagrams showing the surface continuity.

2 Study showing how the Klein bottle can take up various programmes.

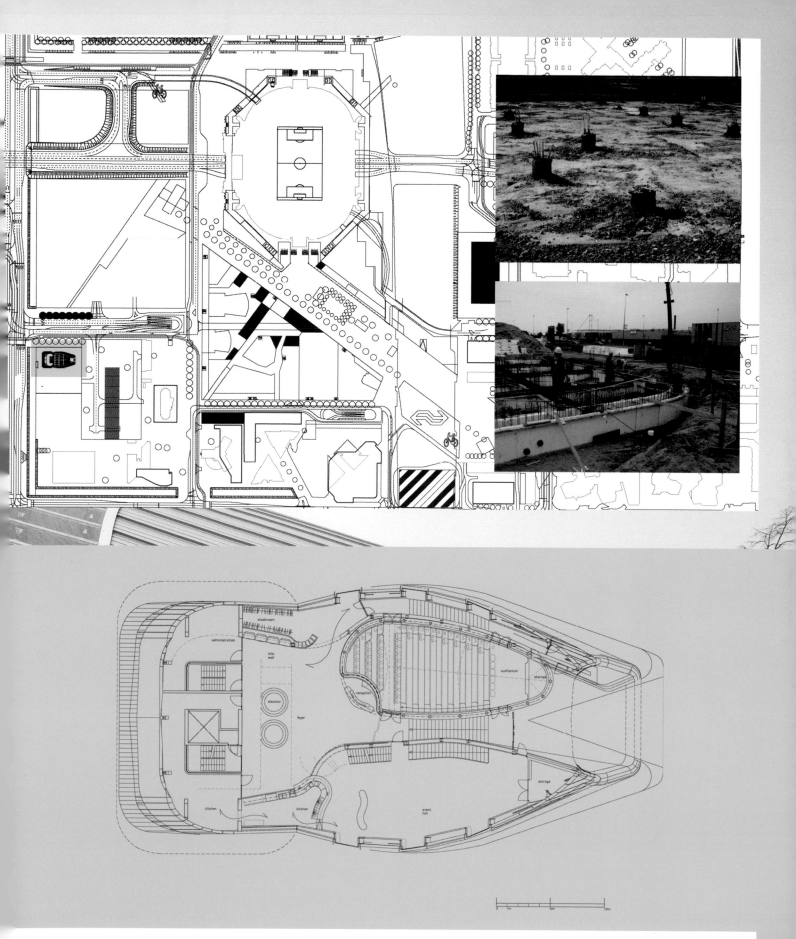

Located in close proximity to the stadium is a new business district; the temporary pavilion occupies a small lot.

The ground floor includes the entrance, atrium, auditorium, café, reception and lifts, with circulation contained in the flipped-over wall surface next to the auditorium.

Tea & Coffee Towers, Alessi
Nested flagons
2001

Silver on silver, super-shiny and not cheap: tea and coffee Alessi style is about reinventing the familiar in a new, must-have way. As an encore to the successful 'Tea and Coffee Piazza' project of 1983, the Italian design house asked twenty-two contemporary architects to participate in an industrial design project, with the aim of creating functional tea and coffee sets.

In our design, the individual containers for tea, coffee, milk and sugar recline in the hollows of a landscaped tray, their low and oblong dimensions contrasting with the conventional upright form of a jug. The sunken handles and internal spouts give the pots and bowls the appearance of smooth stones that interact with the tray like pebbles in a river; separate elements which together form a new unity.

The four containers are all based on the principle of the Klein bottle, although each has been individually transformed according to its specific requirements. Multiple prototypes were made to test proportion, functionality and ergonomic potential. The coffee pot, distinguished from the teapot by its fish-like mouth, has been the catalyst for the design. It is a pot for the ritualistic presentation of coffee: a flat, iron-like flagon made from a continuous surface that flips over from outside to inside, and fluently metamorphoses from inner surface into spout, outer surface into handle. The continuous surface of the coffee pot combines all functions, and the integrated handle allows for natural and controlled pouring. The smaller milk jug and sugar bowl are ergonomically shaped to fit into the hand, enabling the contents to be tipped out without the aid of teaspoons or tongs.

Built-in flexibility in the tray design allows for stability of the pots and bowls, as well as accommodating other objects, from biscuits to house keys. The mirroring quality of the material instantaneously registers the surrounding room, while the reflections add the appearance of liquidity as they dance across the surface.

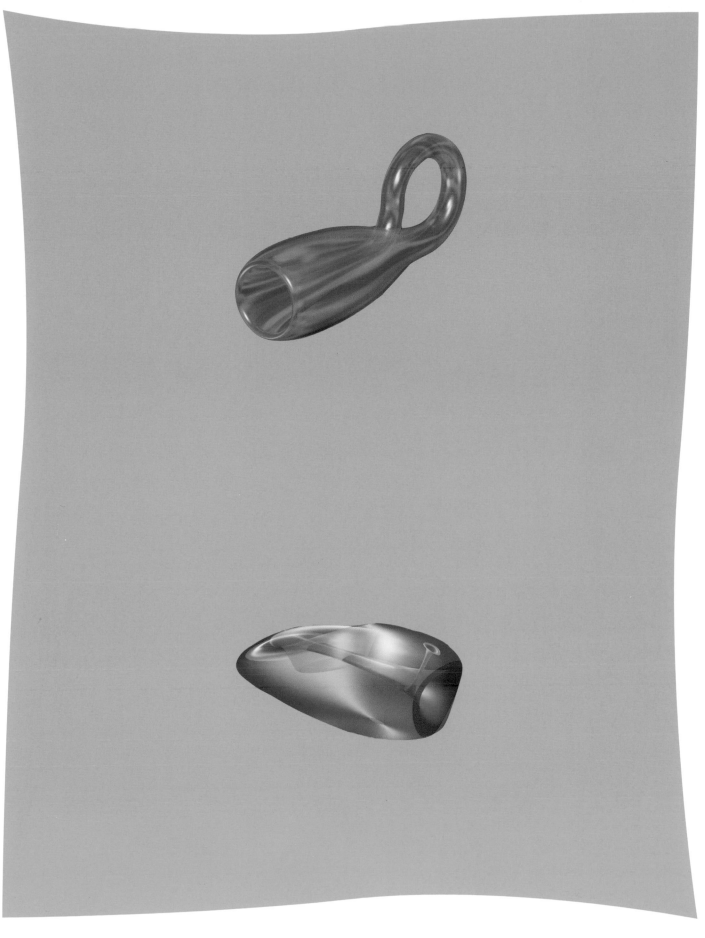

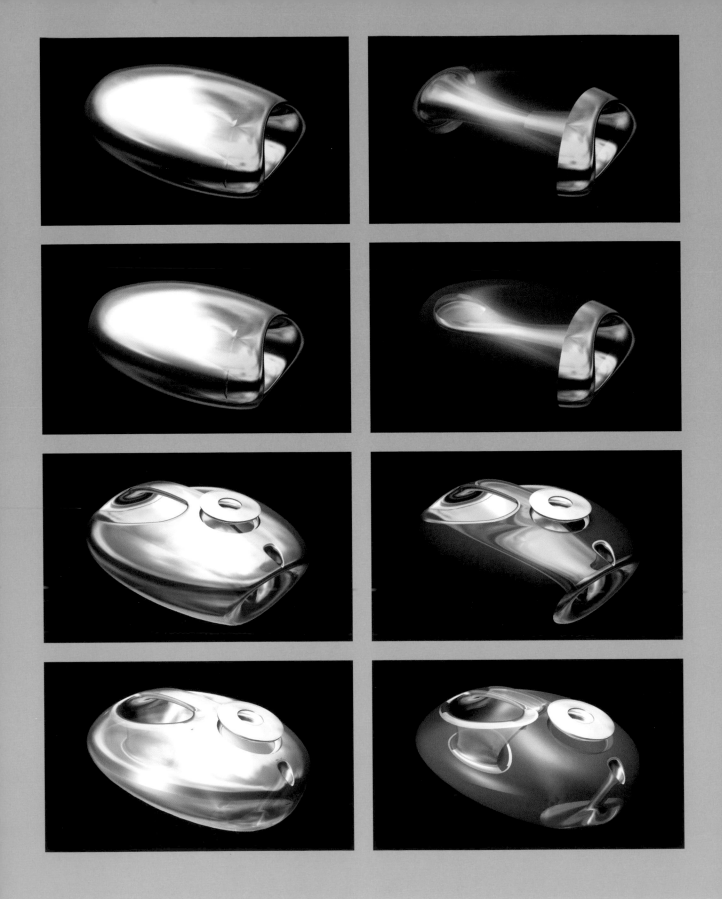

The inner and outer surfaces of the pots and bowls flow continually into one another.

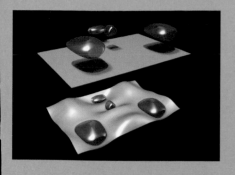
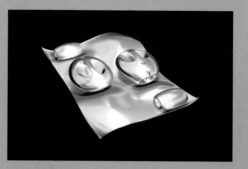
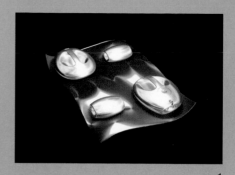

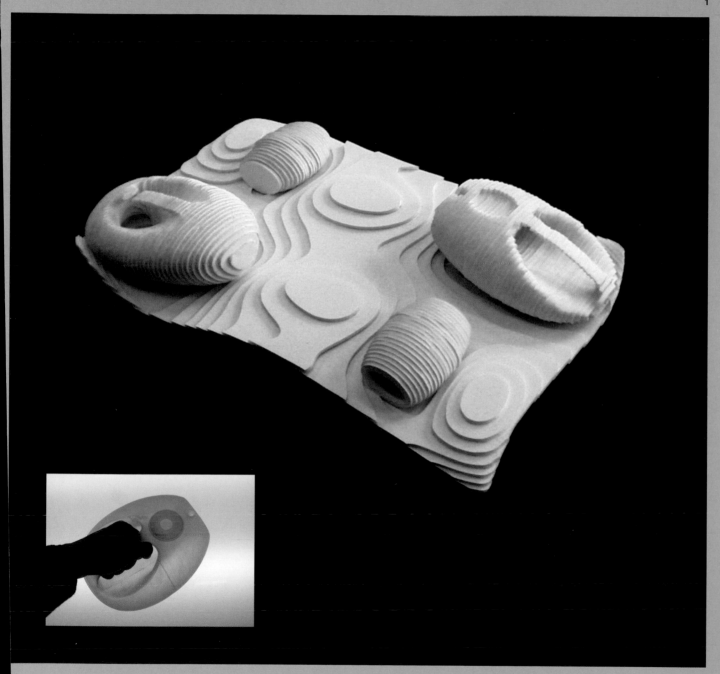

1 Renderings illustrate the variation potential of the containers on the landscaped tray. By reversing the tray, the objects recline in different hollows of the contours.

2 Prototypes made from foam board examine proportion, ergonomic qualities and pouring potential.

Reflections of the objects combine with reflections of the surroundings, animating the collection. A layer of coloured plastic on the tray causes the objects to appear to float.

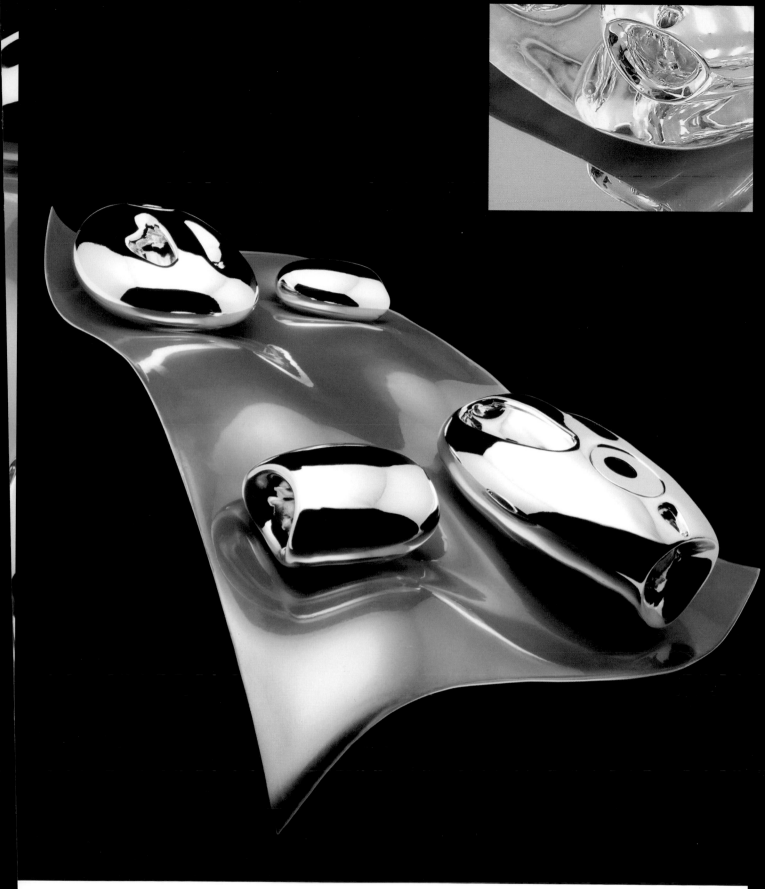

The distortions caused by the overlaying reflections of the silver surface add to the
dynamics of the tray's design.

Positive note 6 Not that everyone loves our work, but the good thing about producing a building is that people keep interacting with it for a long time, much more so than with a new film or novel. But then they have to, don't they? They may moan about the awful environment that contemporary architecture (or the building industry?) has created, but they can't ignore it, and none of us can step outside it, except by removing our lives completely from the 'giant department store' and sacrificing all that exists within that sphere. The product of architecture can at least be partly understood as an endless live performance. The project transforms, becomes abstracted, concentrated and expanded, diverse and ever more scale-less, all of which happens in interaction with a massive live audience. Today, more than ever, we feel that the specificity of architecture is not itself **contained** in any aspect of **the object**. The true nature of architecture is found in the interaction between **the architect, the project** and **the public**. The generative, proliferating, unfolding effect of architecture continues beyond its development in the design studio, and into its subsequent public use.

Mercedes-Benz Museum, Stuttgart
Trefoil organization
2001–2006

The new museum, located next to the Daimler-Chrysler Stuttgart plant, has been designed to exhibit the company's ever-growing collection. A synthesis of structural and programmatic organizations, the building's geometry responds to the car-driven context of the museum.

The geometric model of three overlapping circles is stretched three-dimensionally, becoming spatial and thus able to accommodate programme and movement. The transformative potential of the model is exploited as line turns into loop, surface, and, finally, volume. The design is accommodated in an intricate package, in which the various exhibits and public services are interwoven. Shifts in the floor levels challenge the symmetry of the trefoil plan in section. The leaves of the trefoil rotate around a triangular void, forming horizontal plateaus which alternately occupy single- and double-floor heights.

Visitors enter the building from the northwest corner of the raised platform that elevates the building, and are then introduced to the organizational system of the museum, which distributes two types of exhibitions over three leaves, connected to a central stem in the form of an atrium. The lobby's escalator leads down to ground level, and three lifts take visitors up to the top of the building.

The museum experience begins on the top floor. From here, visitors may descend via one of two ramps; the first chain-linking the collection of cars and trucks, and the second connecting the 'legends' rooms, secondary displays related to the history of Mercedes-Benz. The two spiralling trajectories cross each other continuously, mimicking the interweaving strands of a double-helix and enabling the visitor to change paths. The downward incline of the trajectories is confined to the ramps at the perimeter of the building; the platforms that function as display areas are level, with the slow gradients of the walkways bridging the height differences. This structure enables a wide range of see-through options, shortcuts, enclosed and open spaces, and the opportunity for cross-referencing and continuity in the various displays.

The collection of automobiles is shown in combination on five platforms. Seven further platforms display the 'legends', or 'Mythen', and the lowest levels house 'Races and Records' and 'The Fascination of Technology'.

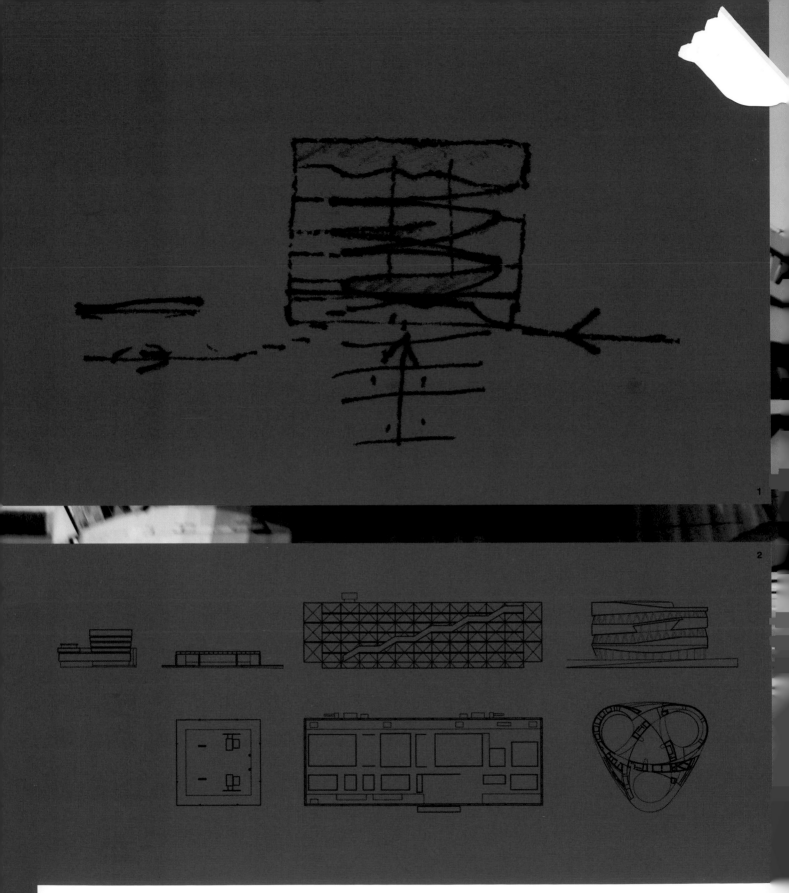

1 Ben's first sketch of the stretched geometric model, made on the back of pantyhose package.

2 Sections and plans of the Guggenheim Museum, the Staatsgalerie and the Centre Pompidou, illustrating the various ways in which visitors circulate. The Mercedes-Benz project incorporates all of these patterns.

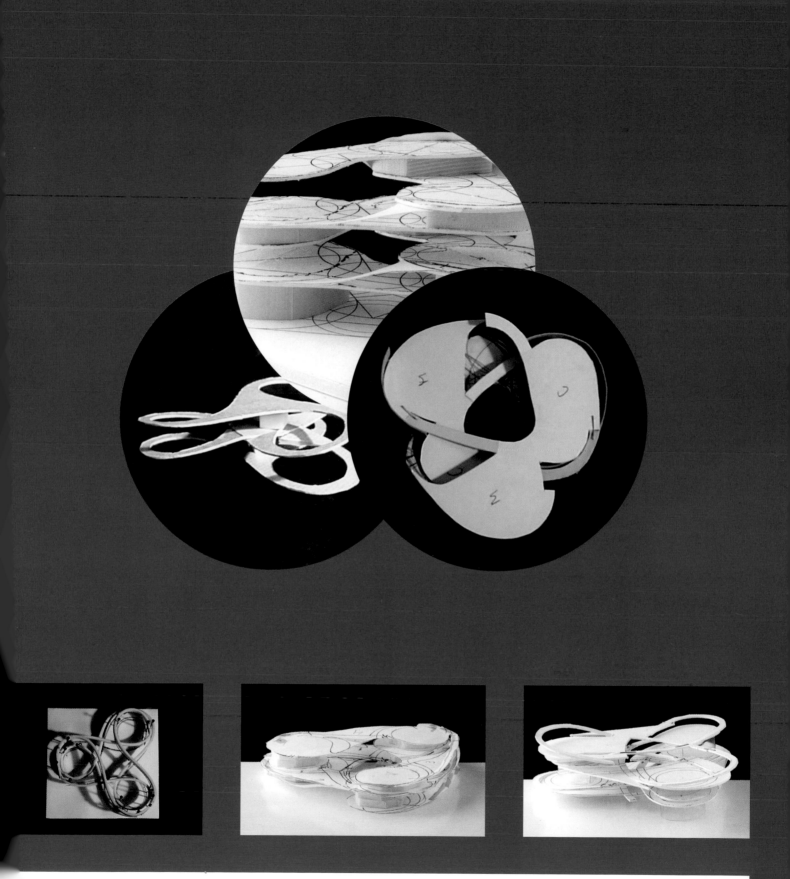

Early sketch models exploring the double-helix circulation.

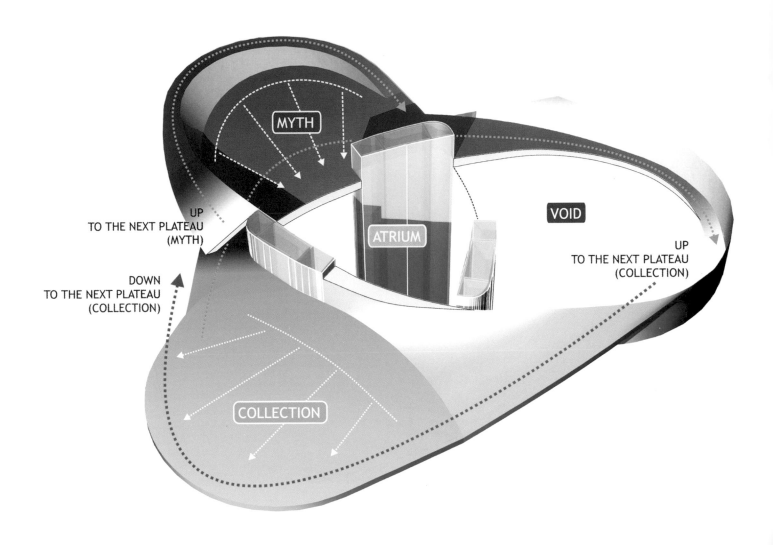

MYTH

VOID

UP
TO THE NEXT PLATEAU
(MYTH)

ATRIUM

UP
TO THE NEXT PLATEAU
(COLLECTION)

DOWN
TO THE NEXT PLATEAU
(COLLECTION)

COLLECTION

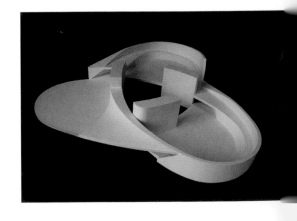

The three-dimensional floor plan shows the intricate package in which the various
exhibits are interwoven and connected.

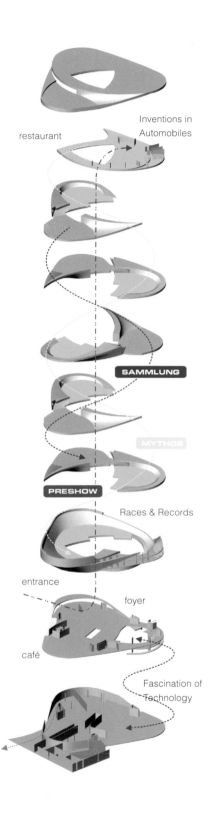

restaurant

Inventions in
Automobiles

SAMMLUNG

MYTHOS

PRESHOW

Races & Records

entrance

foyer

café

Fascination of
Technology

Exploded view of the 7.7-metre (25-ft) double-height 'legends' rooms and
4.5-metre (15-ft) single-height collection rooms, which are intertwined and
connected by two spiralling walkways.

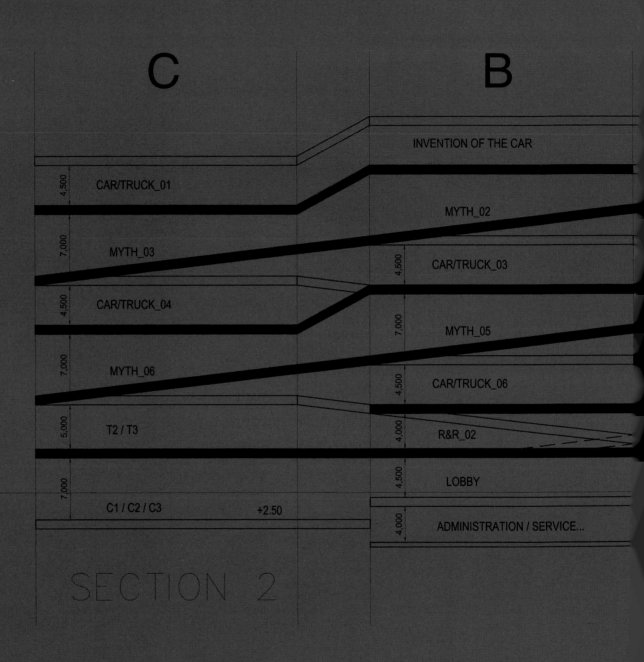

C

B

INVENTION OF THE CAR

CAR/TRUCK_01 — 4.500

MYTH_02

MYTH_03 — 7,000

CAR/TRUCK_03 — 4.500

CAR/TRUCK_04 — 4.500

MYTH_05 — 7,000

MYTH_06 — 7,000

CAR/TRUCK_06 — 4.500

T2 / T3 — 5,000

R&R_02 — 4,000

LOBBY — 4.500

C1 / C2 / C3 — 7,000 — +2.50

ADMINISTRATION / SERVICE... — 4,000

SECTION 2

Unfolded section of the trefoil leaves placed side-by-side to provide an overview of the organizational structure.

Legend:
A: Northwest wing
B: Northeast wing
C: South wing

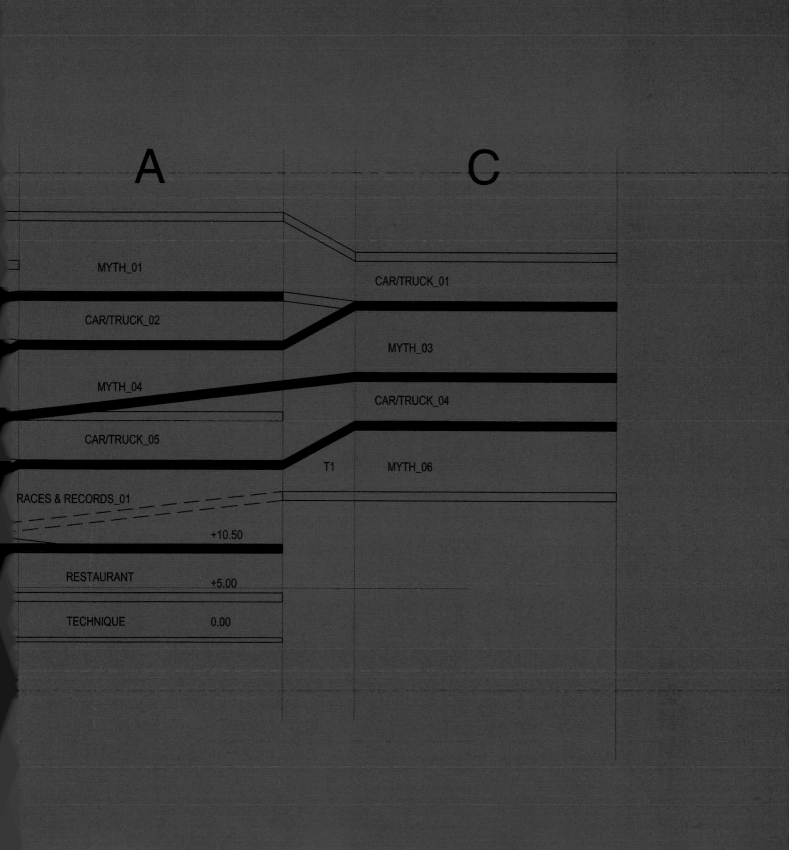

A

C

MYTH_01

CAR/TRUCK_01

CAR/TRUCK_02

MYTH_03

MYTH_04

CAR/TRUCK_04

CAR/TRUCK_05

T1 MYTH_06

RACES & RECORDS_01

+10.50

RESTAURANT +5.00

TECHNIQUE 0.00

The smooth curves of the Mercedes-Benz Museum echo the rounded vernacular
of the nearby industrial- and event-spaces. The metaphor of the car and driving
connects the building to the meandering landscape.

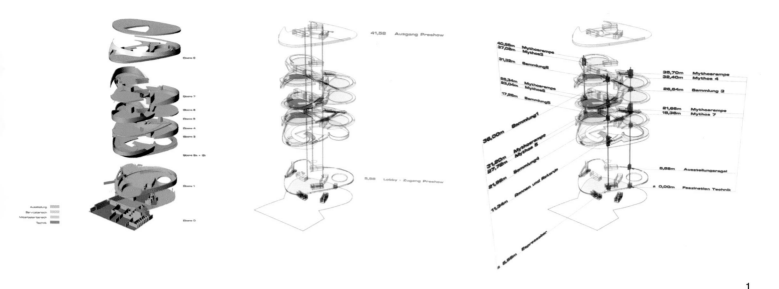

1

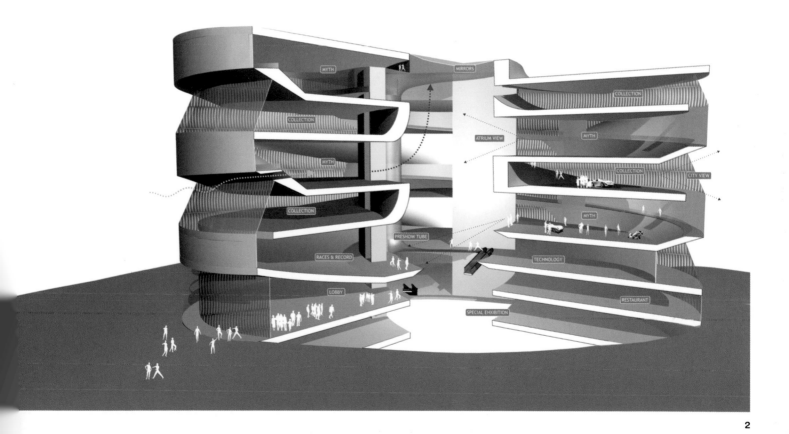

2

1 Schematic diagrams illustrate programme allocation, public access and emergency exits.

2 This sectional drawing highlights the trefoil organization and the role of the 'twist', a 30-metre (98-ft) long double-curved element that connects the collection rooms.

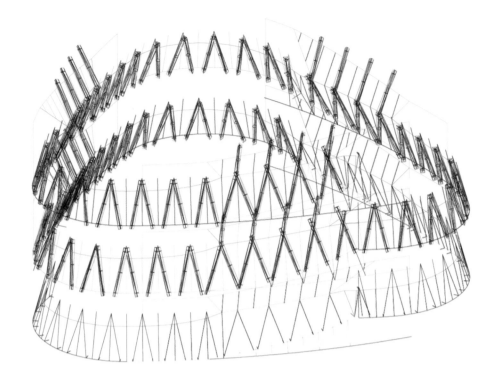

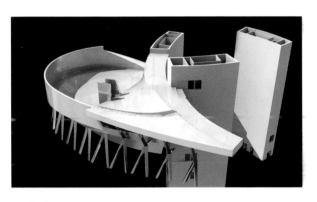 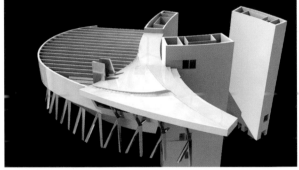

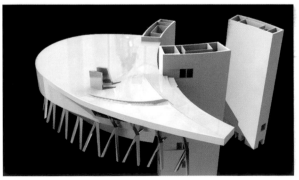 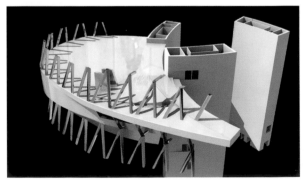

The individually shaped columns form one half of the support structure, while the atrium core forms the other. Just as the floors are continuous, there is also only one enveloping window.

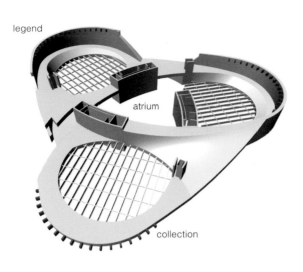

legend

atrium

collection

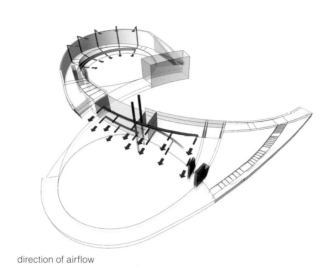

direction of airflow

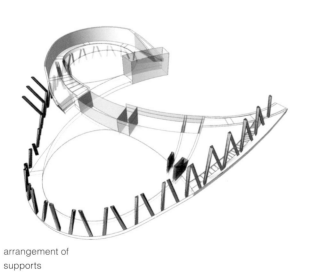

arrangement of
supports

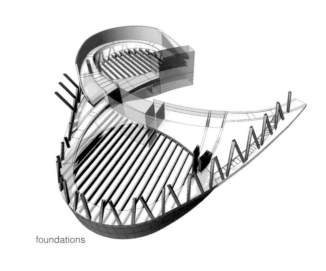

foundations

Diagrams illustrate the integrated construction, ventilation and installations.

1 Model used by H.G. Merz for the exhibition design.

2 Concrete shutterings for the 'legends' ramps were constructed off-site.

Variously scaled models were used to test lighting, display and infrastructure.

Start of construction: 02–11–03.

Highest point: 03–03–05.

Photo taken: 06–06–04.

Opening: 19–05–06.

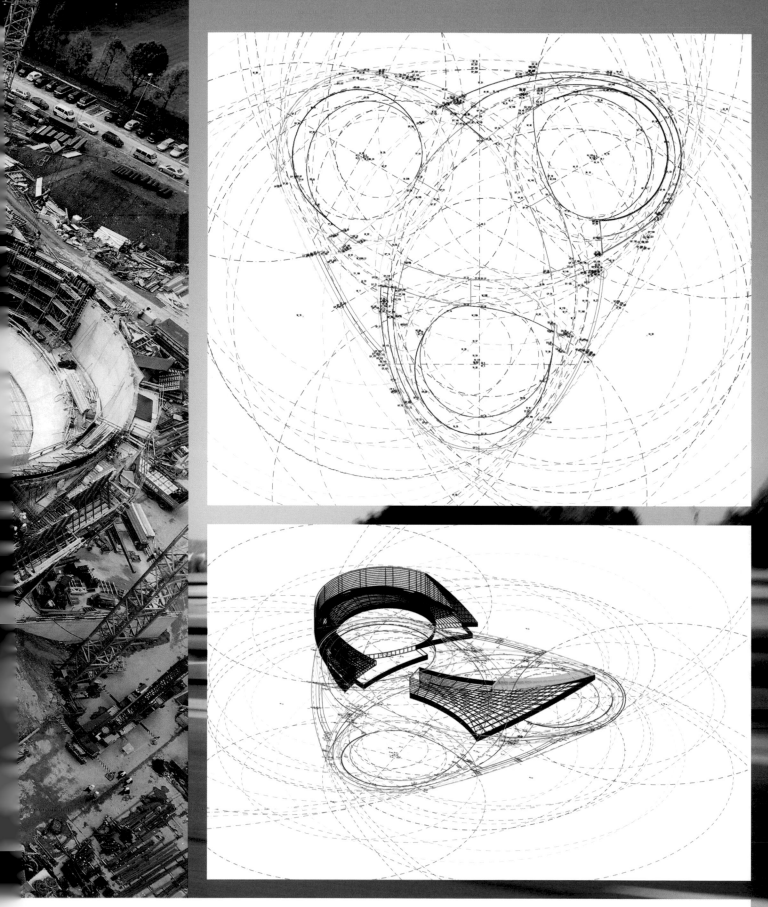

The underlying geometry of the building consists of tangentially interlocked circles and arcs. The system was later programmed with the idea that changes could more easily be carried through, and the geometry of the building controlled.

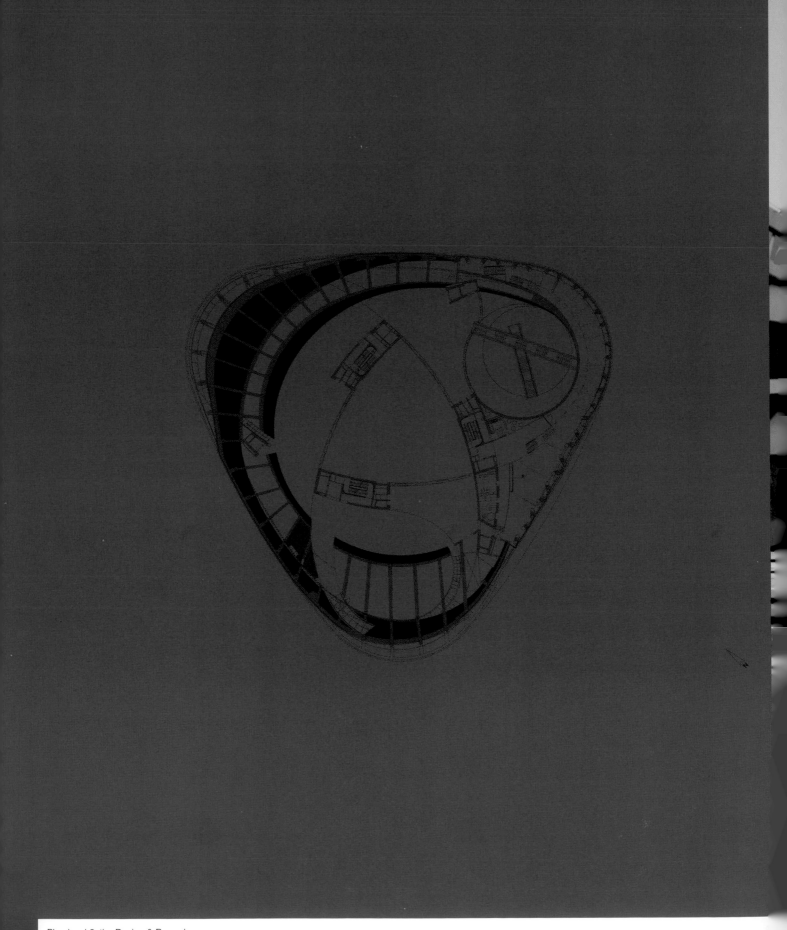

Plan level 2: the Racing & Records room.

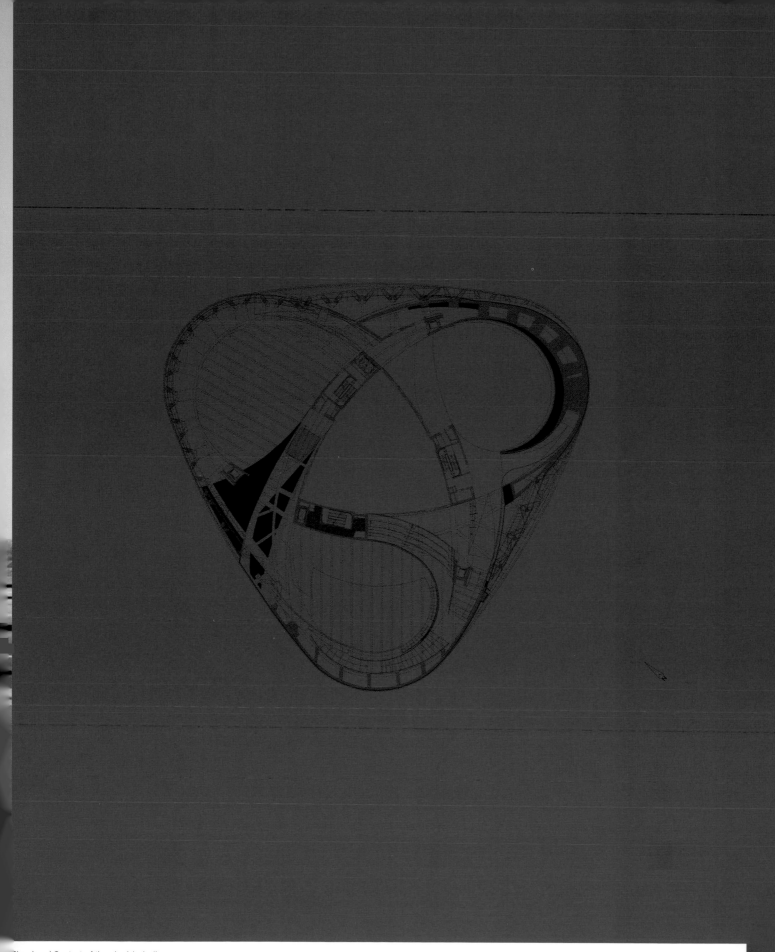

Plan level 3: start of the double-helix.

Above View of the building site, showing the upper façade's steel-covered columns and the concrete columns of the ground-floor façade.

Below Aerial view illustrating the three-dimensional architectural design.

PHASE I

Rohbau im Bau / fertiggestellt

Glasfassade im Bau / fertiggestellt

Technik / Ausbau

Dach
E8
E7
E6
E5
E4
E3
E2
E1
E0

C   B

PHASE II

Rohbau im Bau / fertiggestellt

Glasfassade im Bau / fertiggestellt

Technik / Ausbau

Dach
E8
E7
E6
E5
E4
E3
E2
E1
E0

C   B

PHASE III

Rohbau im Bau / fertiggestellt

Glasfassade im Bau / fertiggestellt

Technik / Ausbau

Dach
E8
E7
E6
E5
E4
E3
E2
E1
E0

C   B

PHASE IV

Rohbau im Bau / fertiggestellt

Glasfassade im Bau / fertiggestellt

Technik / Ausbau

Musealer Ausbau

Dach
E8
E7
E6
E5
E4
E3
E2
E1
E0

B

A 1:1-scale test construction, consisting of one-third of the 'twist' to determine shuttering technology and concrete quality.

Construction phases.

Details of the structural 'twist', displaying the patterns of the shutter drawings.

Battersea Weave Office Building, London
Rotational transformation
2004–2010

Located near Victoria Station, the 'Weave' office building fulfils a linking role within the master plan for the development of the Battersea Power Station site by Ove Arup. The office building is situated along the southwestern perimeter of the location. The presence of the railway line determines the composition of the adjacent façade, incorporating elements for sound and wind screening, while the next layer of facet articulation hints at the unfolding geometry of the rest of the building. The variability of future tenants is taken into account, as the design allows for maximum occupancy flexibility and strategies of identity.

The depth and width of the footprint necessitates the introduction of voids within the building, which enable enough daylight to penetrate deep within the envelope. The slight rotation of the floor plates around a number of pivot points was the strategy based upon a play with geometry deployed to accomplish this. The twisting office wings connect and disconnect floors and building slabs. This new typology generates distinctive voids and vertical connections. The locations of the pivot points are used to facilitate vertical elements, such as lifts and escalators. Structural investigations of an external frame have made column-free office spaces possible. Although the weaving strategy created strong dynamic spaces, the façade grid and office layout are designed in a standard 1.5-metre (5-ft) grid structure.

The building touches down onto the site with exhibition, retail and showcase levels. The soft transition between building and landscape causes a blurring between interior and exterior as landscape elements are pulled into the courtyards and exhibition areas. The interplay between the building and the rest of the site continues with the weaving of media technologies across the internal façades, animating the main square and furthering the building-site dialogue.

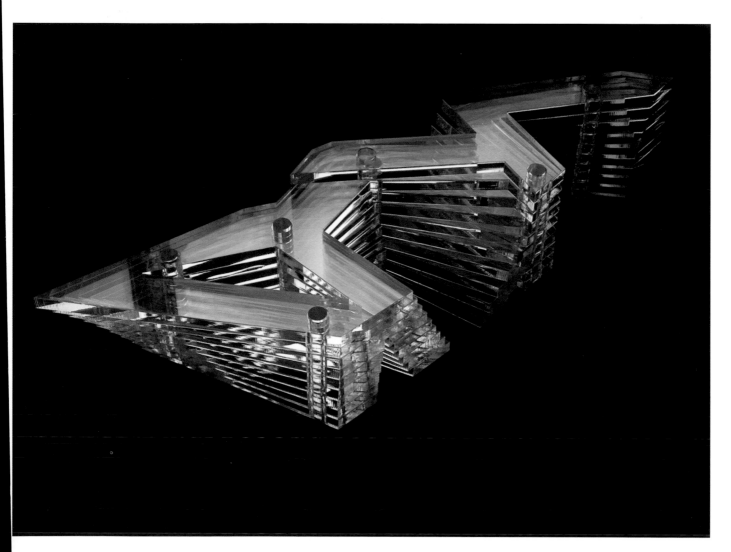

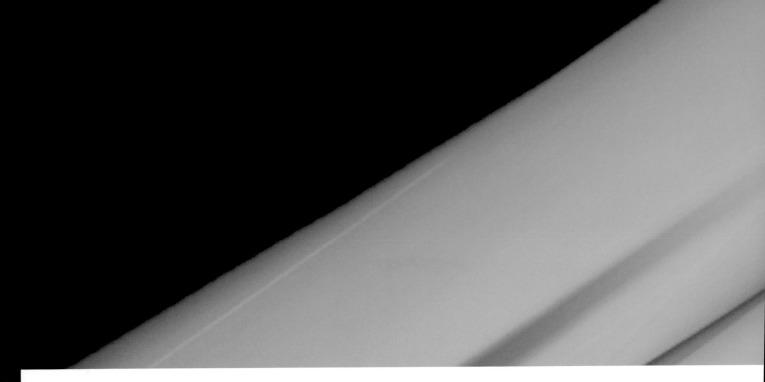

Blob-to-box
model

Blob-to-box model

The principle of an organization that can change from a strict, unit-based system (the box) into a freer, more fluent system (the blob) can be applied on many levels and scales. At an abstract, almost metaphoric, level, it provides a way of thinking about cities and their infrastructural fluxes and built-up grids of high-rises (IFCCA; see p. 326). At the scale level of an individual building, it gives the model for connecting disparate systems through sectional transformation. We are opposed to fragmentation, so what we want the foyer (loose, flux-based system) and the concert hall (strict, black-box system) to do is to work together as one efficient system, without the unnecessary waste of adding secondary systems for installations, construction and circulation (Music Theatre, Graz; see p. 254). But this design model can equally be applied to a house (VilLA NM; see p. 76), or to a large detail, as the pylon of a bridge (Prince Claus Bridge; see p. 242).

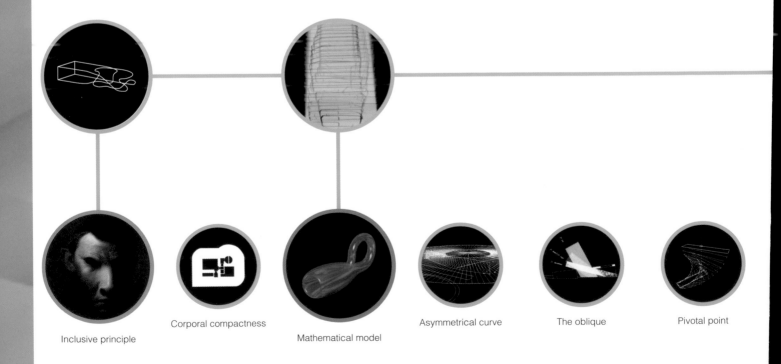

Inclusive principle

Corporal compactness

Mathematical model

Asymmetrical curve

The oblique

Pivotal point

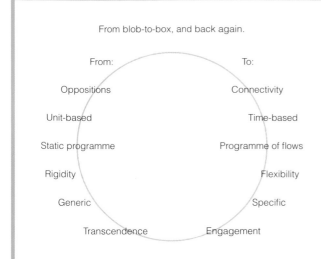

From blob-to-box, and back again.

From: To:

Oppositions — Connectivity

Unit-based — Time-based

Static programme — Programme of flows

Rigidity — Flexibility

Generic — Specific

Transcendence — Engagement

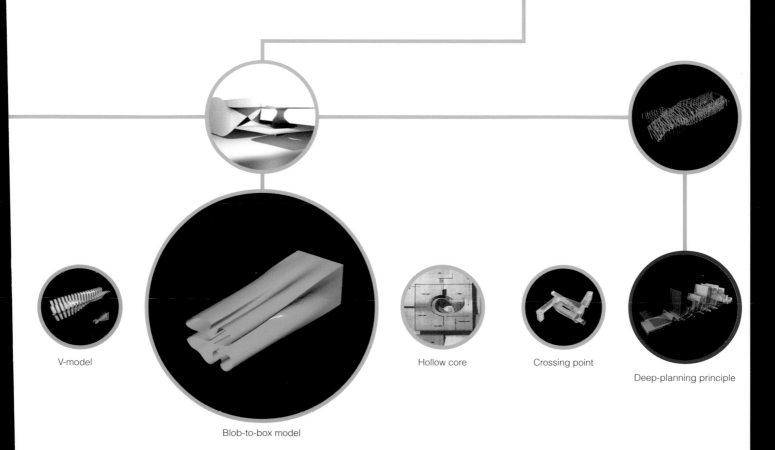

V-model

Blob-to-box model

Hollow core

Crossing point

Deep-planning principle

Electrical Substation, Amersfoort
Electricity diptych, part 1
1989–1994

Urban substations, despite rarely being entered, even by maintenance staff, are frequently disguised as houses, complete with fake windows and doors. This strategy of camouflage has been abandoned, and instead we have approached the project for what it is: a skin surrounding an electrical appliance.

This skin, which is wrapped around three large electrical transformers, consists of two interlocking, asymmetrical roofless containers, which are materialized as polar opposites. The light volume is situated in the dark corner of the site, next door to the town hall, where the shadows of massive trees have turned the substation into a popular backdrop for wedding photographs. The opposite, darker side, facing the railway tracks, catches the sun. The black basalt and aluminium-lined panels are articulated with a pattern of stainless steel that incorporates the same tropical hardwood inlay used for the substation's large doors.

Karbouw, Amersfoort
Asymmetrical curve
1990–1992

At first sight it was nothing much, just a rather small office and workshop for a contractor on a nondescript industrial estate. But from the beginning there were twists in the story; those relating to a smart, driven and exacting client, and those that we applied to the composition of the building.

The first of these twists consisted of the rotation of the corrugated aluminium first floor in relation to the red-bricked orthogonal base. From this shift, the rest of the organization followed. The entrance was allocated to the nook at the side elevation, rather than to the front. Since the basement floor was originally dedicated to the building workshop, and the offices were situated upstairs, the entrance gives way immediately to a staircase leading to the first-floor reception desk. An asphalted internal corridor forms the transition between office zone and workshop, ending in the protruding 'eye' of agglutinated green glass in the opposite façade. Sliding doors separate the different offices from each other and from the second eye made of slanting, green glass that horizontally defines the upper front.

Nothing much, but somehow it worked. The secret was in the balance of the materials and colours, and, most of all, in the balance of line and curve. The asymmetrical curve, our design model of those years, returns in plan and section, as seen in the vaulted roof that follows the same line as the curved façade.

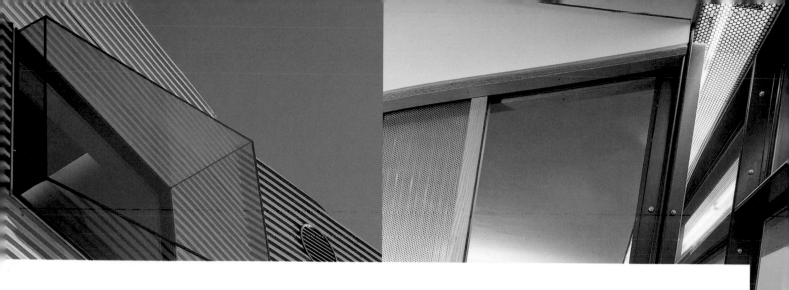

Positive note 7 Not to say that the cliché of the megalomaniac misanthropic architect is never encountered in the real world, but architects more often than not are disciplined and relatively humble. Being closely related to engineers, the traits of perseverance and patience run deep in the architectural personality. If you allow your true self to come forward, you will discover a surprisingly accommodating, even faintly servile (and yes, don't be afraid to be slightly ridiculous), side to yourself that finds pleasure in servicing the infinitely more complex character of the Client. The Client, the ultimate archetype being a Pope, will always remain that unfathomable Power That Must Be Obeyed to his architect, whose archetype is, after all, only that of a simple stonemason.

We all need someone to tell us what to do, and this is why we spend most of our time trying to induce lacklustre Senior Project Managers to play **Julius II** to our **Michelangelo**.

Church Hall, Hilversum

Modesty to the point of starkness

1995–2000

The simple, low-cost building is located in a leafy suburban area, with Victorian villas set well back from the street. The church occupies the same withdrawn, detached position of these houses, leaving a large space between the street and its entrance. According to the beliefs of the Rainbow Church (an amalgam of two types of mainstream Protestantism), this space forms a transitional route between the everyday bustle outside and the quiet repose inside. The façades, with their frosted glass, reflective screens and layered materials, mediate between the interior spaces and the green surroundings.

The initial design concept was a formal interplay between diagonally inclined surfaces and the arrangement of the four skylights. The building's programme organizes itself around the elements of the church hall, offices, meeting rooms and services, all of which are distributed over two interwoven floors. The principal space of the 6-metre (20-ft) high hall and its interconnected areas are situated on the ground level, with the secondary spaces on the upper level. The hall's skylights raise the ceiling of the hall another 4 metres (13 ft) at these points. These skylights are also structural elements, whose placement and shape allow varying amounts of daylight into the interior.

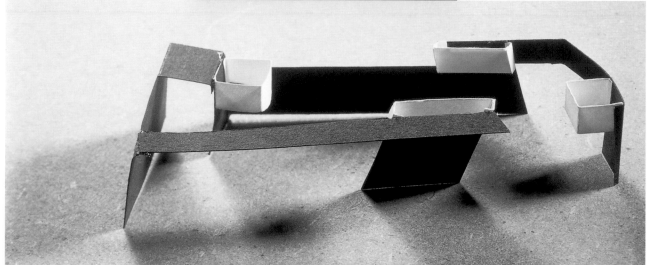

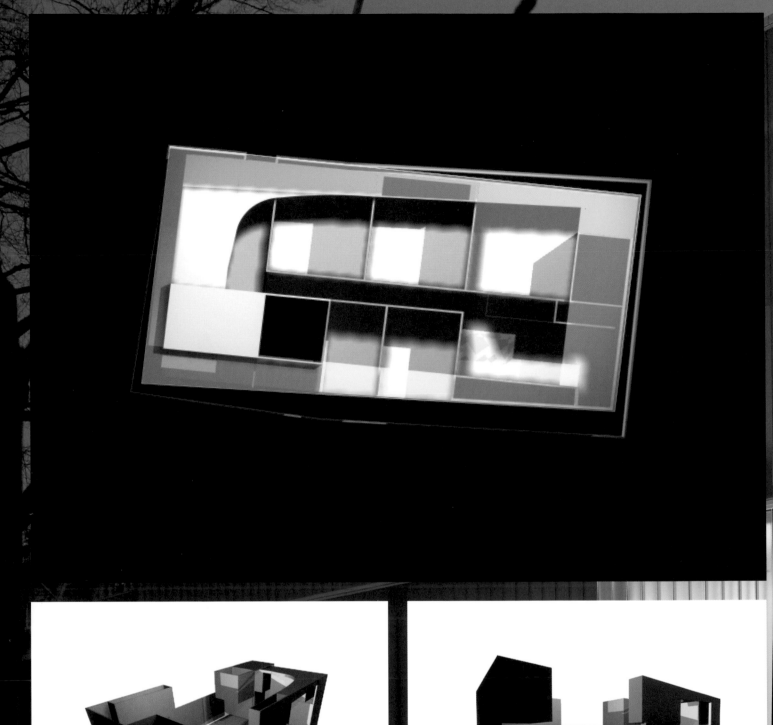

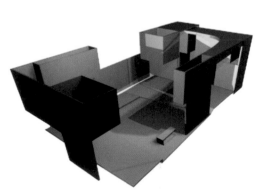
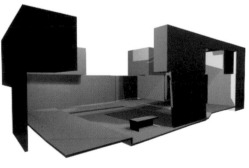

Renderings illustrate the positioning of the four structural skylights.

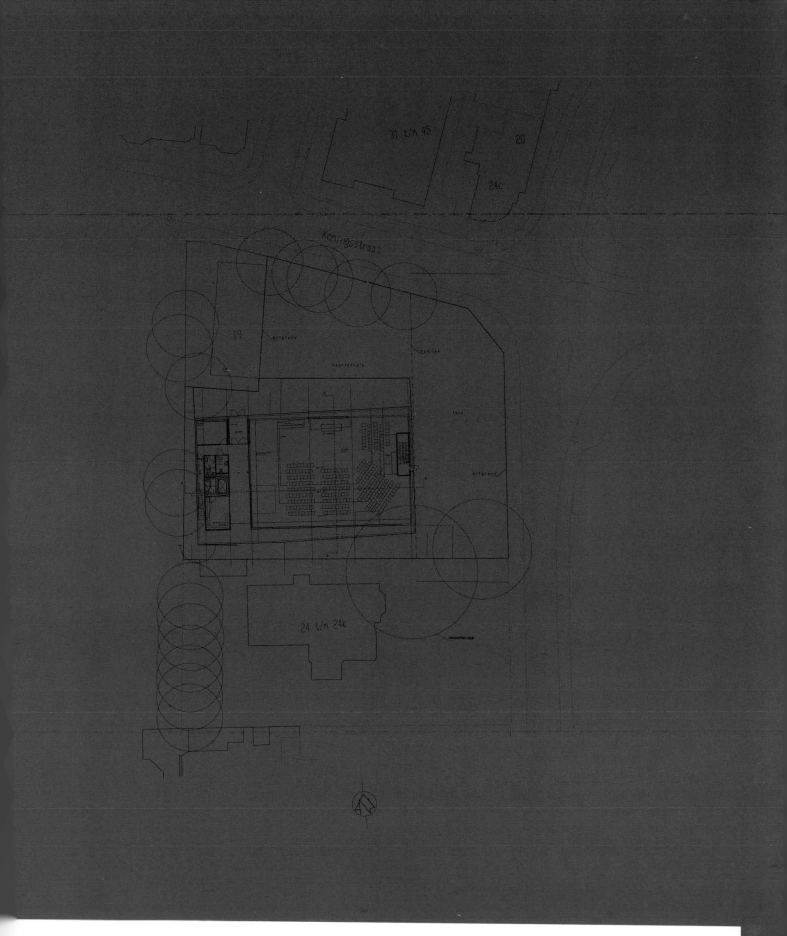

Site plan.

Skylights funnel in daylight at different angles, according to the time of day.

234 Church Hall, Hilversum

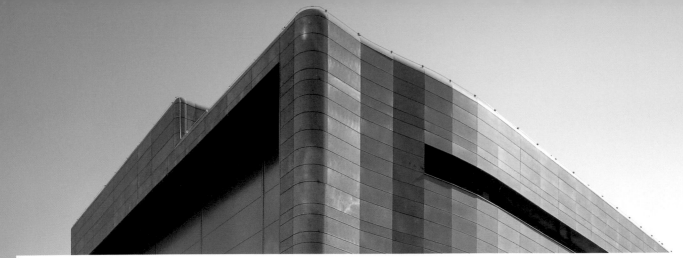

Electrical Substation, Innsbruck
Electricity diptych, part 2
1996–2000

Basalt lava is used again, as in the earlier electricity substation (see p. 218). And why not? These buildings, despite their necessity to our culture, usually have nothing to distinguish them. We decided that in the future we would make all commissioned electricity buildings in basalt lava, and so far there are two. It is a great material, dark, heavy and durable, and suitable for some kind of temple, which – after a fashion – is what an electrical substation is.

Having designed two similar substations, we can play the game of compare and contrast. We can learn that the later building is more expensive and therefore better detailed, is more regularly inspected and used by workers, and thus has a larger interior and greater transparency. This second substation is smoothly incorporated into the surrounding plateau, like a hump in the landscape. Glass strips, which illuminate the building from within, contribute to the chameleon-like nature of the building. Instead of being an alien technical object that poses a threat to its surroundings, the substation is integrated, almost domesticated, in its placement within the town.

Positive note 8 God forbid that we succumb to facile disparagement of account managers and vice presidents in the more diaphanous regions of the service sector. But perhaps it is time for us to realize how fortunate we are to have a profession that is grounded in real knowledge and tangible skills. The practice of architecture occupies a privileged position in the roving, capitalist-driven contemporary world of work. You can be an architect on your own, with a small atelier, with a huge factory-type design studio, or operate within a network. You can be good, bad, or mediocre. However you choose to perform your profession, you are sustained by your training and your unique expertise, which still comes down to a combination of ancient ways of thinking and modern material knowledge.

Prince Claus Bridge, Utrecht
Design and construct
1998–2003

This project represents the first realization in the Netherlands of the American system, whereby the contractor guarantees a fixed price and in return is given free rein in working out the details of the concept design. This method of 'design and construct' is controversial, and is usually applied in the most pragmatic civil constructions, in which architectural ambition is of no concern.

Yet here it worked. The design that we handed over to the contractor does not depend upon refined details. The important elements that give the bridge its character were already fixed in the concept design. These include the knot at the bottom, which fulfills three functions as it stabilizes the pylon, carries the bridge decks, and defines the urban space underneath; the elliptical attachment of the stay cables to the pylon, giving the bridge a dynamic, swirling, almost tent-like profile; and the mobile shape of the pylon itself, as its diameter gradually metamorphoses from slender to sturdy, from cubic to oval.

We were able to define these principles at such an early stage because they are the same principles of transformative geometry that we work with in other projects. It is not style or design, therefore, that is carried over from one project to the next; it is your own way of streamlining complexity.

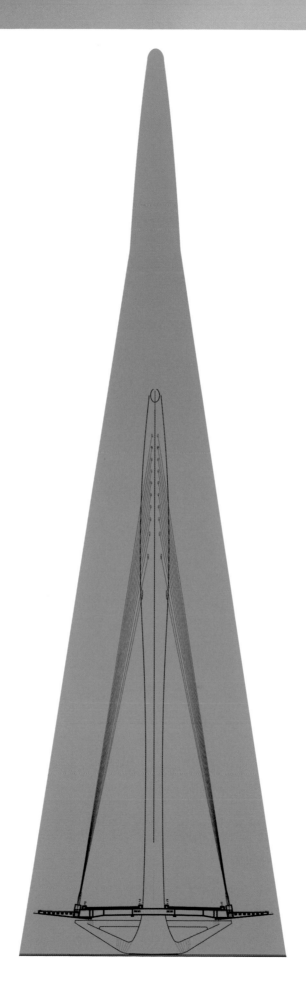

Top The structural elements to be emphasized at night are highlighted in this lighting study: the fan-like shape of the stays, the flanks of the pylon, and the continuous line connecting the pylon and the space below the bridge.

Above This visualization investigates the compositional effect of the elliptical attachment of the stays.

244 **Prince Claus Bridge, Utrecht**

Thirty-eight cables, varying in length between 8 and 160 metres (26 to 525 ft), are attached to the pylon, which transforms from cubic to oval.

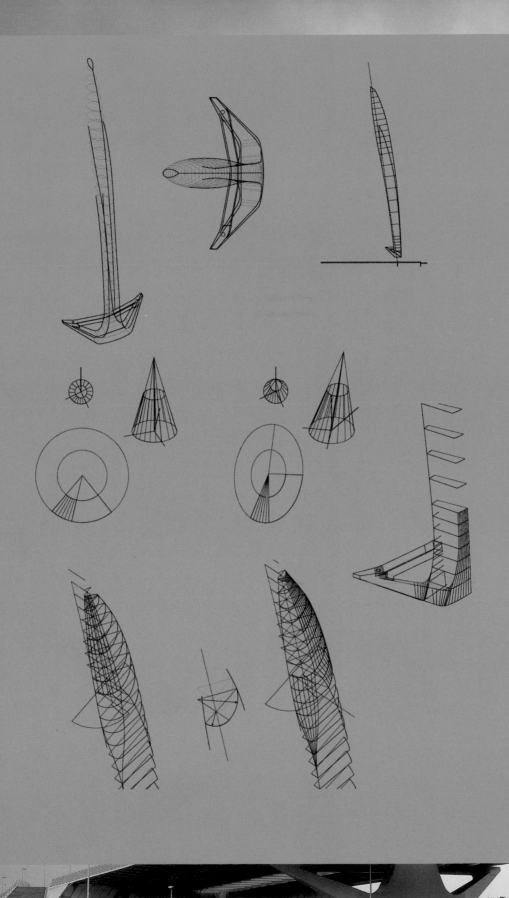

Geometric figures show the construction parameters of the blob-to-box model.

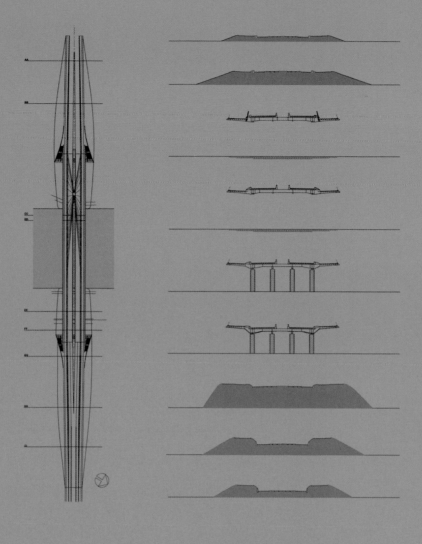

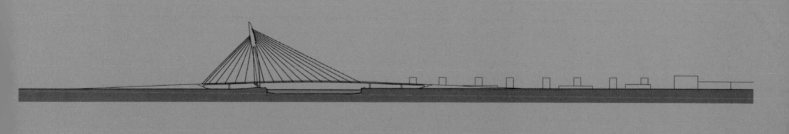

1 Sectional plans illustrate the transformation from road to embankment, to viaduct, and back again, which entails height differences and the splitting up of the bridge decks to allow for different types of traffic.

2 Total span: 115 metres (377 ft)
Pylon height: 91 metres (300 ft)
Back span: 75 metres (245 ft)
Clearance: 9.15 metres (30 ft)

The constructive pylon with its steel cladding, which ranges in thickness from 2 cm (.75 in) at the top to 6 cm (2.25 in) at the bottom, and in width from 2.75 to 4.5 metres (9 and 15 ft).

The steel knot stabilizes the pylon, carries the bridge decks, and defines the area underneath. The split allows light to penetrate the space, creating a public square.

250 Prince Claus Bridge, Utrecht

Music Theatre, Graz
Blob-to-box mother model
1998–2007

The competition for the music theatre of the University of Graz was initially held in 1998. After UN Studio won the second phase, the project was developed further over the next two years before being put on hold, and design revisions were implemented before the project was delayed for a second time. Work has recently resumed on the building.

The design model for the competition entry became one of the most significant and widely applied models for our work, and conveys the simultaneous and interconnected presence of two contrasting typologies, blob and box, within one structure.

The blob-to-box model consists of a horizontally directed spiral, whose ends are interwoven with its middle part to generate the internal organization. The spiral transforms itself from blob to box, and vice versa, in an endless composition; simple, orthogonal and horizontally oriented on one side, and turning into a complex, smaller-scaled principle on the opposite side. Like an octopus, the spiral divides itself into a number of smaller, interconnected spirals that take on a vertical and diagonal direction. Because of this constructive, organizing principle, a fluid and column-free internal spatial arrangement is actualized, efficiently connecting spaces to each other.

The archetypal figure of the spiral has associated characteristics that are closely related to music, such as rhythm, continuity, channelling, directionality and intersection.

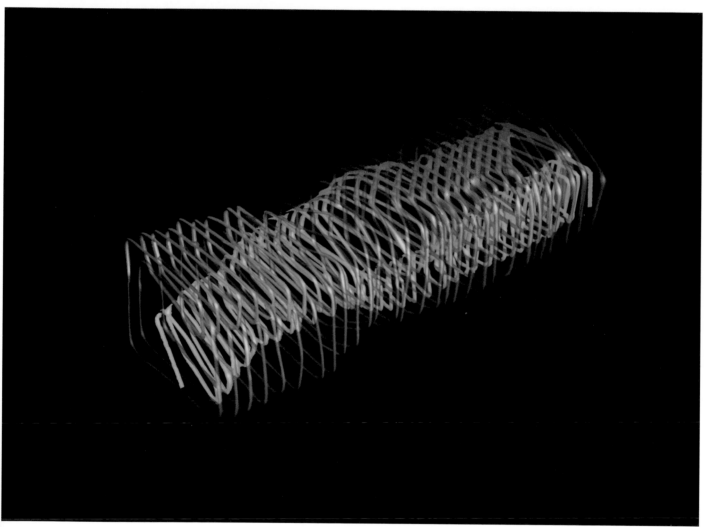

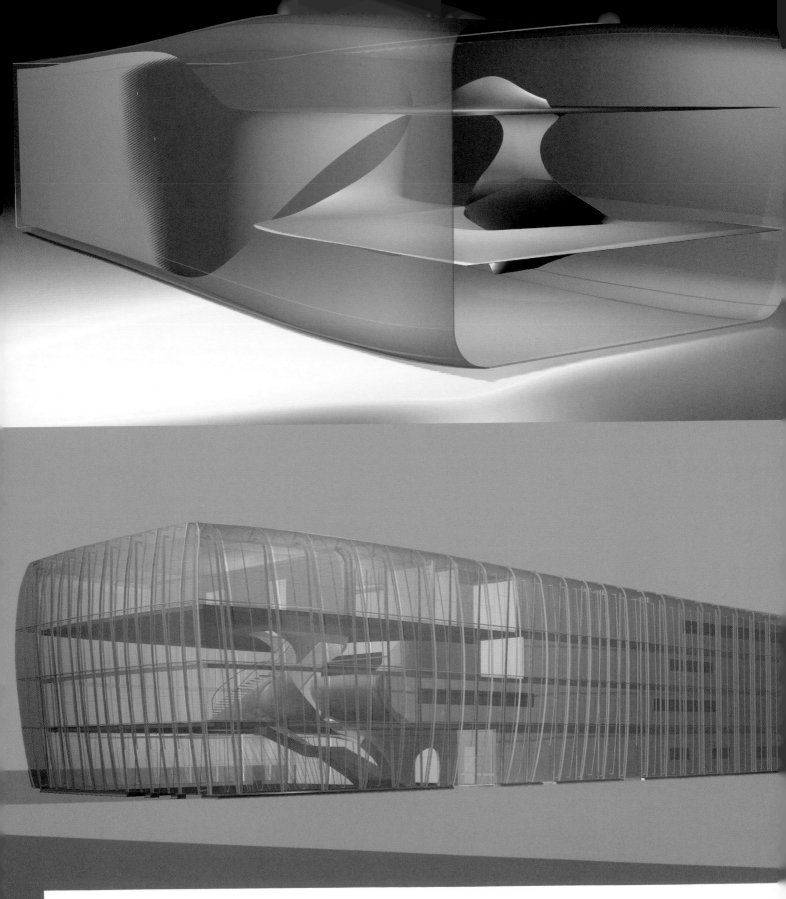

Music Theatre, Graz

Theatre, Lelystad
Kaleidoscopic experience
2002–2006

This successful competition entry for a theatre is part of the new design for Lelystad's city centre, and belongs to a cluster of cultural and social focal points that will bring liveliness to the new quarter. At the scale of the city, the theatre is visually accessible from numerous locations, and, when illuminated at nightfall, allows the building to function as a point of orientation.

It is an inside-outside building, beginning with the element of touch that is manifested by the staircase's handrail, which leads you up to the auditorium. Actually, this winding handrail is nothing but the public inauguration of the celebratory experience of going to the theatre. The traditional, orthogonal distribution of space is transformed by the handrail as it cuts through the entire building as part of the vertical foyer, connecting the various performance rooms situated on different floors. When the handrail finally touches the roof of the building, it spills over into the outside walls, which are of the same warm and festive colours as the interior, and faceted to reconstruct the kaleidoscopic experience of the world of the stage. The theme of the construction, therefore, is that drama and performance are not restricted to the stage, but are extended to the urban experience.

Inside, the theatre contains different types of public and performance spaces. The large auditorium has an intimate character with a semicircular seating arrangement, emphasized by the horseshoe-shaped balcony and the short distance between the stage and the back. The small auditorium has a flat floor and flexible stand, making this room suitable for a wide variety of uses. The event space on the second floor has walls that can be moved aside, enabling the room to flow into the foyer.

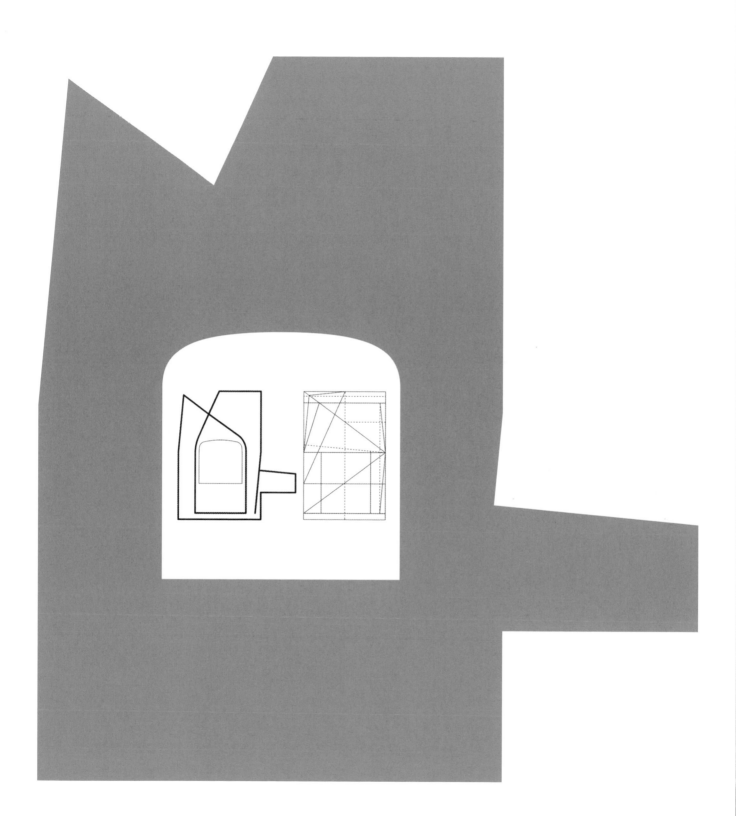

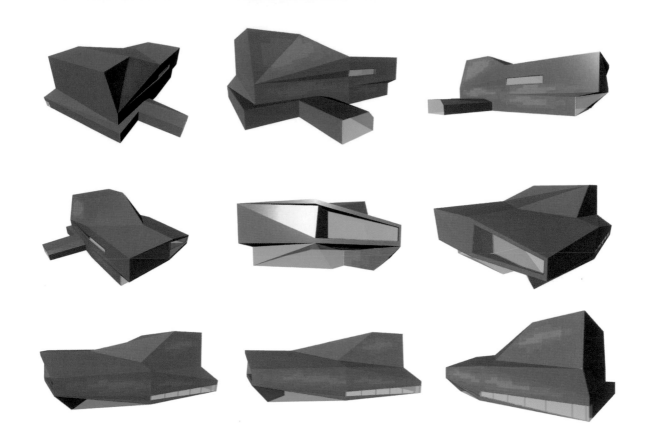

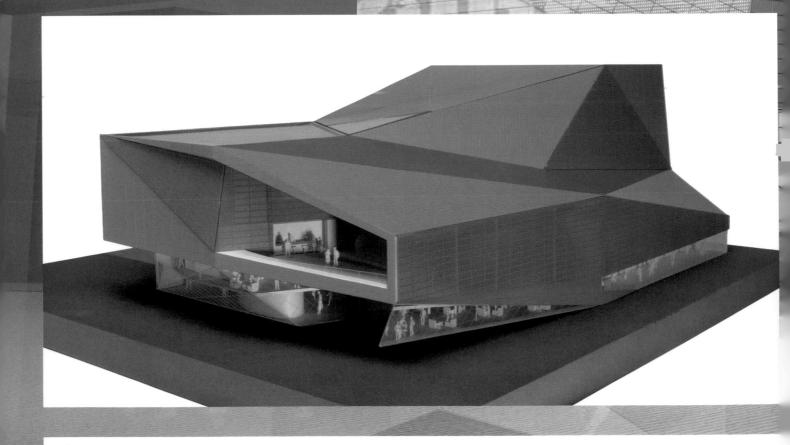

Volume studies of the theatre, showing the integration of the two boxes within a faceted, malleable envelope.

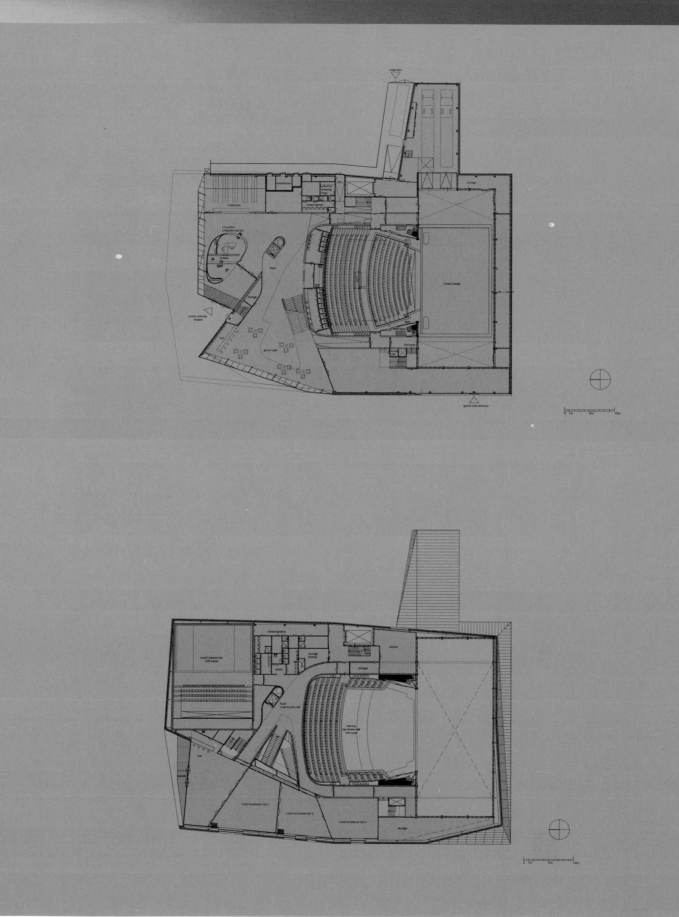

Plans of the ground floor and first floor illustrate the conceptual diagram that organizes the distribution of programmes and spatial events.

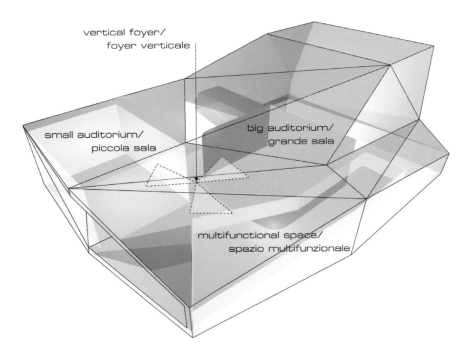

vertical foyer/
foyer verticale

small auditorium/
piccola sala

big auditorium/
grande sala

multifunctional space/
spazio multifunzionale

Above Interior of the 720-seat auditorium, showing the geometric transformation from the stage tower through the faceted walls. All of the technical equipment is incorporated into the curved back wall.

Below Study of the allocation of the programme in relation to the vertical foyer.

Study showing how the handrail develops to embrace the volume of the entire theatre.

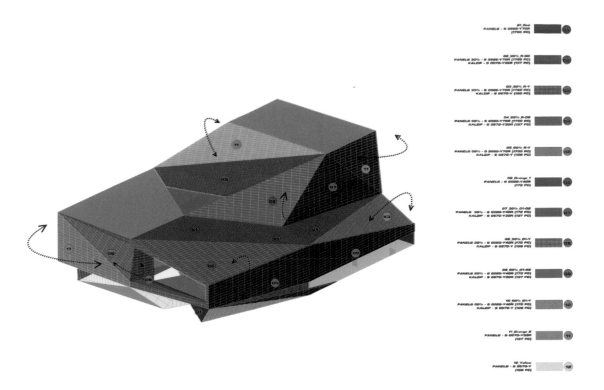

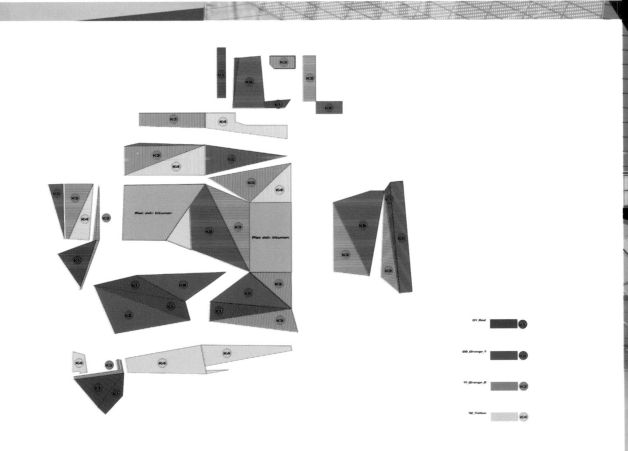

Analysis of the kaleidoscopic effect of the façade. The façade surfaces are
set at different angles to each other, resulting in various grids, perforations
and colour schemes.

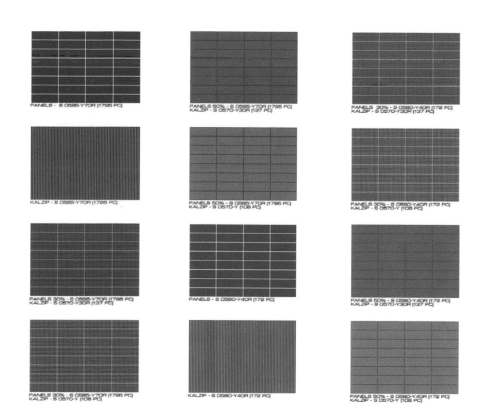

PANELS - S 0585-Y70R (1795 PC)	PANELS 50% - S 0585-Y70R (1795 PC) KALZIP - S 0570-Y30R (137 PC)	PANELS 30% - S 0580-Y40R (172 PC) KALZIP - S 0570-Y30R (137 PC)
KALZIP - S 0585-Y70R (1795 PC)	PANELS 50% - S 0585-Y70R (1795 PC) KALZIP - S 0570-Y (108 PC)	PANELS 30% - S 0580-Y40R (172 PC) KALZIP - S 0570-Y (108 PC)
PANELS 30% - S 0585-Y70R (1795 PC) KALZIP - S 0570-Y30R (137 PC)	PANELS - S 0580-Y40R (172 PC)	PANELS 50% - S 0580-Y40R (172 PC) KALZIP - S 0570-Y30R (137 PC)
PANELS 30% - S 0585-Y70R (1795 PC) KALZIP - S 0570-Y (108 PC)	KALZIP - S 0580-Y40R (172 PC)	PANELS 50% - S 0580-Y40R (172 PC) KALZIP - S 0570-Y (108 PC)

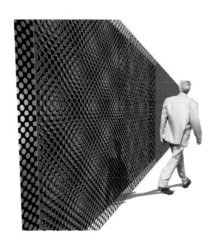

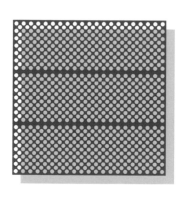

Studies showing the different grid densities and effects of coloured, perforated and layered façade panels.

V-model

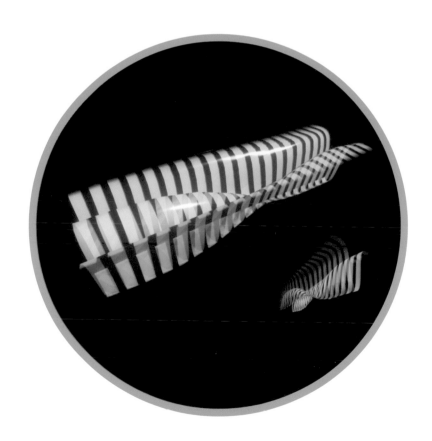

V-model

An early interest in the oblique, realized in the concrete piers of the Erasmus Bridge (see p. 140), developed over time into a particular organizational typology, as we looked for ways to intensify the use of diagonally inclined, architectural forms. A competition entry for an Olympic boxing hall in Berlin (1992) shows the first instance of a V-system; the arena is supported by a concrete structure of high corridors with slanting walls, resulting in an oblique, permeable space that lets in daylight and is filled with programme and circulation.

A second competition entry for an ethnological museum in Geneva (1996) shows the V in an inverted way, as a series of connected pyramids. In the same year we began Arnhem Central (see p. 272). In this project, the vertical slant of the V addresses the issue of stacking a series of different programmes, each with its own grid. The V is used here as a morphing technique to fuse together the typologies of parking, offices and public space, while still being a constructive and usable space, in this case forming the sunlit, pedestrian access to the parking garage.

Finally, with the Ponte Parodi pier in Genoa (see p. 292), the V-structure has loosened up and become part of a transformative system. The Vs, in their increasingly multidirectional arrangement, persist as integral elements that connect between different vertical layers.

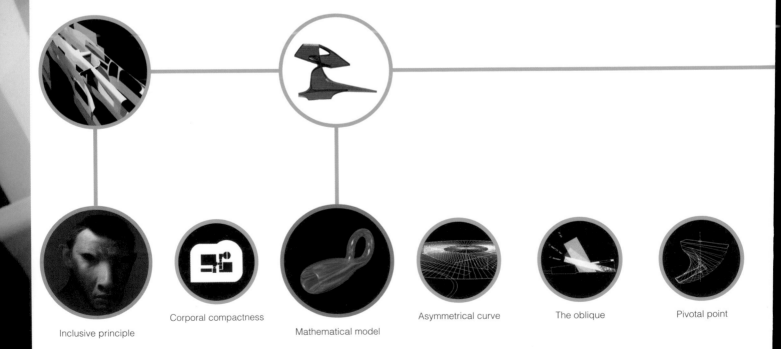

Inclusive principle

Corporal compactness

Mathematical model

Asymmetrical curve

The oblique

Pivotal point

Separate
unit-based grids:
grid 1. office
grid 2. public space
grid 3. parking

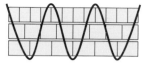

Superimposition of
integral principle

Integration of all
relevant parameters
into one system

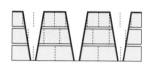

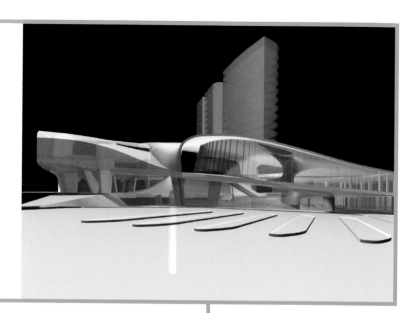

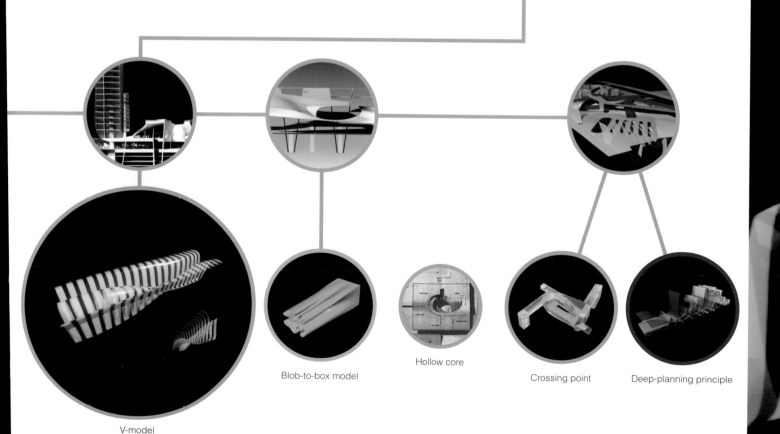

V-model

Blob-to-box model

Hollow core

Crossing point

Deep-planning principle

Arnhem Central, Arnhem
Three models
for a life's work
1996–2008

It has taken a chunk out of our lives and has formed the conceptual and material basis for UN Studio. Arnhem Central, begun only weeks after Queen Beatrix opened the Erasmus Bridge (see p. 140), has been both a mind-altering experience and an endurance test. While we dislike the convention of describing projects in terms of 'problems' and 'solutions', the task of devising a new master plan for the small railway station, hastily erected as a temporary measure after World War II, had already tripped up several generations of architects.

It was not the station itself that constituted the problem, but rather the combination of the bus station attached to it, the road system surrounding it, and the demand for extensive urban expansion that resisted standard planning. The instinctual desire to break up the various elements to achieve order was the one thing that was impossible here, as we found out several weeks after being invited to join the team already in place and at work. Once again, we found ourselves inching our way into a project from the starting position of a vaguely defined consultant.

Over the course of a summer we defined the approach to Arnhem Central as an integrated public transportation area; a roofed-over, climate-controlled plaza that interconnects and provides access to trains, taxis, buses, bicycles, parking, office spaces and the town centre. With this approach came the awareness that we were dealing with a new type of project with enormous public and political potential, requiring vision, ideology and communication skills, together with an understanding of the contemporary role of the architect.

The deep-planning method was employed to develop a coherent set of site- and programme-specific organizational principles, expressed through three design models: the V-model, the Klein bottle and the blob-to-box. The materialization of the V-model is a structural element combining a carpark, public space and offices, whereas the Klein bottle is used as an organizational model for passenger movement throughout the project, efficiently stitching together internal and external programmed spaces. The blob-to-box model becomes the formal transition between the rectilinear offices and the transfer hall knot.

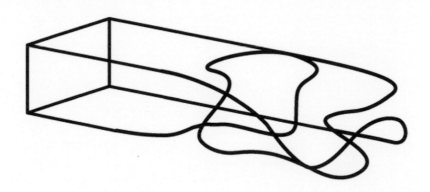

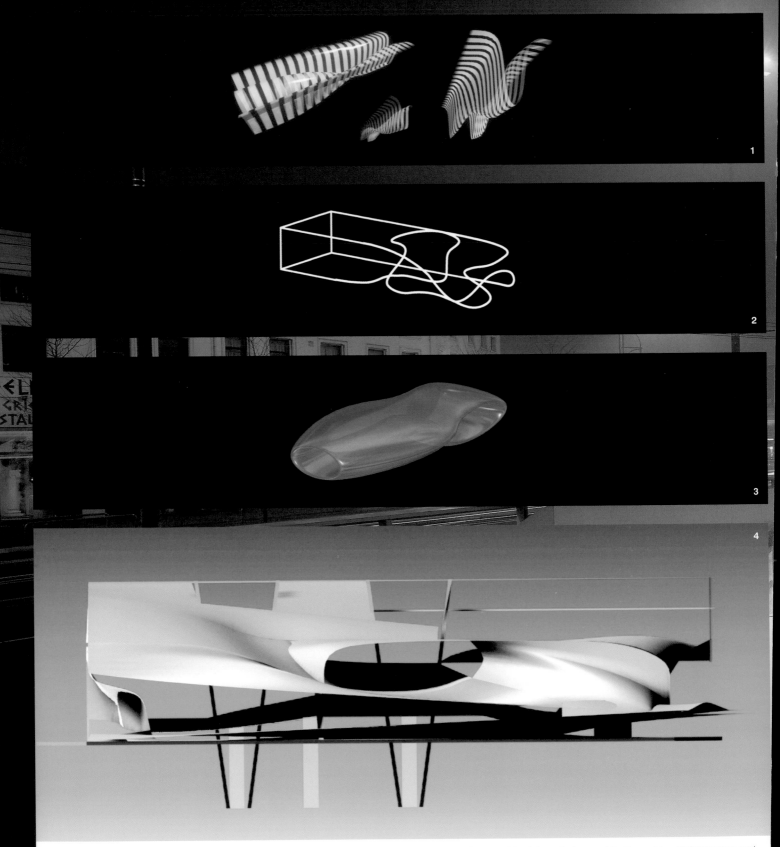

1 V-model: conceptual rendering of the transformation of the Vs as the result of grid constraints relating to the programme.

2 Blob-to-box model: wire model of the formal transition between programme requirements.

3 Mathematical model: the flattened Klein bottle.

4 Prototype of the combined three design models. Ground-level infrastructure and upper-level office programmes are interlinked by a raised topological mezzanine.

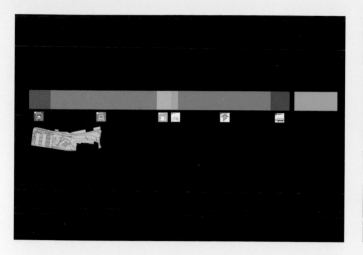

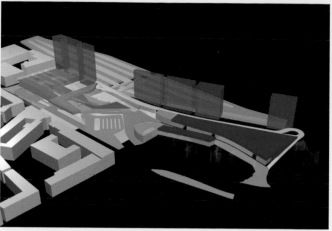

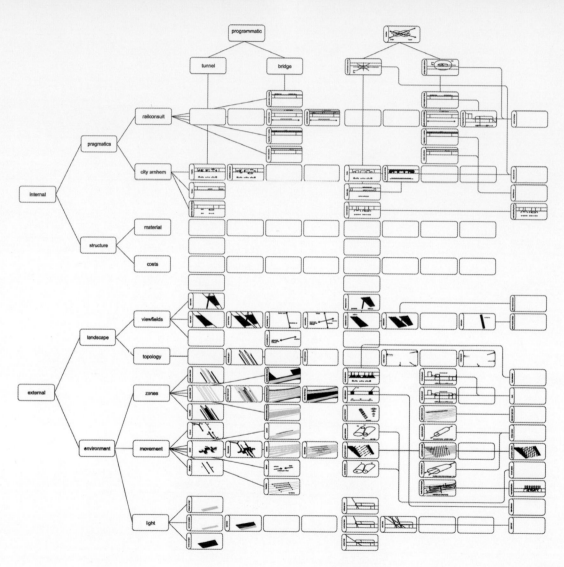

Visualization of 160,000 m² programme projected onto the 40,000 m² site.
Red: living
Orange: offices
Yellow: shops and restaurants
Blue: transportation
Green: public space

Schematic matrix of internal and external forces, regulations and other constraints, generating an overview of the potential of combining different parameters.

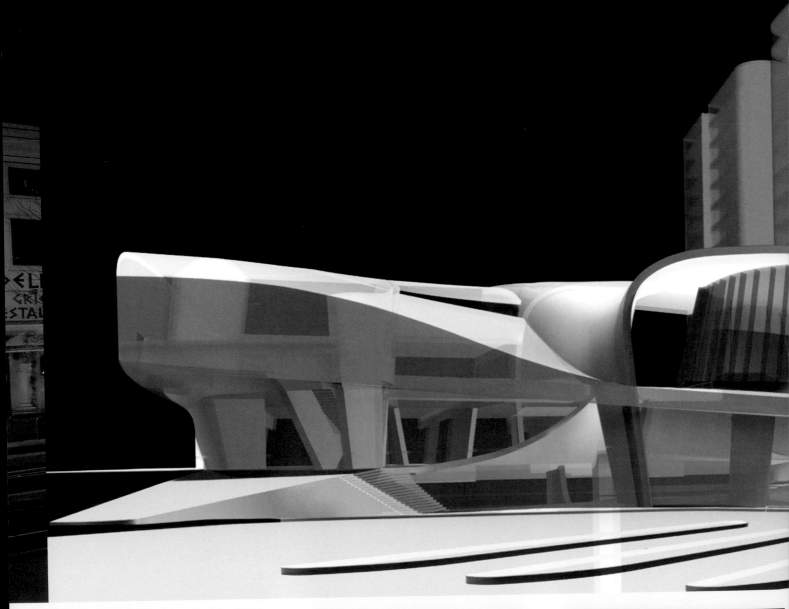

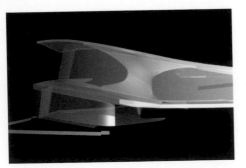
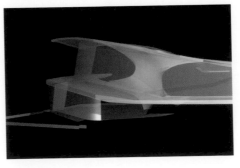
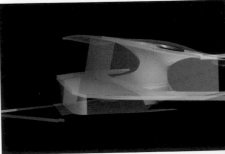

This series of renderings show the constructive element that brings the forces down from the 40-metre (131-ft) span of the transfer hall roof. A vital part of the master plan, the twisted element lets in daylight, directs movement and connects the Vs to the roof.

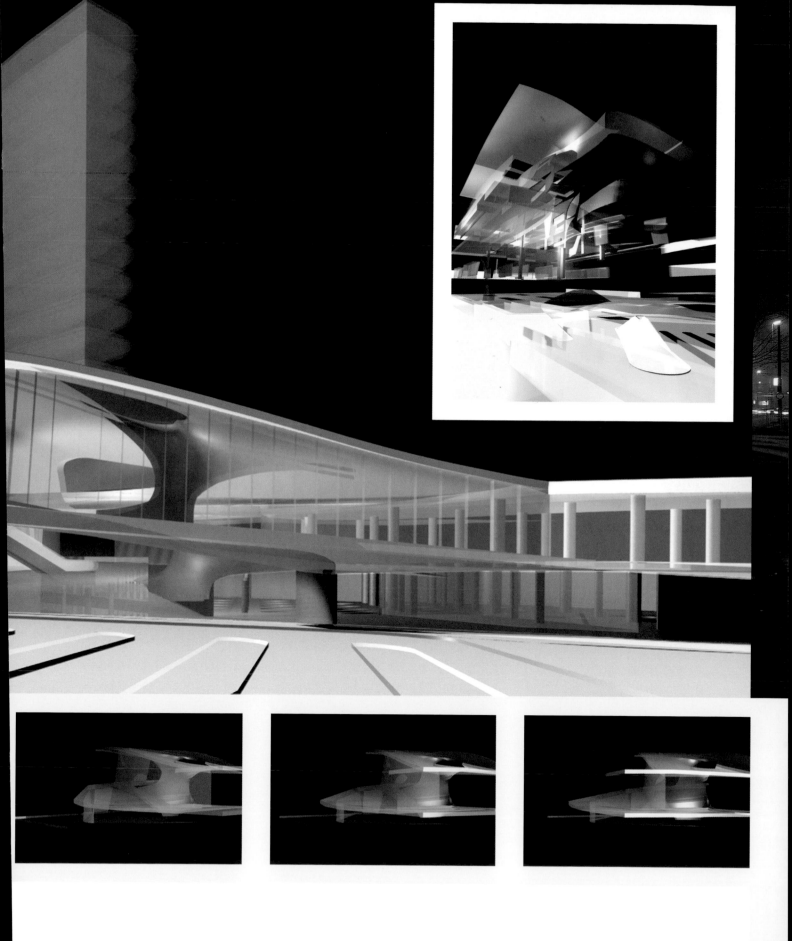

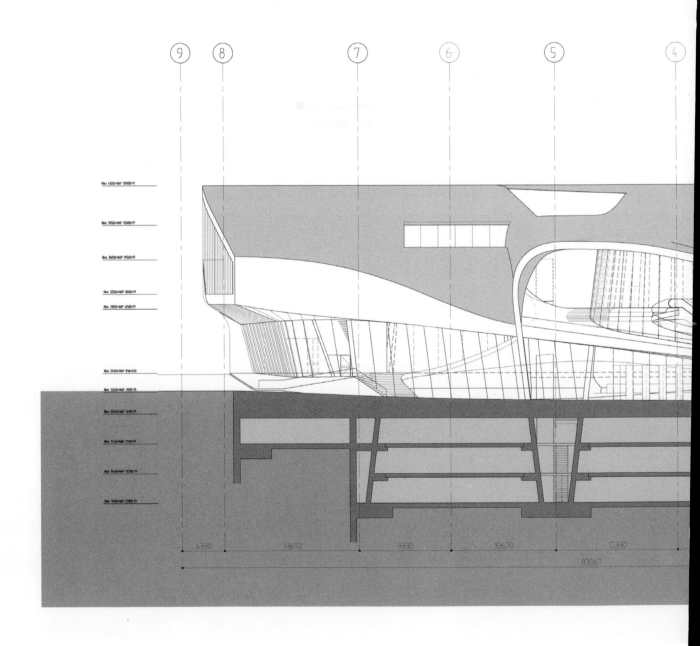

Section through the transfer hall, showing the eastern elevation and underground carpark and bicycle storage.

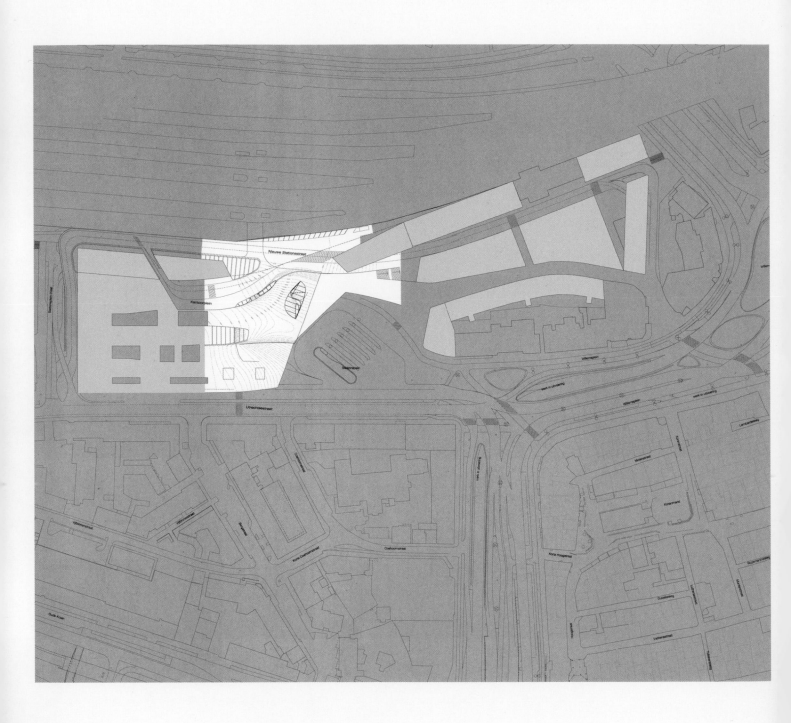

Plan of the station area illustrating the transfer hall, which acts as a hinge between
the western and eastern developments of the master plan.

1 May 2005: the Park and Rijn Offices are realized.

2 Aerial rendering of the location, showing the transfer hall centrally located as an infrastructural knot.

February 2000: the parking garage is completed and in use.

1 Plan of the underground carpark, showing the Vs as integral connectors, containing circulation, allowing in daylight and forming construction.

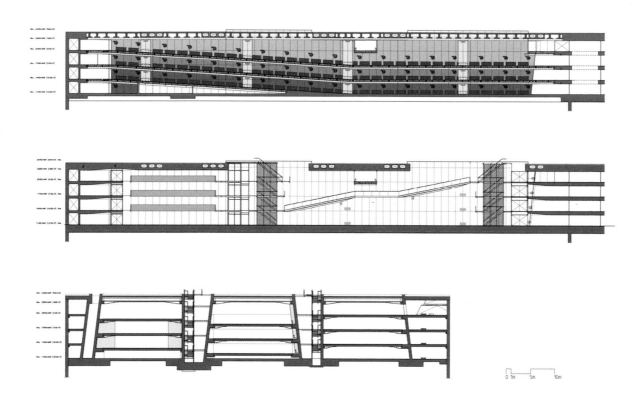

2 Sections:

1. Longitudinal section of the parking bay

2. Longitudinal section of the V

3. Cross section

The V-model under construction: the V will continue the public circulation space
from the future transfer hall.

July 2002: fashion show held in the parking garage by the Arnhem Fashion Institute.
The V-construction allows a column-free parking space.

The V-construction at the bus deck level (above) and parking level (below).

WILLEMSTUNNEL
2000

Positive note 9 A 'network practice' means only that everyone is a supplier to the end product; their individual roles are a matter of contractual particulars. You might supply the ideas for the architecture, the calculations for the construction, the glass panels for the façade, or the styling for the photos at the end. We don't hear those archaic terms 'concept', 'sketch', or even 'design' very much any more; they are deliverables, and lists are drawn up and distributed as to what these deliverables are and when they should be in the client's possession. In this constellation, the definition of competences is vital. This dispassionate, business-model view of architecture as a Gesamtkunstwerk of contractually binding competences might at first seem unattractive. But think again:

the **supplier-model** of architecture encourages (well, forces, really) architects to find **new ways of control**. Architects will be increasingly hired as consultants, providing design concepts that may or may not be translated into reality in the way they had **envisaged**. The risks of this working mode are **obvious**; you may find your name associated with a finished product that is **horrendously embarrassing**. But never mind, sooner or later that will happen anyway, whether you are in control or not.

Ponte Parodi, Genoa
Diamond cuts: the grid pulled apart and made deep
2000–2009

This project is part of the city's plan to revitalize the harbour and to extend the city centre towards the waterfront. As industrial activities relocate, the city is reclaiming the vacated area by adding public attractions and creating a new focal point.

Formerly dominated by a massive silo, the pier has been cleared and prepared for transformation into a three-dimensional 'piazza sul mediterraneo', a low-slung, faceted structure designed to bring the liveliness of the city to the waterfront, and vice versa. Four main clusters complement the pier's continuing function as a cruise terminal. Each cluster addresses a different theme: entertainment, wellness, technology and commerce. In order to stimulate pedestrian circulation, the clusters cater to the different user groups that frequent the pier and its surroundings. The precise clustering has been calculated by factoring in the attractiveness of the views, time of day and time of year. This time-based clustering of themes entails a distribution of activities throughout the day, with the aid of a 'programme-finder'.

This diagram of the 360-degree circle of experience, representing the perspective of a future visitor, conveys the potential of site-specific, topological conditions together with time- and use-related variables. As the project emerges by relating these values to each other in order to find the optimal combination, it is clear that the focus of the design throughout has been to create the ultimate user experience. This focus has been given a concrete manifestation by articulating a clear structural vision from the beginning to accompany the user-oriented developmental strategy. The structural vision, a variation on the Vs, warrants the spatial and organizational continuity of the pier. The structure is based on the conceptual device of pulling apart a grid, with the result that diamond-shaped cuts begin to emerge. The diamonds organize vertical circulation, allow views of the waterside, and let daylight penetrate deep into the structure.

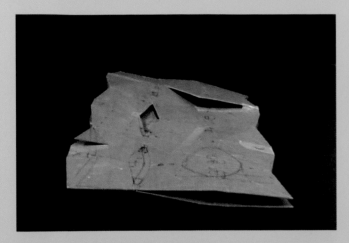

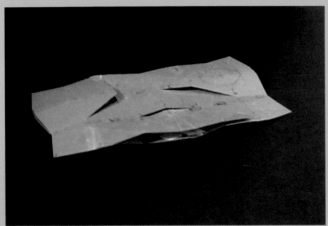

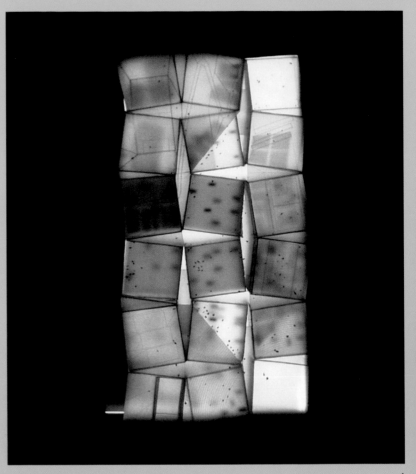

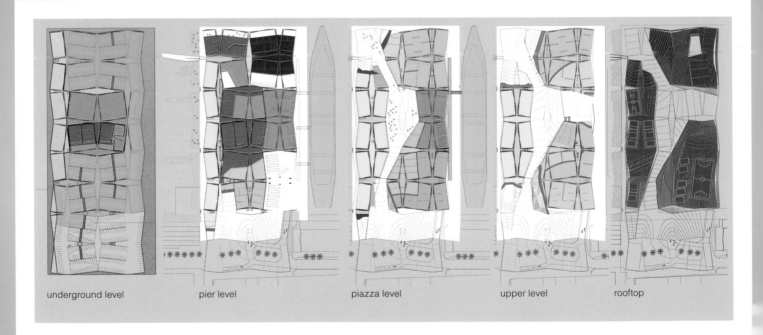

| underground level | pier level | piazza level | upper level | rooftop |

1 Study models illustrate how the diamond-shaped cuts show the gradients of the landscape.

2 Diagrams depict the clustering of the programmes around the different pockets. The organization of programmes contained within 16,000 m² volume generates 36,000 m² of public space.

Aerial view of the three-dimensional plaza. The new development will attract almost two million people, including passengers from the arriving cruise ships.

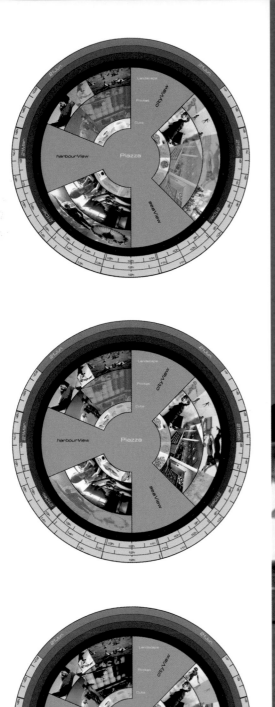

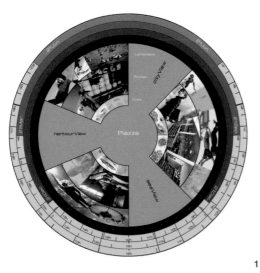

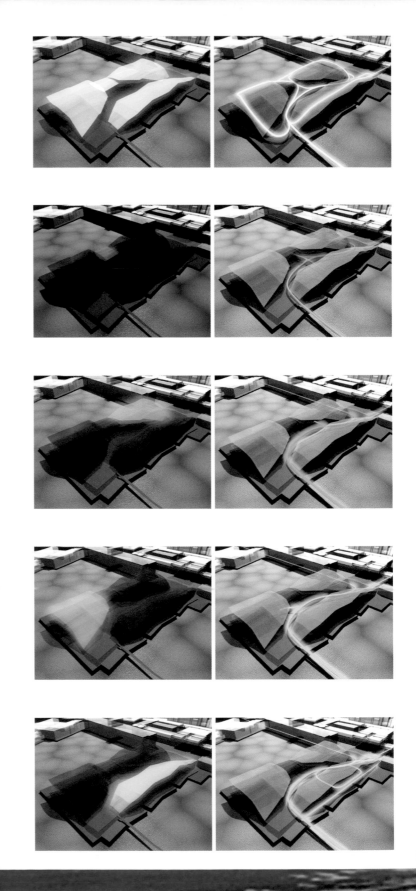

1 'Circular programme finder' as a site- and climate-specific device for hypothetically programming the Ponte Parodi.

2 Schematic diagram of visitor flow, moving to and from the surrounding attractions.

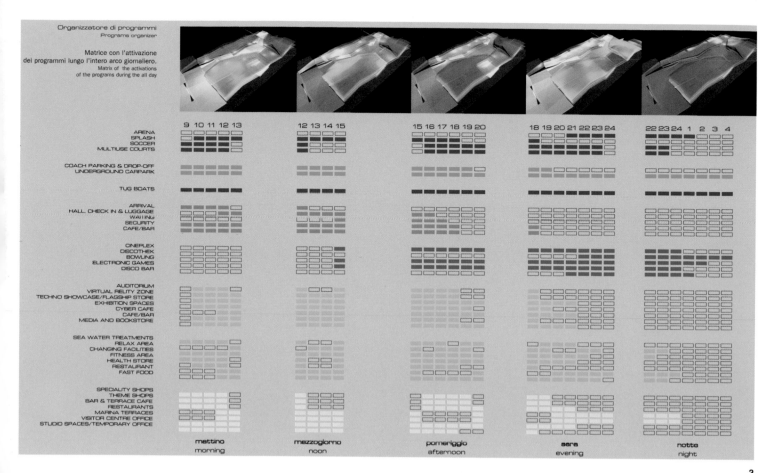

Organizzatore di programmi
Programs organizer

Matrice con l'attivazione
dei programmi lungo l'intero arco giornaliero.
Matrix of the activations
of the programs during the all day

	9 10 11 12 13	12 13 14 15	15 16 17 18 19 20	18 19 20 21 22 23 24	22 23 24 1 2 3 4
ARENA					
SPLASH					
SOCCER					
MULTIUSE COURTS					
COACH PARKING & DROP-OFF					
UNDERGROUND CARPARK					
TUG BOATS					
ARRIVAL					
HALL, CHECK IN & LUGGAGE					
WAITING					
SECURITY					
CAFE/BAR					
CINEPLEX					
DISCOTHEK					
BOWLING					
ELECTRONIC GAMES					
DISCO BAR					
AUDITORIUM					
VIRTUAL RELITY ZONE					
TECHNO SHOWCASE/FLAGSHIP STORE					
EXHIBITION SPACES					
CYBER CAFE					
CAFE/BAR					
MEDIA AND BOOKSTORE					
SEA WATER TREATMENTS					
RELAX AREA					
CHANGING FACILITIES					
FITNESS AREA					
HEALTH STORE					
RESTAURANT					
FAST FOOD					
SPECIALTY SHOPS					
THEME SHOPS					
BAR & TERRACE CAFE					
RESTAURANTS					
MARINA TERRACES					
VISITOR CENTRE OFFICE					
STUDIO SPACES/TEMPORARY OFFICE					
	mattino / morning	mezzogiorno / noon	pomeriggio / afternoon	sera / evening	notte / night

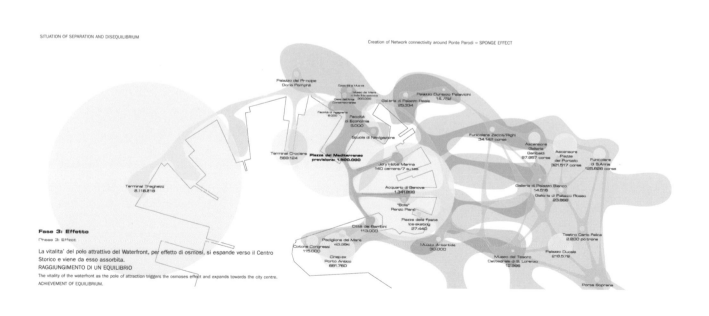

SITUATION OF SEPARATION AND DISEQUILIBRIUM

Creation of Network connectivity around Ponte Parodi = SPONGE EFFECT

Fase 3: Effetto
Phase 3: Effect

La vitalita' del polo attrattivo del Waterfront, per effetto di osmosi, si espande verso il Centro Storico e viene da esso assorbita.
RAGGIUNGIMENTO DI UN EQUILIBRIO

The vitality of the waterfront as the pole of attraction triggers the osmoses effect and expands towards the city centre.
ACHIEVEMENT OF EQUILIBRIUM.

3 Diagram of the forecasted cross-fertilization of visitor attendance. The vitality of the waterfront as a magnetic pole of attraction triggers an osmosis effect, and expands towards the city centre.

4 Schematic drawing analyzing links and access as a catalyst of urban regeneration.

Wien Mitte Urban Competition, Vienna

Dynamic exchange

2004

This competition entry for Vienna's central station sets out to meet three basic conditions: connecting the interests of the city, transportation authorities and private investors; impacting positively on the surroundings while respecting the historic city; and, finally, offering a meaningful public experience to both local residents and visitors.

Vienna Central is a formidable transit hub, housing both undergound and commuter rail lines, trams and buses, in addition to a future rail connection to the airport. The site analysis, which focuses on both usage and flow, demonstrates that the site's most vital prospects occur at the corners of the site. For this reason, a relatively low volume is proposed, with strongly articulated corners.

The inside of the urban block is the focal point of the project, and is where the strongest urban and iconic qualities are found. Views and sightlines help users navigate their way through this open space towards their destinations. The project uses the crossing-point model in order to develop a system that supports the arrangement of traffic and helps locate the various programmes. The ground level is conceived as an intense node of transportation exchange systems, made possible by extending and elevating the existing subway entrances in a northerly direction.

The central void dissects the urban block with three stepped and interrelated public spaces at different altitudes. The main hollow core is funnel-shaped, establishing visual connections between the different levels, as well as permitting daylight deep into the building, creating open areas with individual characters. Below ground level, the open space is situated in the southwest corner and forms a central arrivals hall for those travelling by train and subway. Travellers ascend via escalators to a public space that widens and opens up to the upper levels. Once at street level, they find an oval plaza with various circuits leading off in different directions and to different levels. The higher levels of the site have commercial functions and a more tranquil organization than the dynamic exchange of the lower levels.

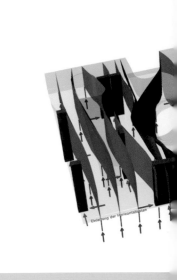

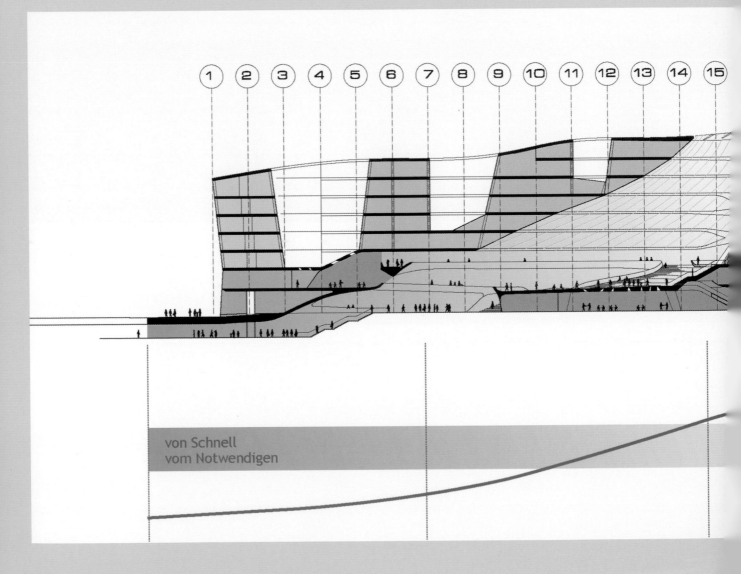

von Schnell
vom Notwendigen

1 Models show the transformation of the massive block into a ribbed structure with large and smaller voids between the crossbeams, which bridge the subterranean station and tracks. The models explore the potential of a structure that must span 60 metres (197 ft) because of limited foundation possibilities along the railway.

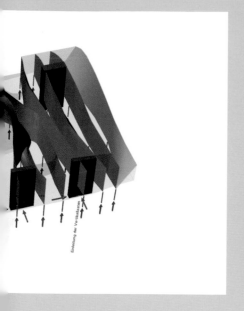

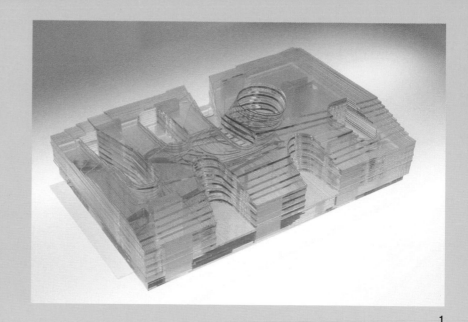

1

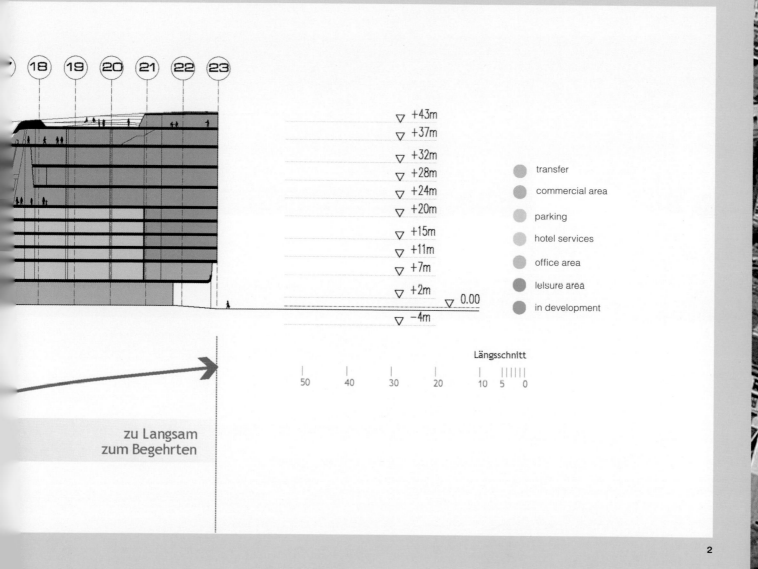

(18) (19) (20) (21) (22) (23)

▽ +43m
▽ +37m

▽ +32m
▽ +28m
▽ +24m
▽ +20m

▽ +15m
▽ +11m
▽ +7m

▽ +2m
▽ 0.00
▽ −4m

● transfer
● commercial area
● parking
● hotel services
● office area
● leisure area
● in development

Längsschnitt

| | | | | | |||||||
50 40 30 20 10 5 0

zu Langsam
zum Begehrten

2

2 Section of Vienna Central Station, an infrastructural node that accommodates
over 50 million people a year.

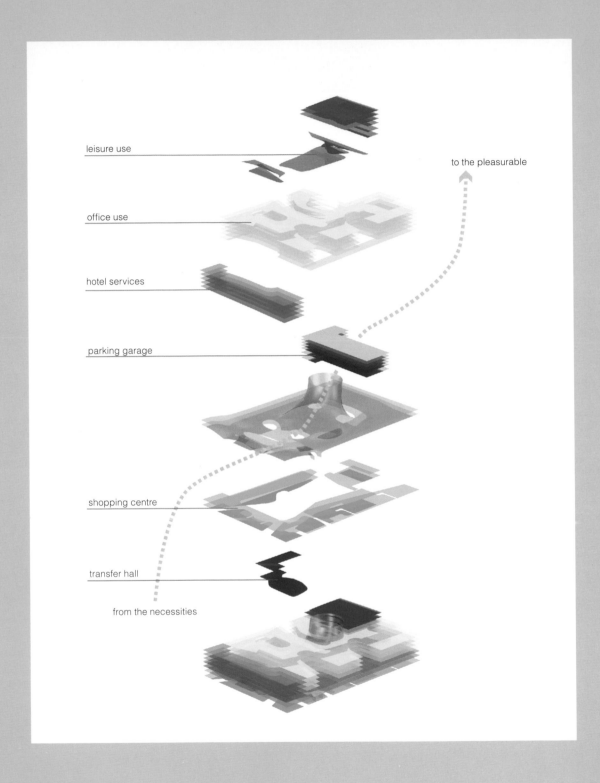

leisure use

office use

hotel services

parking garage

shopping centre

transfer hall

to the pleasurable

from the necessities

Exploded view illustrating the juxtaposition of programmes, including leisure and commercial destinations, public spaces and transportation systems.

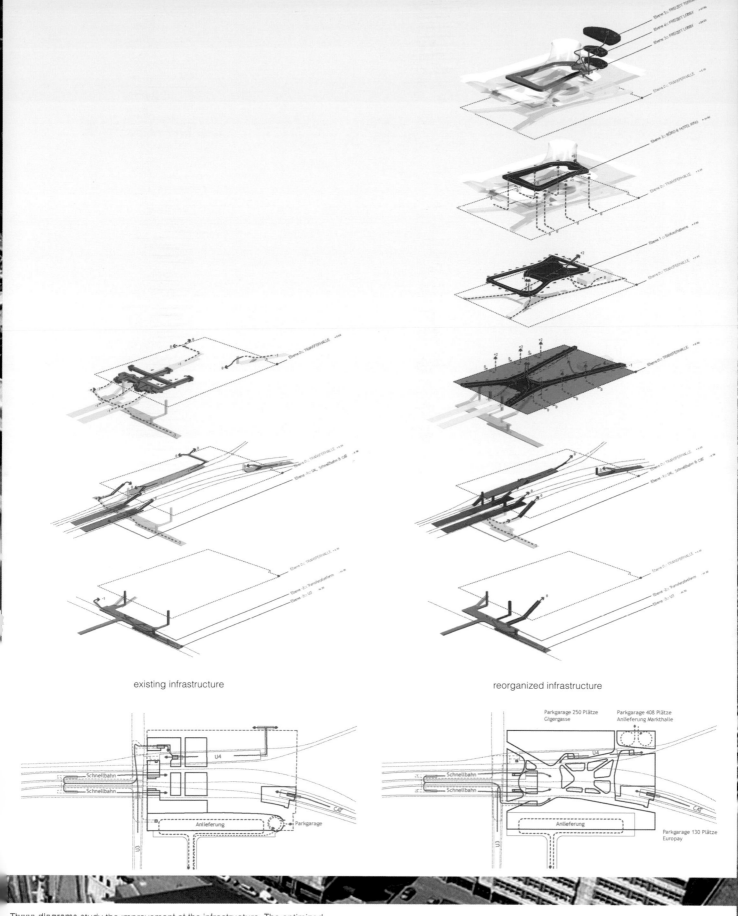

existing infrastructure

reorganized infrastructure

These diagrams study the improvement of the infrastructure. The optimized
hub organization targets a barrier-free connectivity for approximately 150,000
movements a day (28,000 per hour).

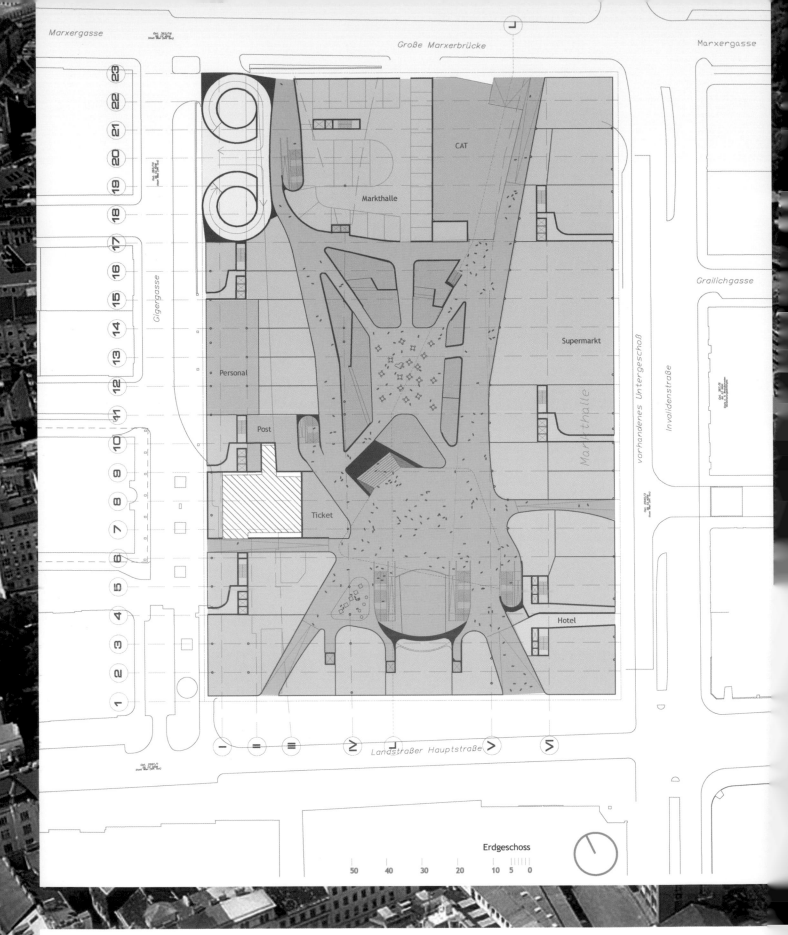

Marxergasse

Große Marxerbrücke

Marxergasse

CAT

Markthalle

Gigergasse

Grailichgasse

Supermarkt

Personal

Markthalle

vorhandenes Untergeschoß

Invalidenstraße

Post

Ticket

Hotel

Landstraßer Hauptstraße

Erdgeschoss

50   40   30   20   10 5 0

Plan of the ground level showing the hub's internal organization, like tentacles
reaching into the city.

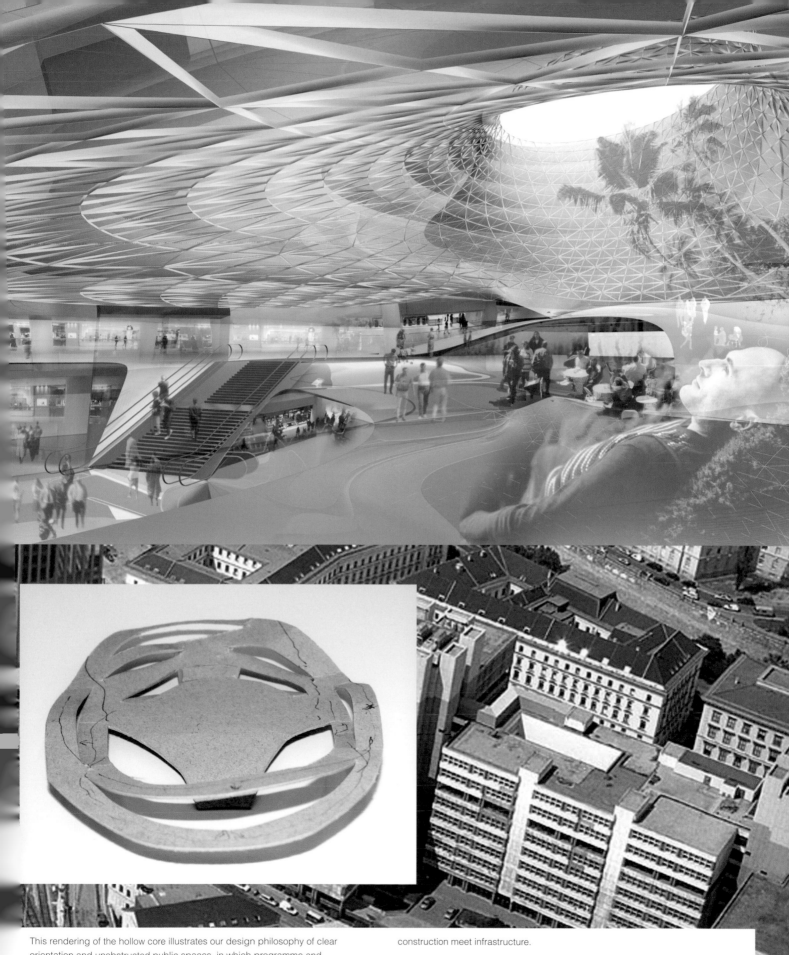

This rendering of the hollow core illustrates our design philosophy of clear orientation and unobstructed public spaces, in which programme and construction meet infrastructure.

The main entrance of Vienna Central Station.

Deep-planning principle

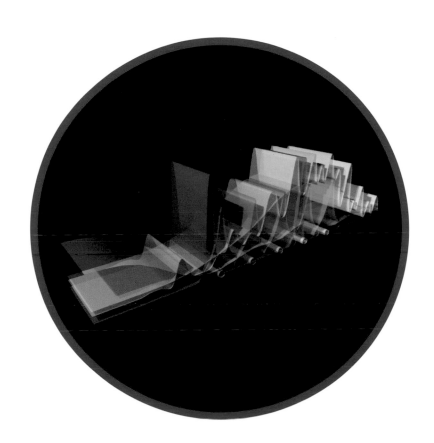

Deep-planning principle

Our early experiences with the 'mobile forces' of large, infrastructure-informed projects on an urban scale (the ever-changing and interrelated forces of construction, politics, money and the city) taught us not only to recognize these elements as the contemporary ingredients of architecture, but also to see them in connection with each other. Balancing these unstable, shifting layers requires the addition of the largest determinant of all: time. Time is introduced both as a binding factor and as a quotient, and allows us to calculate values related to use. Time-based planning, as we might also call deep planning, delivers images of locations as transformative models that address relationships vital to development potential, such as programme and distance, public access and attraction.

A view of the contemporary city as a material organization of time-sharing social practices, working through flows, lies at the basis of deep planning. Flows are sequences of exchange and interaction in the economic and symbolic structures of society. The space of flows is made up of localized networks that link up with global ones. The flow of the physical movement of people and goods reveals the relationship between duration and territorial use. Movement studies are important in determining the composition of a location; analysis of types of movement includes the direction of the various trajectories, their prominence in relation to the forms of transportation on the site, their links to different programmes, and their interconnections.

All this began in 1995 when we were asked, along with many other Dutch architects, to provide a vision for Rotterdam in 2045. We suddenly realized that architecture does not dispose of the means for designing in the future. Intrigued, we started to build a model forecasting future developments in the form of a rubber mat. The mat was the first model, albeit admittedly a rough and primitive one, to comprise change, instead of being a mere architectural or urban plan.

The rubber mat consists of four layers: dwelling, work, leisure and green space. The mats are projected into future time, in which movement is generated by the following factors: value of land, building and habitation density, and the growth of enterprises. By superimposing the four mats, one can see how changes in each of these factors will permeate different fields. The rubber mat shows an allotment structure, an architectural organization principle in four dimensions; the whole area suitable for building lies between the mats, moving in time.

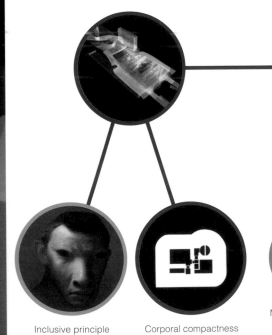

Inclusive principle   Corporal compactness   Mathematical model   Asymmetrical curve   The oblique   Pivotal point

Urban planning from industrial age; equal potential grid

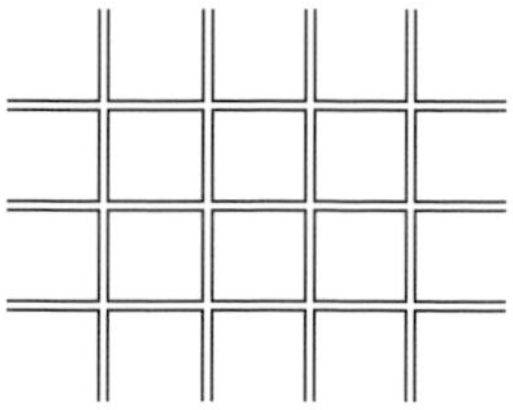

Time-based planning; entailing selection of critical programme package, contemporary user groups and a relational approach to access and publicness

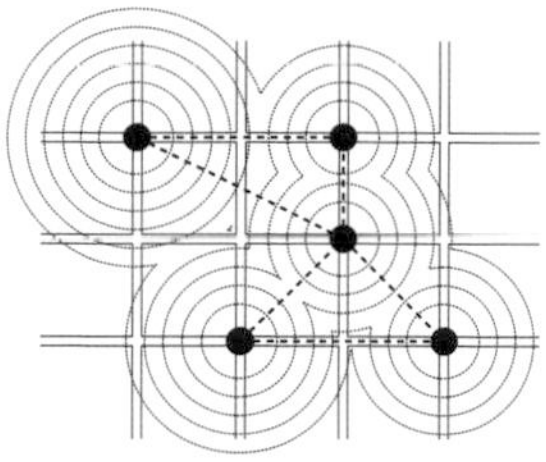

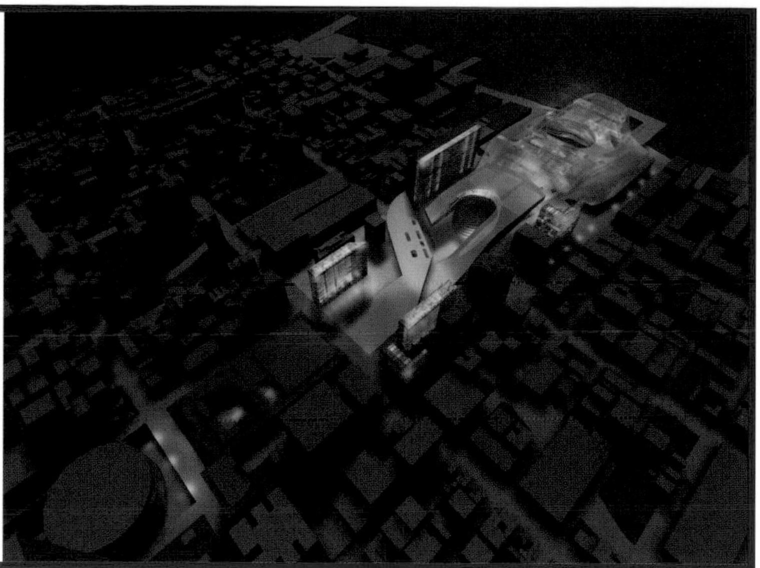

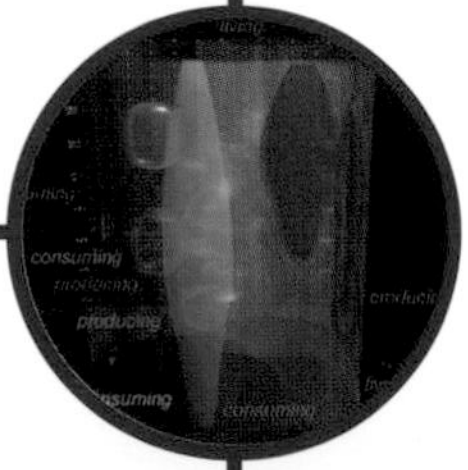

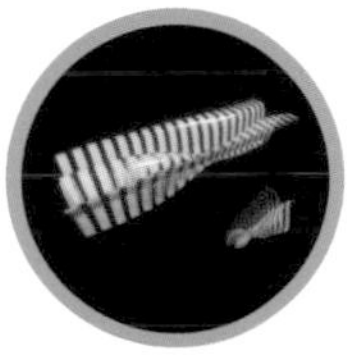

V-model

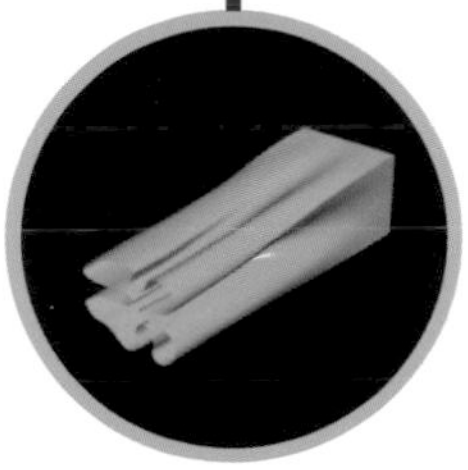

Blob-to-box model

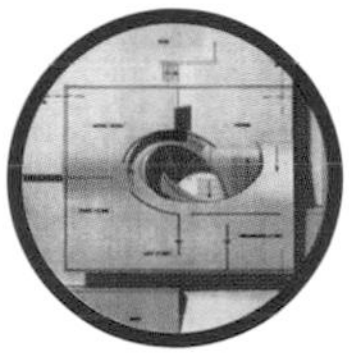

Hollow core

Crossing-point model

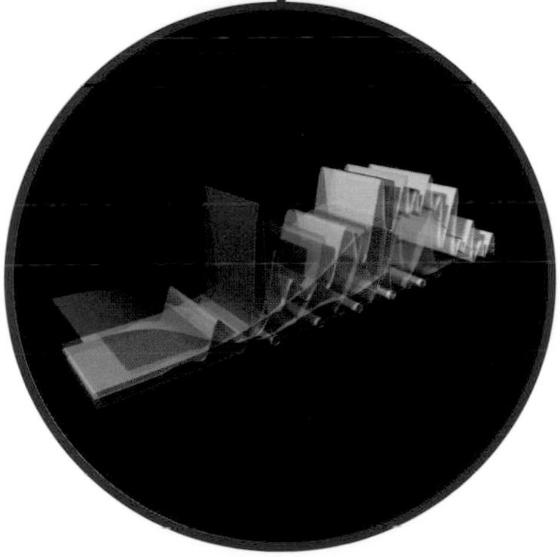

Deep-planning principle

Shopping Centre Renovation, Emmen
Image upon image upon image
1994–1996

The 1960s concrete-panelled façades of the department store have been replaced by a lighter, glazed cladding. The store has also been reorganized internally, with the addition of a gallery, apartments, and smaller shop outlets. A new public passage on the ground floor changes the arrangement of the shopping centre, giving it a stronger directional structure than the original, meandering one. The façade takes on a new role, becoming the skin that keeps the complex together and produces different effects. It can be reflective, transparent, or translucent. As demonstrated by the curved, glazed façade of the gallery, it can be all of those at the same time, too, generating a surface for the fleeting appearance of various images and messages, like a natural, non-digital, unprogrammed media wall.

Bridge and Bridge Master's House, Purmerend
Open and closed
1995–1998

The municipal commission for an infrastructural node between the Pumerend city centre and a new residential neighbourhood is an integrated design based on studies relating to the synchronization of the traffic flow it is to support, a 'crossing-point' model. Conclusions drawn from movement studies, which incorporate related transport systems, time-based usage and connection to the existing city grid, determined the scale, form and location of the programme's elements.

The bridge has been designed with three individual decks, one for cars and two for pedestrian and bicycle traffic, which open and close independently and at different rhythms. The undersides of the decks have been completely steel-encased, showing no ribs. Structural elements are controlled from the bridge master's house, a small edifice that is perched 8 metres (26 ft) above sea level. Technical facilities are placed at ground level, and upstairs are the domestic spaces and workrooms of the bridge master.

The modest structure has been wrapped in stretched-metal plates, which are applied to the concrete core of the building, and reveal, from certain angles, the interior of the lower half of the structure. Depending on the viewpoint, the building appears transparent, semi-transparent, or closed, with moiré effects gleaned from specific perspectives.

Positive note 10a Be glad that you will **never be famous**. Even the most stellar architect is nothing compared to a movie star or president. You are free; there is no need to set yourself up as a **slave to the media**. If you do, the reflection of your success in publicity will boost your chances of acquiring new opportunities. For this reason, you try to **play the game**. But where will you draw the line? After becoming a **minor kind of star**, you may find (and here this positive note transforms into a **cautionary tale**) that you have begun to produce for the media. You cultivate a **media-savvy persona**, with a provocative quote always at the ready. And, sadly, your work loses all **cultural meaning**. Like the newscasts for which it is now produced, although ever wittier and more ironic, it is also empty, shallow and detached. So we say: choose culture as the focus of your production.

Positive note 10b Then again (not to contradict ourselves), don't be shy! When all is said and done, architecture does take up a lot of space, so the least you can do is to **say something**. Make a statement, put across an idea. One of the reasons why we feel that Mies van der Rohe is the **most overrated architect** of his time is that, besides having only one idea and continually repeating it, he said too little. Loos, Semper and **Le Corbusier** may have spoken into a void, but their opinions **still resonate**. It is the construction manager's role to be the silent hero, and that of the architect to be the **desperate chatterer**, full of **bright ideas**.

Time-based urbanism
1997

We consider this competition to be one of our key projects, because of the urban ideas that were developed as a result of extensive studies into user movements, and because of the shifts in urban uses of the postindustrial city. Principles developed for this entry would later be added to those established at Arnhem Central (see p. 272), constituting a number of the fundamental elements at the heart of the deep-planning method. Our proposal was presented as an integral strategy, which allowed fragmentation and differences to be absorbed into a coherent, continuous approach.

The subject of this study is the area around Pennsylvania Station, between 42nd and 23rd Streets. This area contains a number of service facilities that form obstacles in two respects: they constitute physical barriers that block fluid connections between locations, and they prevent further development and full land use of several districts. Diagrams were made which map the performance of Manhattan in order to extract parameters for the development of the site. At the basis of the 'critical package' (a term chosen to indicate relational qualities), lies the question of which combination of factors is optimal for the site to function effectively with respect to programmes, construction, economy, community concerns, and political and managerial feasibility.

The answer is to develop and implement a new urban package for the postindustrial, global city. Affected by the decline of the harbour area since the 1960s, the site now acts as an infrastructural link within a broader network of sites of attraction, consumption and major transportation nodes. It has the potential to function as a 'lobby' for Manhattan.

The consideration at the basis of this scheme concerns the future of this part of Midtown in the face of the increasing homogenization of cities. All over the world, similar metropolitan conglomerations cater to a transnational population of urban travellers. These non-places of the business élite all seem based on the original prototype of Manhattan, inviting the question of what steps the borough will take to distinguish itself from replicas, and to once again set the tone for the future.

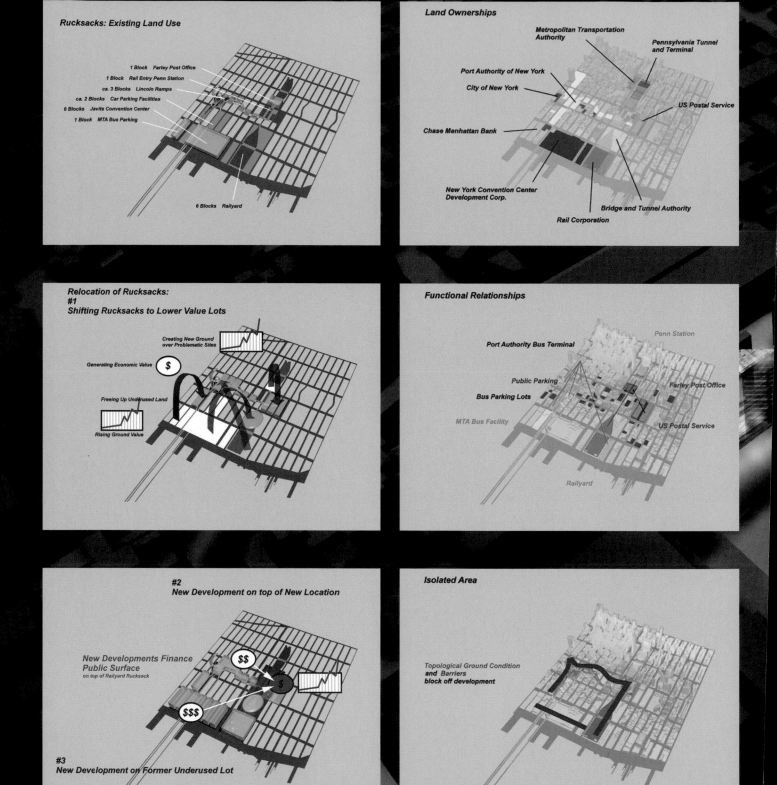

Rucksacks: Existing Land Use

1 Block   Farley Post Office
1 Block   Rail Entry Penn Station
ca. 3 Blocks   Lincoln Ramps
ca. 2 Blocks   Car Parking Facilities
6 Blocks   Javits Convention Center
1 Block   MTA Bus Parking

6 Blocks   Railyard

Land Ownerships

Metropolitan Transportation Authority
Pennsylvania Tunnel and Terminal
Port Authority of New York
City of New York
US Postal Service
Chase Manhattan Bank
New York Convention Center Development Corp.
Bridge and Tunnel Authority
Rail Corporation

Relocation of Rucksacks:
#1
Shifting Rucksacks to Lower Value Lots

Creating New Ground over Problematic Sites
Generating Economic Value $
Freeing Up Underused Land
Rising Ground Value

Functional Relationships

Port Authority Bus Terminal
Penn Station
Public Parking
Farley Post Office
Bus Parking Lots
MTA Bus Facility
US Postal Service
Railyard

#2
New Development on top of New Location

New Developments Finance
Public Surface
on top of Railyard Rucksack
$$
$
$$$

#3
New Development on Former Underused Lot

Isolated Area

Topological Ground Condition
and Barriers
block off development

Diagrams of the 'rucksack' strategy: this strategy of negotiation involves reorganizing and densifying facilities, rather than replacing them.

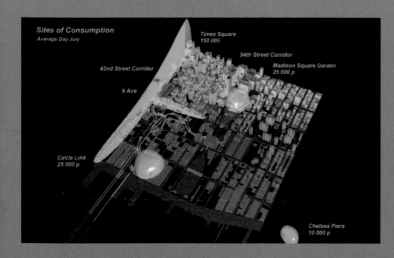

Sites of Consumption
Average Day July

Times Square
150 000

34th Street Corridor

42nd Street Corridor

Madison Square Garden
25 000 p

9 Ave

Circle Line
25 000 p

Chelsea Piers
10 000 p

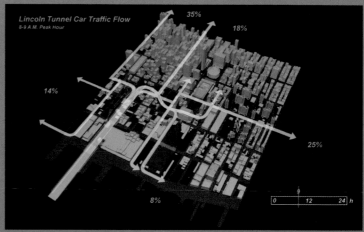

Lincoln Tunnel Car Traffic Flow
8-9 A.M. Peak Hour

35%

18%

14%

25%

8%

0   12   24 h

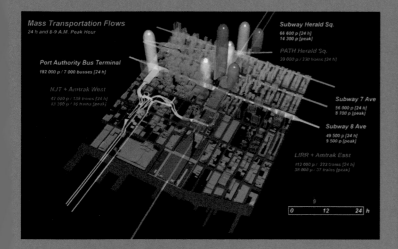

Mass Transportation Flows
24 h and 8-9 A.M. Peak Hour

Subway Herald Sq.
66 600 p [24 h]
14 300 p [peak]

PATH Herald Sq.
39 000 p / 230 trains [24 h]

Port Authority Bus Terminal
182 000 p / 7 000 busses [24 h]

NJT + Amtrak West
42 000 p / 138 trains [24 h]
13 200 p / 16 trains [peak]

Subway 7 Ave
56 000 p [24 h]
8 700 p [peak]

Subway 8 Ave
49 500 p [24 h]
9 500 p [peak]

LIRR + Amtrak East
112 000 p / 223 trains [24 h]
38 000 p / 27 trains [peak]

0   12   24 h

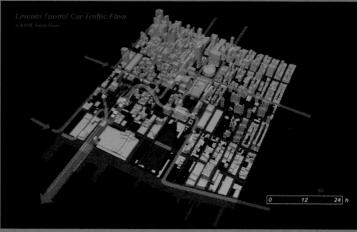

Lincoln Tunnel Car Traffic Flow
5-6 P.M. Peak Hour

0   12   24 h

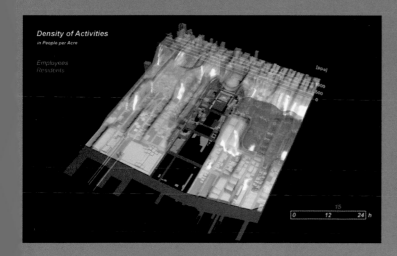

Density of Activities
in People per Acre

Employees
Residents

[ppa]

1000
500
0

15

0   12   24 h

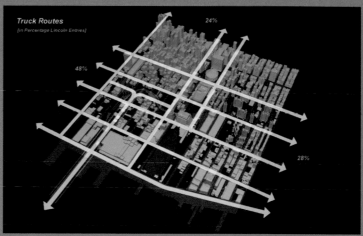

Truck Routes
[in Percentage Lincoln Entries]

24%

48%

28%

Diagrams of the 'critical package' for the global city, which is built up using
scenarios, diagrams, parameters, formulas and themes.

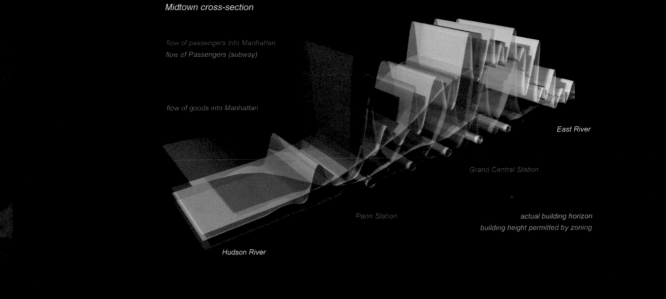

flow of passengers into Manhattan
flow of Passengers (subway)

flow of goods into Manhattan

East River

Grand Central Station

Penn Station

actual building horizon
building height permitted by zoning

Hudson River

1

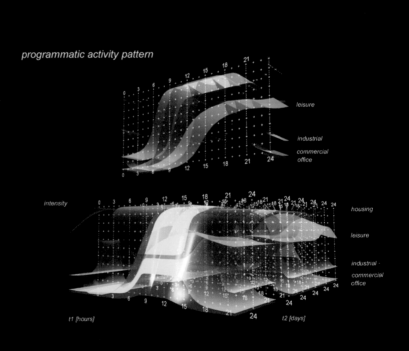

programmatic activity pattern

leisure

industrial

commercial
office

intensity

housing

leisure

industrial

commercial
office

t1 [hours]

t2 [days]

2

1 This diagram of the Midtown cross-section shows that the commuter influx (red) of Grand Central Station is balanced by the building volume (white) and subway traffic (blue), whereas the commuter influx at Penn Station is an isolated peak.

2 Diagram illustrating the programme activities throughout the day.

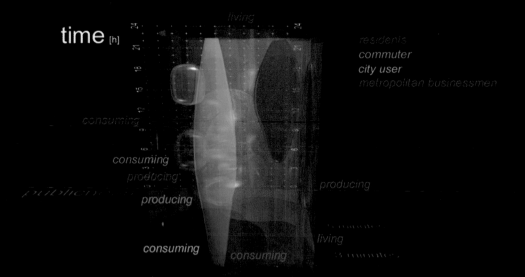

time [h]

living

residents
commuter
city user
metropolitan businessmen

consuming

consuming
producing

producing

producing

living

consuming

consuming

access

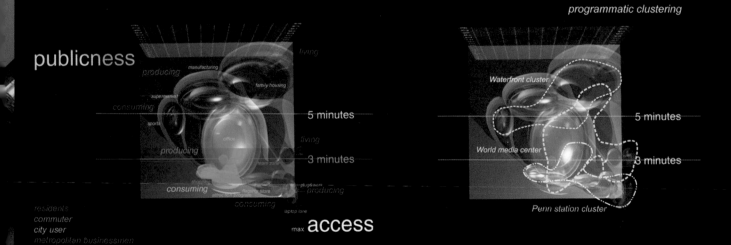

programmatic clustering

publicness

living

producing   manufacturing

family housing

supermarket

consuming

sports

office

producing   living

5 minutes

3 minutes

shopping

consuming   flagship store

plug&work
producing

consuming

laptop lane

max access

Waterfront cluster

World media center

5 minutes

3 minutes

Penn station cluster

residents
commuter
city user
metropolitan businessmen

3

3 Analysis of the relational parameters at the location. The
'seven-dimensional' diagram relates access to proximity and time
to different programmes and different degrees of publicness versus
privacy.

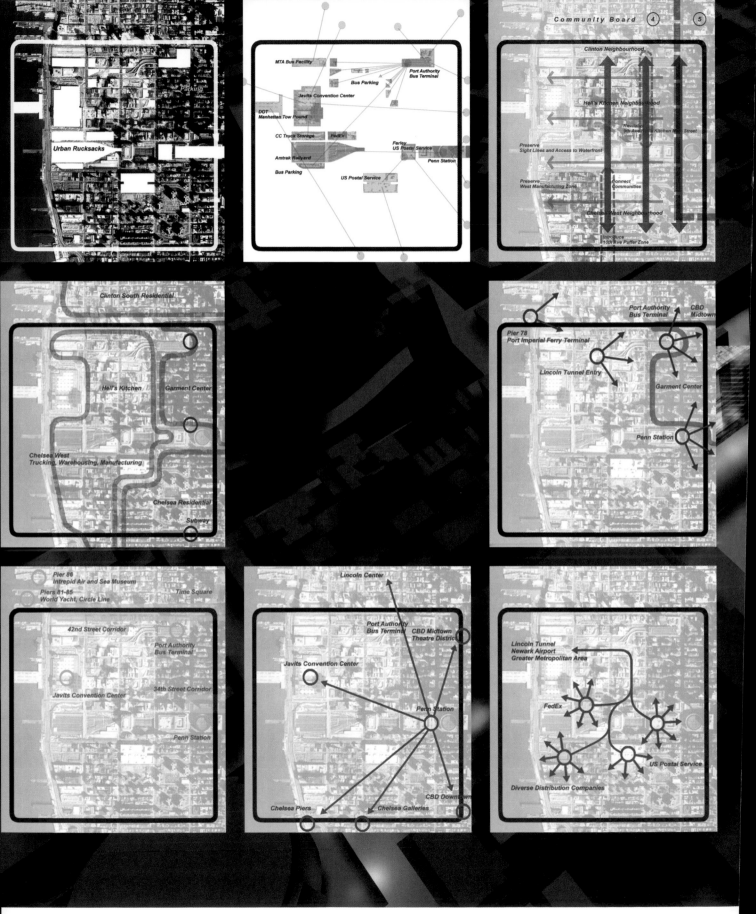

Diagrams showing user groups in relation to the critical package.

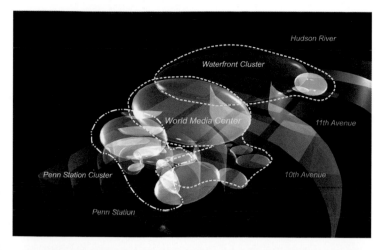

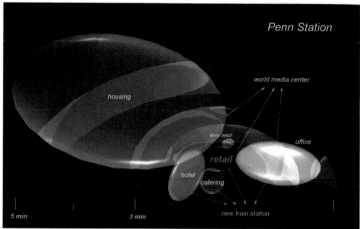

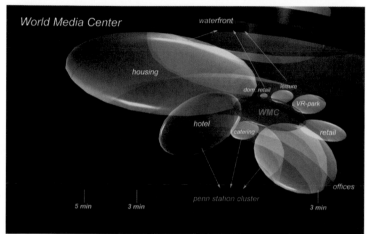

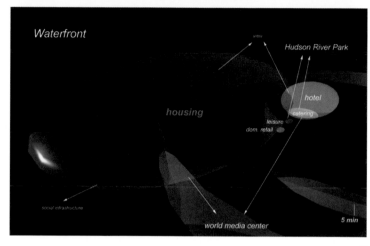

1

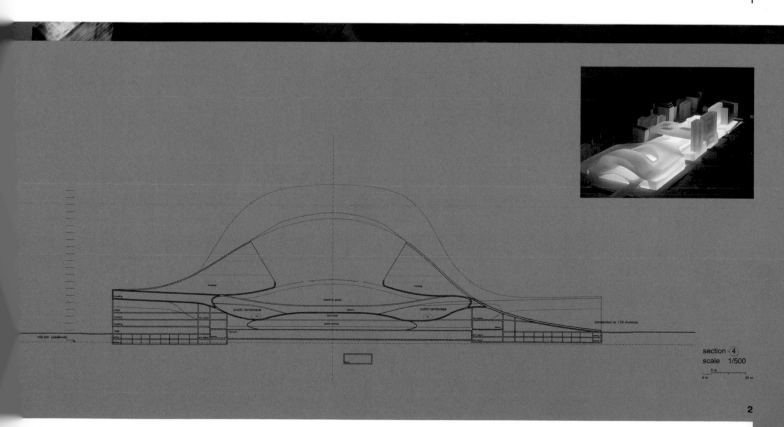

2

1 Renderings of programme clustering at Midtown locations.

2 Section and model of the media centre.

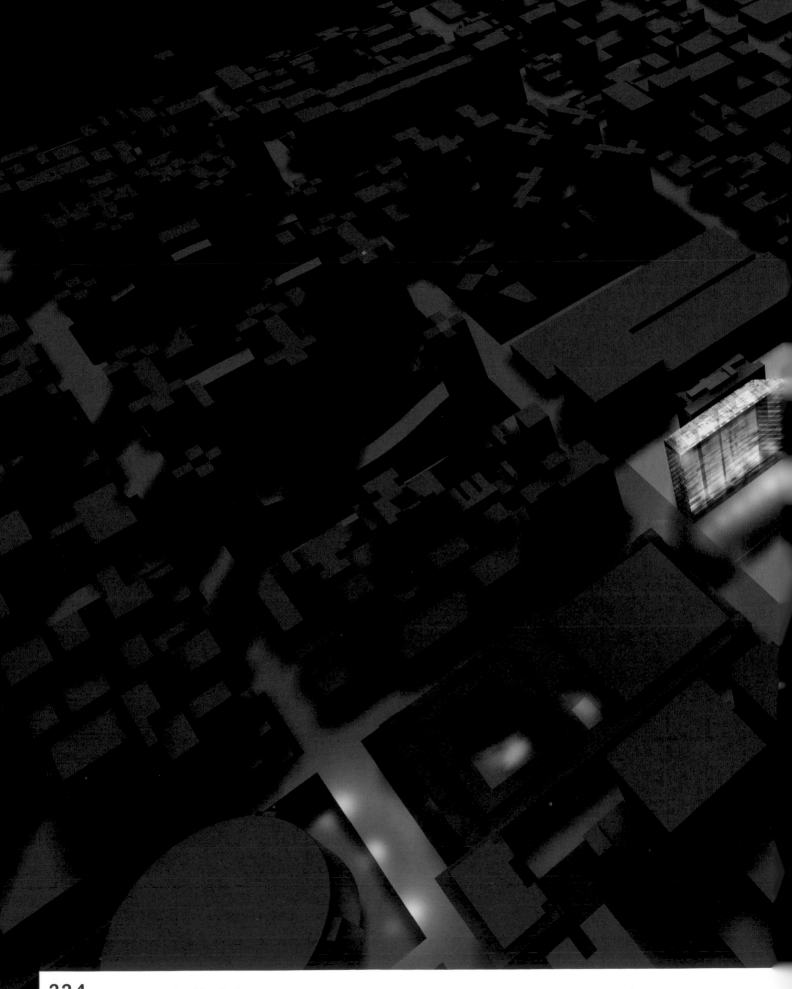

Offices La Defense, Almere
Dynamic abstraction
1999–2004

The iridescent inner walls lining the courtyards comprise the machine that invigorates this project; the flat, glazed membranes are treated with a special film that destroys any iconic semblance by generating continuously changing images.

The offices consist of four partly interconnected blocks of varying lengths, ranging in height from three or four, to five or six stories, with the differences in height resulting in sharply sloping angles. Conclusions drawn from site investigations dictated the placement of the inner courtyards' two entrances at points that tie in with the larger urban plan, linking park and street.

The materialization of the outer elevations, clad with aluminium and silver-coloured glass, also relate to the urban setting, whilst localized variations of the façade treatment respond to the programmatic distribution, as well as to acoustical and wind-load parameters. In contrast to the protective outer shell, flashes of the flame-like internal walls can be seen through two large openings. These internal courtyard elevations feature glass sheeting, covered with a film that changes colour depending on both light and the viewer's perspective. Investigations into various materials and effects were carried out with both office tenants and environmental concerns in mind. The desire is to create spaces that animate daylight by producing ever-changing atmospheres in the office environment.

Developed in collaboration with 3M, the film was specially produced for this project in Japan. TNO-tested and based on an existing packaging material, it is covered with additional layers that render it suitable to serve as transparent wall-cladding, shielded from the sun. Depending on the position of the sun and the viewer, the wall will turn blue, yellow and red; in the evening, the complementary colours will show up as a result of the indoor lighting. The reflection is so intense, at 99 per cent, that the adjacent paving takes on the same colour.

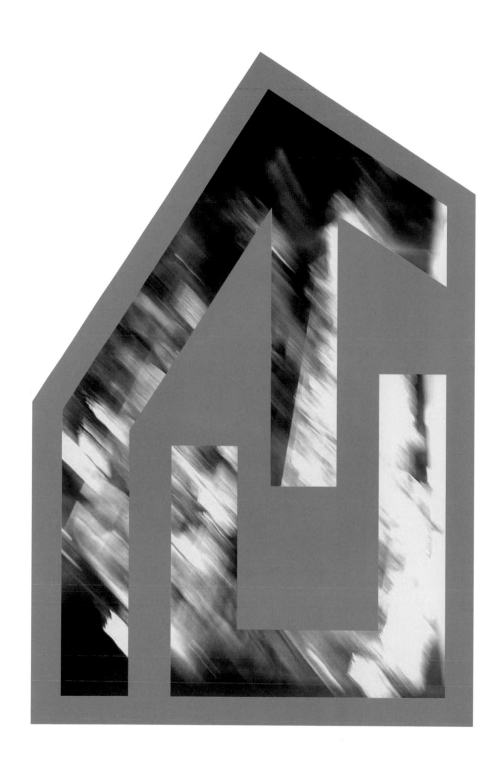

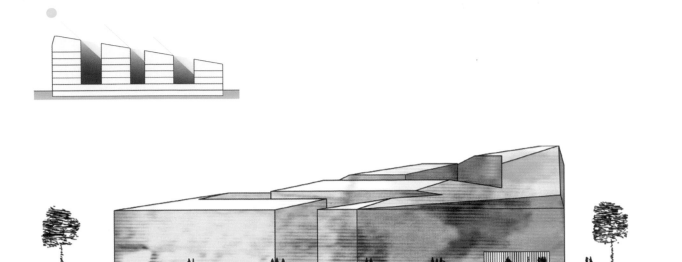

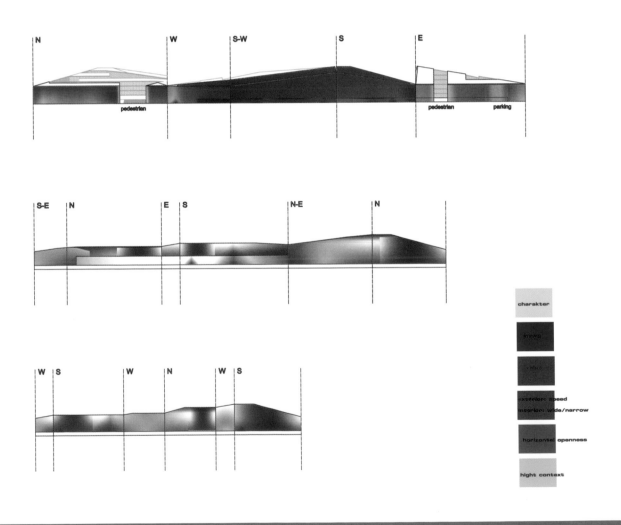

charakter

??????

????? ??

exterior: speed
interior: wide/narrow

horizontal openness

hight context

Studies analyze daylight and the building's volume, as well as light and colour
reflections of the façade.

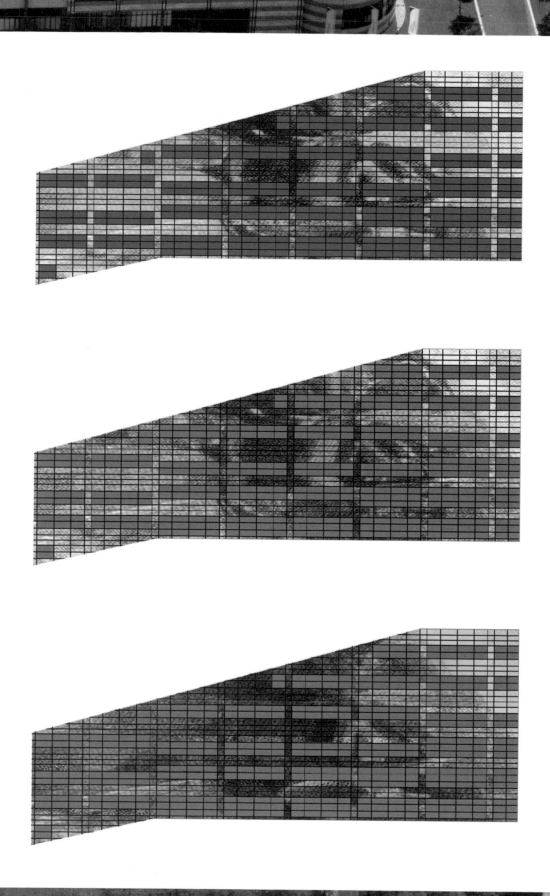

Schematic analysis of the climate façade, showing variables in the incidence of
sunlight over the different seasons.

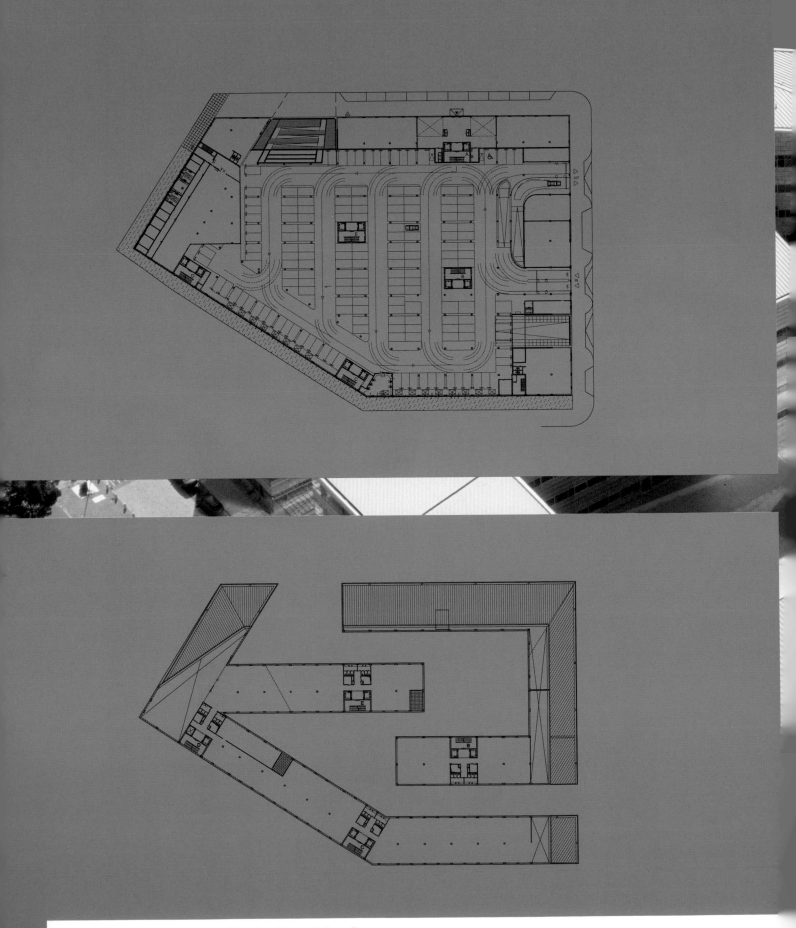

Plans of the ground-level parking garage (above) and the fourth-floor office
spaces (below).

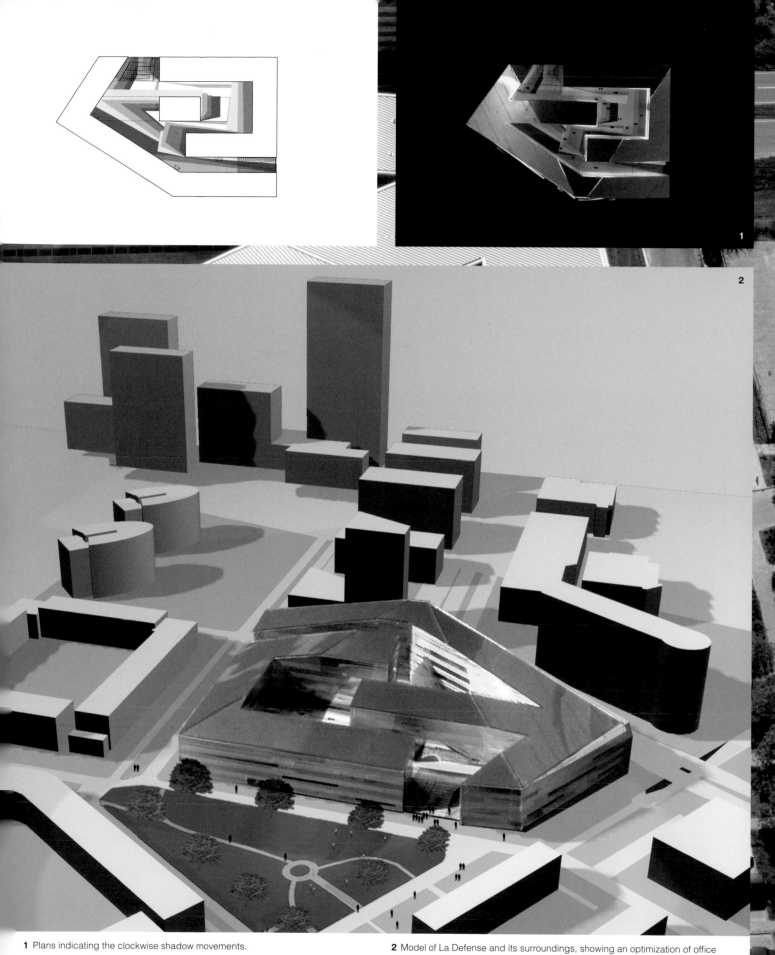

1 Plans indicating the clockwise shadow movements.

2 Model of La Defense and its surroundings, showing an optimization of office space directly linked to the parameters of light and technical requirements.

Study models investigating light effects and the differences between the internal
and external courtyard façades.

From red to blue: lit from the inside, the foil takes on the same complementary shade as when lit from the outside.

Inside façade, with the foil that we first discovered on the cover of a science magazine. Although recognized for its sunscreen properties, the foil's diachronic effect was considered undesirable. The foil has since been used as packaging material and its original purpose neglected – until revived by UN Studio.

Shadows and reflections interact with the building's surroundings.

After-effects: the world of work at different times of the day.

Positive note 11 It's over; you may never have to do another project, another building, again. In the present day, the 'building' is a rarity. In seventeen years we brought to fruition only three houses and two museums; the other projects that made it into reality (over twenty of them) were all hybrids, complex packages of needs and desires relating to urban life, transportation and mixed-programme uses. But that doesn't mean you have to disappear as an architect. The wonderful paradox is that the product of architectural vision is valued and in demand. Few people have been trained to cultivate the encompassing imaginative powers that architects possess. In the complex situations that characterize today's densely populated, urbanized sites, which are increasingly striated by infrastructural connections and hubs, those imaginative skills are vital. Focused architects, ready for the future, will invest in increasing their **connective imaginative** capacity, alongside the ability to express and communicate their **collective vision**.

Galleria Department Store, Seoul
Magnetic geometries
2003–2004

As with the project for Almere (see p. 336), the building re-imagines itself in moving colours. The invited commission for this department store renovation encompasses the introduction of a new façade and integrated interior. The guiding force behind the façade is the desire to create an envelope that, in a similar manner to fashion, can change over time and reinvent itself. The renovation consists of the application of 4,330 glass disks on an aluminium substructure that is directly attached to the existing concrete elevations. A great deal of time was spent exploring different materials, sizes and surface treatments in order to achieve the desired results. The conclusion of these studies indicated that the façade would be made of sandblasted, laminated glass disks onto which a special dicroic foil is applied, causing constant changes in perception according to the angles of view and light.

By night, a lighting scheme designed in collaboration with Ove Arup interacts with the material condition of the glass disks. The placement of three digitally controlled LED-light sources behind each one results in an infinite variety of colour and lighting schemes. Clouds of saturated colour, alternating with messages, chase along the scale-like screen and contrast with the more subdued, enigmatic daytime image.

The interior renovation is focused in the shared public zones between the individual concessions. UN Studio has sought to streamline the circulation spaces, providing 'catwalks' of glossy, light-coloured and coordinated walkways and ceilings, which improve orientation and give the store a super-bright, fresh image. Moving through the store, the visitor, like a model, is the focus of the fashion world. The hotchpotch of superfluous and outdated details is removed, replaced instead by two new 'big details': the escalator, which is conceived as a moving event space, and the ceiling lighting, which doubles as a device that provides fluent directionality and dynamism to the shop floors.

Top left Individual disks are fixed to the façade construction by three clamps, which are attached to an aluminium substructure.

Façade studies test various foils and the degree of translucency, colouring, diffusion of light and reflection.

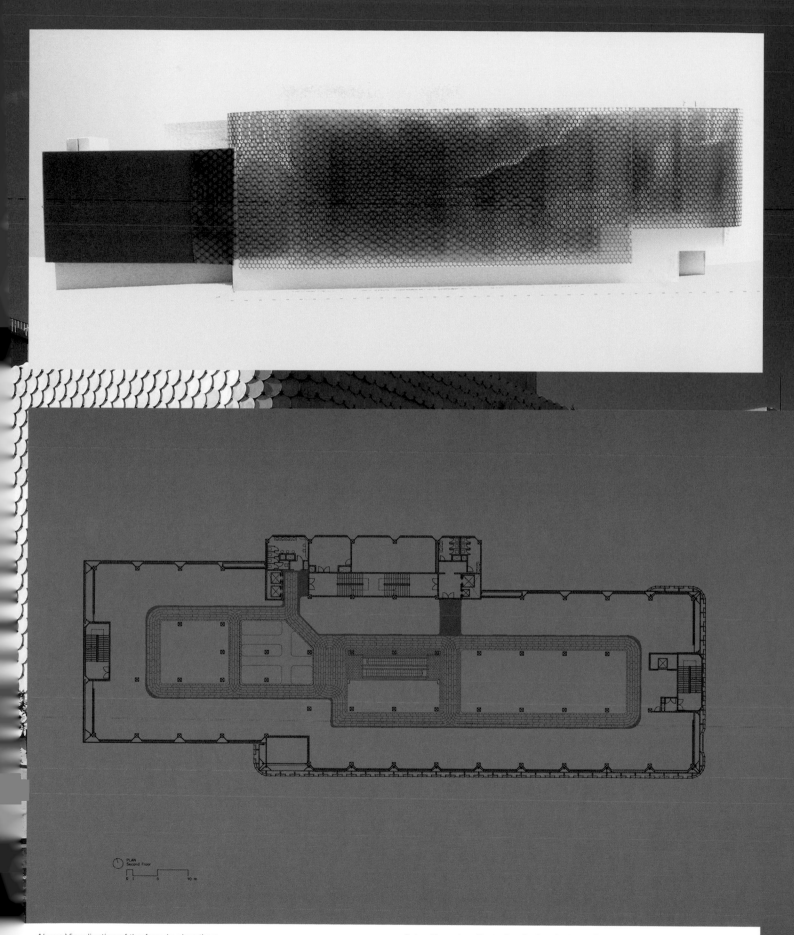

Above Visualization of the façade elevations

Below Floor plan, illustrating the interior 'catwalk' and external position of the new façade.

Application of double-layered glass with a 20 per cent mirror-articulating foil enclosing the escalator shaft.

The reflective floor and ceiling together generate the 'catwalk'; lines within the
light bands emphasize circulatory patterns. Furniture elements are seamlessly
integrated into the overall concept.

The continually changing appearance of the façade is achieved by programmed
LED-lights of the three basic colours that illuminate each individual glass disk.

Port, Las Palmas
Reductive expressive
2005

The 'flower island' (or Isla de la Luz), the centrepiece of the competition proposal for the port of Gran Canaria's capital city, is the 'after image' of the project, the picture and the idea that you will take home with you. This artificial island, designed for large-scale events and fiestas, addresses matters of structure and island identity. Its uncomplicated outlines are informed by a packed set of performance-, view- and utility-driven constraints.

The question at the heart of the redevelopment proposal is how to amalgamate port and city, in the face of both the need for expansion and shifts in the harbour territory. The competition area concerns the isthmus that forms the hinge between the existing centre of Las Palmas and future developments. The western side of the isthmus, formed by the public beach of Las Canteras, is transformed into a pedestrianized waterfront that provides various spaces for cultural and leisure activity.

Improved connections and a direct relationship with the waterfront are at the core of the proposal. The location is characterized by two exceptional morphologies, which are natural in origin: the isthmus and the isleta. We have added a third morphology, Isla de la Luz. The 'flower island' is a new link in the chain of island-related configurations. It provides more civic space in which to enhance cultural opportunities and activities.

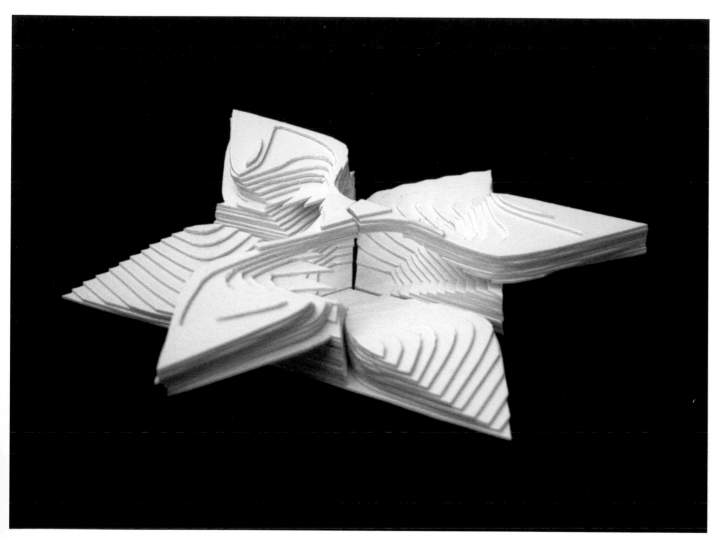

After image

In this essay we set out to explore the problems surrounding the visual manifestation of architecture. How buildings are experienced visually is, and will always remain, central to architecture, but the topic of the image is almost impossibly loaded. Yet architects have inherited a discipline that mixes the constructive and the reflective, progresses through words as much as through works, and must therefore address this delicate subject, beginning with the question of why it should be considered so delicate in the first place.

We attempt to specify some of the problems of the architectural image, such as the processes leading to its commodification. One predicament is the pervasiveness of signage; images give rise to signs, but today signs have come to control images. Whether as visitors to architectural sites or as readers looking at pictures, we are habitually confronted with repetitive, flat, empty images.

These images are even situated stereotypically; it is often the outside face of a building that is photographed and becomes loved. But why should the face of a building always be on the outside? Why, for that matter, can the face not be replaced altogether by a moving picture gallery, a changing kaleidoscope of images?

We question, too, if and how we can replace the manipulative, one-dimensional image with something far more advanced and intangible: the 'after image', the one you take home with you, an inexhaustible, ever-renewing composite of perceptions, memories and thoughts.

No design, no style

The question of image is rarely confronted today. It is the most suspect terrain of the arts and is therefore avoided. Image in all forms of art, including architecture, has been abused too much, reflecting, justifying and inciting commercial manipulation, oppression, and even violence. But circumventing the issue of image can result in a discursive tour de force, imposing a silence on the topic of the work produced while pursuing an intense, but imperspicuous, alternative discourse. Architectural communication can appear self-absorbed, and jargon-laden by outsiders. Even those with connections to the profession are regularly exasperated by the hermetic attitude of architects who insist on carrying out an impenetrable conversation amongst themselves and refuse to address what everyone sees.

The problem with talking about the image of architecture is that it is both hard to describe and dangerous to fixate. One of the pitfalls of the image in architecture is that it quickly becomes defined in terms of style; all efforts to rethink the image in art are turned into architectural styles with disturbing ease. The syntactical rudiments of these styles are fixed with exaggerated force because an entire industry, with its own inexorable procedures and regulations, is amassed around them. Once the relentless downward pull of manufacture and distribution has taken hold of a facet of architectural imagery, it, in convergence with the processes of mediatization, turns the image into a black alter ego, a dark, nihilistic shadow of itself. Every detail is broadcast almost as soon as it is invented, and turned into the décor of another, shabbier performance than the one for which it was originally intended.

Ruptures with previous styles become new styles; the dissonance and asymmetry of modernity are frozen into style, in the same way that the order and symmetry of neoclassicism had been. In this way, the formal elements and methodical relationships that compose a style eventually pose an ontological problem. For if, as we believe, the role of architecture is to make us see ourselves and the world around us in a new way, then the idea of the architectural image frozen into style is a disaster. Its effects are diametrically opposed to our aim of intensifying the gaze, inspiring thoughts and images, and making it attractive for people to linger and return to the places we make for them. Style makes the image of architecture all too familiar, and causes people to turn away in boredom and disgust. Trying to prevent their work from becoming frozen into a style in the face of an avalanche of industrial and media-driven misappropriation, architects' strong sense of alienation reverberates in almost every word, spoken or written.

The everyday construction of images and icons

At the same time, everyone is more preoccupied with the image than ever before. Almost every architectural competition requests a landmark or iconic building, and from the moment that you begin your practice, you are aware that your work must convey the right imagery. Municipalities use architecture to attract companies and population groups that can stimulate their economy. They want to provide the facilities that a discerning urban audience requires, but these theatres, museums and conference centres are also intended to present, or so the cities hope, an attractive image. Museums especially fulfill this role. The art world has accepted that some of the new iconic museums compete with the artworks they house; instead of providing neutral settings for art, these museums dictate which artworks and artists can fill them. In these instances, image, in the sense of deliberate sign-making, has become a question of utility, just as function is. For this reason alone, the question of the role of image deserves to be reconsidered.

Although not a new concept, the recent attempts to create explicit focal points certainly constitute a radical break with recent history. Most of the prime image-making architects active today came along at a time when the prevalent issues, such as structuralism, represented a much more introverted interpretation of architecture. Little or no debate on this topic, therefore, has occurred for many years, and the realization of icons and images takes place almost surreptitiously, under the cover of other concerns. Not being firmly embedded in current design practices makes the question of image extremely difficult to evaluate. Ironically, as a result its importance can be overrated.

Yet there are landmark buildings that have come to

represent not just a particular place, but also the implicit values connected to their surroundings. These values, such as technological advancement and a modern and daring spirit, lend the icon its emblematic significance. More important than any particular representational aspect or purely aesthetic consideration is the fact that its complex history, including discord and failure, is well known and closely associated with its image.

Consequently, it seems to us that icons, and not just architectural ones, are not consciously designed at all. The construction of an icon takes many years, occupies many media, and yet reverberates with a continuous message or theme. Given these conditions, it can even be questioned if the architect should want to be involved in the construction of an icon at all. The spectre of Albert Speer is never far away. Even in the most democratic and enlightened societies, negative icons resound, kept fresh and alive in the public imagination through television, print media and the internet.

Contemporary iconographic practices

How then are we to respond to the resulting dilemma? On the one hand, our culture craves images and demands the shock of the new every five seconds, hence the ubiquitous requests for icons; requests that are impossible to resist, as witnessed by the plethora of landmark buildings recently completed or under way. The opposition to an image culture that still was feasible only a few years ago is no longer an option. The demand for new images cannot simply be rejected; we must acknowledge that the 'new' fulfills an important role in our culture. To reject it seems to be a sign of problematic societies.

On the other hand, just another funny form will not fill the void. What is needed is an attempt by architects to strategize the images generated by their work, just as they do other aspects of design, to bring them in line with a conscious ambition. Already it is possible to distinguish different approaches. Some contemporary architects return to an almost Boullée-like sense of unfolding drama to convey a state of enhanced meaningfulness. The unfinished narrative becomes an aspect of the architecture. This is what, as United Architects, we attempted to infuse into the memorial part of our proposal for New York City's Ground Zero. We incorporated into the design a spatialized version of the high placement of icons in Russian Orthodox churches, generating a devotional upward gaze.

But drama is not the only option, nor is it advisable to opt for sublime and baroque effects frequently as the situation rarely warrants it. Keeping it light and almost scientific is our policy; the ploys invented to intensify the gaze are directly related to the traditional ingredients of architecture: construction, light, circulation, and so on.

Learning from artists, we like to expand the genre of the icon. We play with it. We try to make ugly icons, ridiculous icons that go with our crazy times and appreciation of the bizarre. Our Living Tomorrow project in Amsterdam (see p. 164) is an example of building that flirts with the absurd and has personality traits that almost, but not quite, qualify for it icon status. An icon needs the patina of time, and the layering of meanings that reinforce each other in different media. Even then, at some point it will stop working.

Architecture and its shadow

Reconsidering image and icon, we aim to respond to the following questions: how can we generate new, interesting and meaningful images for architecture? And how can we incorporate aspects of time if we accept that images and icons are subject to time-related transformations?

Newness, even short-lived newness, entails a form of temporary autonomy, as is sometimes seen when a new industrial product is introduced. The alien object cannot be placed; it has no clear lineage, no style, but is both fresh and enigmatic. It provokes wonderment: where did it come from, what is it for? The impression of autonomy, in fact, is ambiguous; this independent new artifact is in reality intrinsically linked to a world of market research and production processes, invisible to the consumer. The image it presents is utterly strange, but with time becomes familiar. The object is no longer alien, and its apparent autonomy revoked.

What is the architectural equivalent of this type of transient yet real and startling newness? Disappointingly, the shock of the new in many cases does not travel beyond the exterior. We confront elaborate shells, intricate surfaces, which, once entered, reveal spaces within that are not so different after all. Or we come across buildings in which every perceptible feature serves one prevailing concept. Get the concept, and there is nothing more to discover. Even the most provocative message does not survive a prolonged tour around this type of building. Another cause of visual discontent is the precipitate descent into style; we recognize the hand of the master almost before our eyes have hit upon the building itself. In all of these cases, the architecture has initiated some form of communication, but does not entirely fulfill its potential of generating strong, interesting, or new spatial perceptions.

The question of the temporariness of newness and the effects of duration leads us to contemplate the meaning of time-based icons. What exactly is the role of time in the perception of architecture? How can we optimize the movement-image? How do we layer the visual meanings to unfold as people move through buildings? Returning to the paradigm of the fresh enigma, we wonder: can we reverse positive and negative? Can we make architectural objects that appear uncomplicated, but generate rich spatial and visual experiences, positive after images, hopeful shadows?

Image and obsolescence: sensation and after image

It is the function of time to render obsolete all forms of utility, including the function of iconography. Eventually all that remains are the mute after images of buildings; over the abandoned constructs of the past only the eye continues to rove, loosened from the bonds of use and signage. The building that is unfinished, like a decayed ruin, has no functional purpose, it is experienced only through its material presence within its surroundings. Sometimes this is when a building will reach its most attractive state, without inhabitants, functioning almost as sculpture. The building site with its frantic activity and the incomplete building confront us with the limitations of the pragmatic and the utilitarian, but also of the conceptual and meaningful; these structures do nothing, nor do they mean or represent anything, but they might still move us.

Images only partly work through meaning; the other side of their effectiveness resides in pure, physiological sensation, which exists separately from the world of signs and mental representations. The nature of vision ensures that the mind responds instantaneously to the activity of the eye, as it senses and adjusts.

This is why we decided to invest in the longevity of our work by endowing it with specific forms of optical intensity, designed to generate the after images that obstruct the onset of perceptual obsolescence. While the ideas, emotions and associations evoked by sensations triggered by the optical system can be both stronger and longer-lived than any consciously created concepts or messages, they are not an intentional part of the architectural répertoire. 'After image' refers literally to the lingering visual impression caused by intense or prolonged stimulation of the retina. To us, the term means something slightly different; we use it to include the entire scale of sensory perceptions caused by intense impressions.

The intensity of the sensation aimed for is achieved by combining different types of image constructions, within the structure provided by the design model. Yet in order to elucidate these images, we have categorized them separately here, although in practice they are not applied in isolation. The variety of images that result in a proliferation of after images can be roughly divided into the following types: those that relate to the stretching and interconnecting of several themes; those that relate to structure and time; and those that relate to movement and future-orientated topics.

Expanded hybridized images

As we argued in the third part of *Move*, perceptual effects can be extended by combining the classical elements of architecture (light, texture, transition, dimension, and so on) with new techniques, insights, constraints and contexts. An example of the lingering sensations that result from this combining of elements is provided by the '1,000 façades' of the Erasmus Bridge (see p.

140), in Rotterdam, which is caused by the contrast between its uncomplicated outlines and the multiple images it generates. The image of the bridge itself was only a peripheral concern; the design, full of illogicalities and tensions, responded to 'mobile forces' (urban and constructive needs) and an ambition to look to the future. We employed such architectural ingredients as viewlines on an equal basis with civil engineering requirements like economy of material; urbanistic concerns formed a third point of departure. The density of images that the design produces is partly the consequence of this hybridization of disciplines.

The 'manimal' was the emblem we chose to represent this effect of hybridization on perceptual intensity and alienation. The monstrous, digitally created face to us talked about transformation and emergence. Devoid of humanity yet still recognizably a face, the manimal was nothing but a pure image construction without essence, capable of transforming itself into any guise, identity, or form; a surface for projections of all kinds. The constructs of architecture are like a face in that they speak to us and change continuously in response to internal and external events, yet contain no predetermined narrative.

Structure time images

One of the reasons why we are captivated by such illusionary mathematic structures as the Möbius strip and the Klein bottle is that they help us realize kaleidoscopic spaces that trigger the eye and brain, while at the same time helping us to fuse spaces of different durational uses. The V-structure of Arnhem Central (see p. 272), running through the entire project and displaying its structural nature, elevates service spaces to the quality of user spaces, and exposes the structural core of architecture. This idea of making structure both visible and accessible, seen also in the transformation of the structural knot into a public square at the Prince Claus Bridge (see p. 242), is not an aggrandizing gesture, but the consequence of the inclusive principle.

We have compared the Mercedes-Benz Museum (see p. 184) to a time machine in that, as the visitor wanders through the building, the sense of sequence is amplified.

The design model of a continuous volume with diagonal, transecting spaces delivers unexpected sensations of spatiality. The geometry of the plan, with its three overlapping circles, is suggestive of a trajectory subject to centrifugal forces which propels the visitor. Orientation is almost impossible, although it is equally impossible to lose your way. The museum engages in contradictions at all levels: it seems smaller from the outside than it does on the inside; its solid, curving masses of concrete embrace voids; and the stage-like exhibition platforms give the impression that you are standing still and that the building is revolving around you.

Future movement images

The multicoloured courtyard façades of the La Defense offices (see p. 336) engender after-effects incessantly through a combination of movement, light, reflections and cross-reflections. This complex play of changing pictures takes place against a backdrop of sober office organization; its expressiveness, therefore, is contained by the reductiveness of the building.

This expressive minimalism also characterizes the department store renovation in Seoul (see p. 354). The department store, neutral and business-like during the day, turns into a display of LED-activated colour at night. Just as the La Defense office walls evoke the world of work, the department store promotes reflections on shopping, spectacle and the pixellation of brands. These buildings offer glimpses of alternative experiences that bear a relationship to the more familiar reality, but how can we conjure up these inverted images? How do we stimulate the particular form of imagination that enables of to 'see double', or to find fresh wonders in banal conditions? To reveal this we use the notion of a figment.

Ghosts are figments of our imagination, but are real in the sense that they are imaginary constructs. The reality of such figments is fuller than that of a concept, idea, or notion, which are vague and verbally articulated. Figments, on the other hand, have a whole history, moving from narrative to narrative, interacting and fully formed. They are explicit, existing in a realm in between the representational and the actual.

When we design, you could say that we create new figments. But we call these unbuilt projects 'designs' (rather than figments), because they are already too real. They belong too much to the everyday world. There have been architects, like Piranesi or Constant, who have devoted themselves to creating a figment world of architecture, a strong and imaginative reality.

But we think that all of us have brief glimpses of figments all the time; they reveal themselves to us at moments when one reality level falls into the next. The potential for the design of figments first occurred to us when we considered the moment a digital camera moves automatically from one captured moment to the next half-captured one. The resulting image is partly generated by the framing of the previous (conscious) instant, and partly by the automatic (unconscious) mechanism of the camera. This figment moment suggests an architecture at its fullest, dissecting the construction, while being loaded with effect.

Conclusion

The need for the architect to balance long-term vision with the opportunity-driven experimentation that is at the basis of the design model is complemented by the turbulent equilibrium between thought systems and the visual world. The close collusion between structural, conceptual and visual thought systems persists in architecture, as in art, to this day. Like Andy Warhol, we tend to take a positive view of business-art, and extend the depersonalized vision this notion implies to the many real and virtual aspects that touch architecture.

Seeing architecture as both thought-made-spatial and business art has provoked many of the questions posed here, and has sparked our investigation of the image, its construct and its potential as a source of displacement, changeability, signification and sensation. Rather than condemn the inescapable image, more prevalent than ever, we believe the answer is to generate multiple and surprising after images by strengthening each image's logic of structure, spatiality and vision.

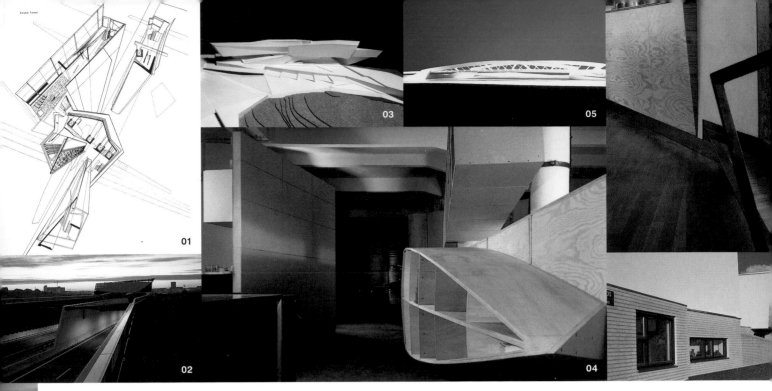

Chronology of projects

Study Projects Ben Van Berkel

1983–1988

1983
The Marathon Project, housing block for physical culture, Isle of Grain, Kent,
   Study

1984
'Intertwining landscapes', Design museum Hockney and Caro Gallery, London,
   Competition

1985
Room as pavilion, Design/realization
Crossing Points, Hyde Park, London, Design
Untitled house, London, Design

1986
Kensington barracks, urban study and housing, London, Design

1987
Docklands, London, final study project with Zaha Hadid, Design **(01)**

1988
Headquarters housing corporation 'Ons Huis', Amsterdam, Study
Penitentiary complex, Arnhem, Landscape design
Urban study and housing Geuzenveld West, Amsterdam, Design

Projects Van Berkel & Bos

1989

Primary school DROS, The Hague, Competition
De Raaks, housing, shopping mall, parking, Haarlem, Design
Gallery Van Rooy, Amsterdam, Design
Apartments in former Marine Hospital, Bloemendaal, Design
'IS in de Hal', exhibition design, Fund for Visual Arts, Design and Architecture,
   Rotterdam, Design/realization
Schellerhoek, 129 single-family houses, Zwolle, Design/realization
Urban plan and housing in former swimming pool Stoop, Overveen, Study/
   design
Urban plan 2,500 houses, Sloten, Amsterdam, Study
Office interior Kunst & Bedrijf, Amsterdam, Design/realization **(04)**
Theatre square, landscape design, Rotterdam, Urban study
Electrical substation, Amersfoort, Design/realization

1990

Apartments for presentation Slokker at BouwRAI 1990, Amsterdam, Design
Piet Hein tunnel and two service buildings, Amsterdam, Design/realization **(02)**
The Bathing Machine, apartments and boulevard, Domburg, Design **(03)**
Harbour Antwerpen, stad aan de stroom ('city on the river'), Antwerp,
   Competition 1st Prize
Karbouw, Amersfoort, Design/realization
Eastern harbour area, western tunnel entrance, Amsterdam, Study
Varkenoordse viaduct, Rotterdam, Design **(05)**
Villa Härtel, renovation and transformation into café-restaurant, Amersfoort,
   Design/realization **(06)**
Erasmus bridge, Rotterdam, Design/realization

1991

Water villas and apartments, Sloten, Amsterdam, Design/realization **(07)**
Hamseweg, 8 single-family houses and office space, Amersfoort, Design/
  realization
Offices Spido boat company, Rotterdam, Design/realization **(09)**
Master plan IJ-banks, Amsterdam, Study
De Kolk, housing, hotel, offices, shopping mall, parking, Amsterdam, Design/
  realization **(13)**

1992

Offices Pakhoed, Maas Boulevard, Rotterdam, Design
Multifunctional centre Kattenbroek, Amersfoort, Design/realization
Street furniture, kiosk at Rembrandt Square, Amsterdam, Design
Boxing hall, Berlin, Competition **(08)**
SWOZ 1, centre for mentally disabled, Amsterdam, Design **(10)**
Apartments Raadhuisplein, Zandvoort, Design
Office building Crea & Activa, Nijkerk, Design **(14)**
Villa Wilbrink, Amerfoort, Design/realization
ACOM, renovation office building, Amersfoort, Design/realization
Parking facilities, Erasmus bridge, Rotterdam, Design/realization
Rijksmuseum Twenthe, Enschede, Design/realization
Electrical substation, Ouderijn, Utrecht, Design
Urban plan South-axis, Jollenpad, Amsterdam, Competition
Water Park, Borneo Sporenburg, Amsterdam, Study

1993

National Freedom carillon, The Hague, Design **(11)**
Street furniture Willemsplein, Rotterdam, Design/realization
Office purifying installation, Kleve, Design
Soundscreen, Wielwijk, Dordrecht, Design
Möbius House, Naarden, Design/realization
Villa Van de Ven, Amersfoort, Design
Office building Wisselwerking, façade study, Diemen, Study
Urban study 'Volkspalast' 'Das Schloß', Gallery Aedes, Berlin, Study/exhibition
  (12)
Villa De Lange, Sukatani, Design/realization
Offices KNP, Hilversum, Design
Interior director's office, Netherlands Architecture Institute, Rotterdam, Design/
  realization
Oostelijke Handelskade, housing and shopping, Amsterdam, Competition
Housing Rijkerswoerd, Arnhem, Design/realization
Entrance lobby Twijnstra Gudde, Amersfoort, Study
Urban plan Zeeburger Island, Amsterdam, Study

1994

Shopping centre renovation, Emmen, Design/realization
Rijkerswoerd 2, 20 single-family houses, Arnhem, Design/realization
Swimming pool, Breda, Design
Offices Schipper Bosch, Amersfoort, Design/realization
Housing Sporenburg, Amsterdam, Design/realization
Boat terminal, Yokohama, Competition **(15)**
Urban plan De Weiert 1, Emmen, Study
Gallery Aedes East, Berlin, Design/realization **(16)**
Wilhelminakade, 44 apartments, Groningen, Design/realization
Diaconessen area, 50 apartments, Arnhem, Design/realization
Offices housing corporation 'Onze Woning', Amsterdam, Design

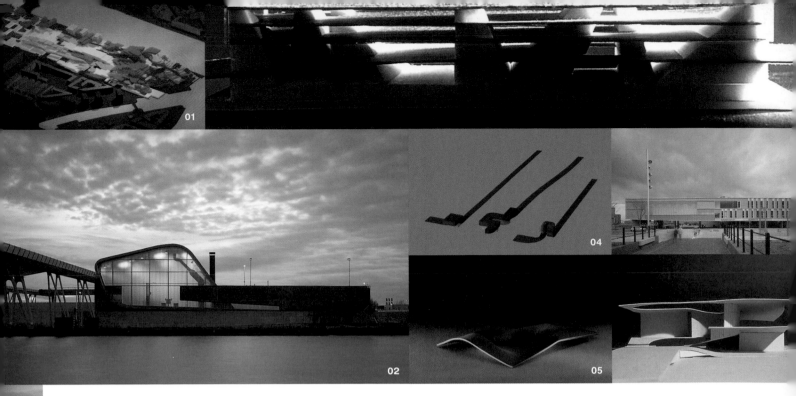

1995

Metro connection North-South, Amsterdam, Design
Key area, 129 single-family apartments and 31 apartments, Nijmegen, Design/realization
'De rubber mat', transformation industrial complex Unilever, Rotterdam, Study/group exhibition **(01)**
Congress hall, Düsseldorf, Design
Urban plan former Saksen Weimar barracks / Menno Coehoorn barracks, Arnhem, Study
Museum Het Valkhof, Nijmegen, Design/realization
Pedestrian bridge, Amsterdam, Design/realization
Police headquarters, Köpenich, Berlin, Competition 1st prize
Dutch pavilion design 'Real space in quick time', 19th Triennial, Milan, Design/realization
Multifunctional stadium, Rotterdam, Design
Infrastructural interventions Highway A27, Design
Kaditz-Mickten, 450 houses, Dresden, Design
Church, Hilversum, Design/realization
Urban plan and houses Rummelsburger Bucht, Berlin, Design/study
Statue of Christ, Troina, Design

1996

Houses Sterpolis / Cito building, Arnhem, Design
De Aker, 3 housing blocks, Amsterdam, Design/realization
Bridge and bridge master's house, Purmerend, Design/realization
Seizoenenbuurt, 28 single-family, Almere, Design/realization
Supermarket and 56 apartments and parking, Emmen, Design/realization
City hall and theatre, Ijsselstein, Design/realization **(06)**
Exhibition design at Royal Palace, Amsterdam, Design/realization
Urban plan Zeeburg, Amsterdam, Study
Electricity station ENECO, Amsterdam, Design
Waste disposal, Delft, Design/realization **(02)**
'De Blauwe Grift', apartment building, Utrecht, Design/realization
Arnhem Central, Arnhem

Master plan, bus deck, transfer hall, Park and Rijn tower, underground parking, tunnel, Design/realization
Dream house, Berlin, Design **(07)**
Randstad, façade renovation and interior office, Dordrecht, Design/realization
'Fragile', spatial container, Gijs Bakker, Design/realization **(05)**
Ethnological museum, Geneva, Competition **(03)**
Erzbischöfliches Diözenan museum, Cologne, Competition
Bridges IJburg, Amsterdam, Competition
Electrical substation, Innsbruck, Competition 1st prize/design/realization

1997

Library, University of Utrecht, Competition
Randstad, façade renovation and office interior, Apeldoorn, Design/realization
Urban plan IBA Berlin 1999, Berlin, Study
NMR Laboratory, University of Utrecht, Design/realization
Bridge, Dresden, Competition
IFCCA, New York, Competition
Double decks, A12 Utrecht-Veenendaal/A2-A4-A10 Badhoevedorp-Holendrecht, Study
Redevelopment centre, Nieuwegein, Design/realization
'Homes for the Future', Glasgow, Competition
'Bridges @ Leidscheveen', Leidscheveen, Competition
Photographer's Gallery, London, extension and renovation, Design
Yacht harbour 't Raboes, Eems, Design **(04)**

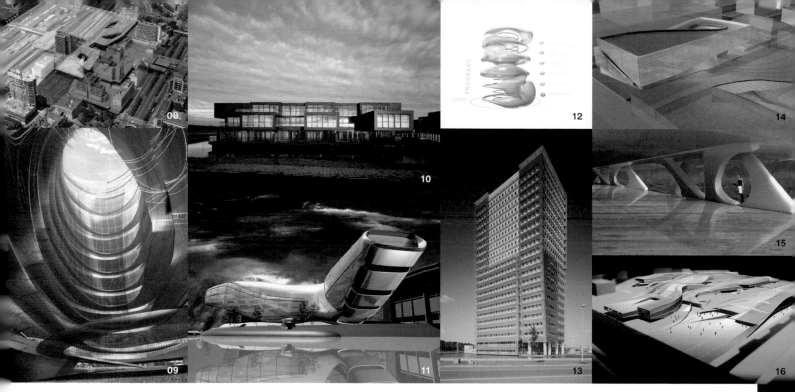

Projects UN Studio

1998

Architecture Faculty, Venice, Competition 2nd prize
Music Theatre, University of Graz, Competition 1st prize
Offices Hoogovens, Beverwijk, Design
Station balcony, Utrecht, Study **(08)**
Prince Claus Bridge, Utrecht, Competition 1st prize/design/realization
Office tower La Tour, Apeldoorn, Design/realization **(13)**
Houses Kolhornseweg, Hilversum, Design
Aquaduct Walcheren, Middelburg, Study
Pavilion Expo 2001, Yverdon-les Bain, Competition 2nd prize
Villa Landheer, Zaanseschans, Design
National Library, Singapore, Competition **(09)**
Urban plan Faulen Quartier, Bremen, Study

1999

De Loswal, apartment building with 40 single-family houses, Amsterdam,
    Design/realization
Museum and cultural centre Las Maretas, Lanzarote, Competition
'(Ge)wild wonen', 48 water villas, Almere, Design/realization **(10)**
Urban plan Amstel station, Amsterdam, Study
Infrastructural interventions, overpass/soundscreens A2, 's-Hertogenbosch,
    Design/realization
Offices La Residence, Nieuwegein, Design/realization
Téxtile Museum, Tilburg, Study
Traffic transfer centre Utrecht-East, Utrecht, Competition
Offices La Defense, Almere, Competition/design/realization

2000

Museum for Space Research, Rome, Competition
Urban plan Playa de 'Las Teresitas', Tenerife, Competition
VilLA NM, Upstate New York, Design/realization
National Library, Quebec, Competition
Carnegie Science Centre, Pittsburgh, Competition 2nd prize **(11)**
Interior Skim.com store, Zurich, Design **(12)**
Living Tomorrow pavilion, Amsterdam, Design/realization
Pedestrian bridge, Venray, Competition
Ponte Parodi harbour redevelopment, Genoa, Competition 1st prize
Window Construmat product design, Spain, Design/realization
Urban plan Olympic games 2008, Paris, Ideas competition
Urban plan former Brewery Liessing, Wenen, Competition
Hotel Castell, apartments, hotel renovation and hamam, Zuoz, Design/
    realization
Smart Apartment Building (SAB), Hilversum, Design
Wadsworth Atheneum, renovation and extension, Hartford, Design
Toledo Art Museum, extension, Toledo, Competition
Office towers Park and Rijn, Arnhem, Design/realization

2001

Infrastructural interventions A2, Eindhoven, Design/realization **(15)**
Pedestrian bridge and landscape design, Las Palmas, Design
Jewish Historical Museum, extension and renovation, Amsterdam,
    Competition/design/realization
Akron Art Museum, Ohio, Competition 2nd prize **(14)**
Tea & Coffee Towers, Alessi, Design/realization
Flyover Randstad rail, The Hague, Design
Factory transformation into Internet company, DaDa Florence, Competition
    1st prize
Public Library, Minneapolis, Competition
Mercedes-Benz Museum, Stuttgart, Competition/design/realization
Multifunctional theatre, Dallas, Competition
Science centre Watergraafsmeer, University of Amsterdam, Competition **(16)**

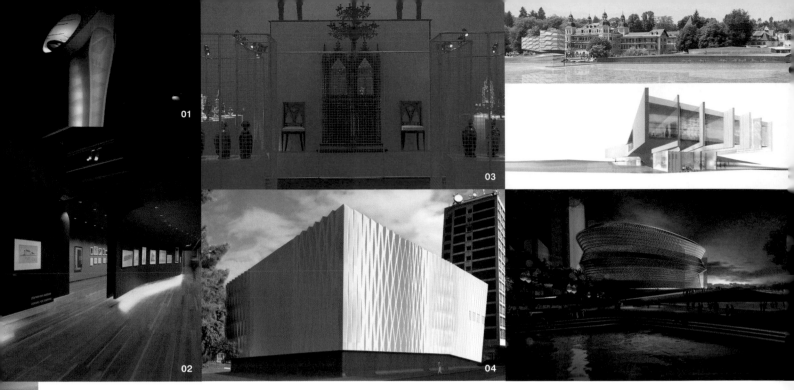

2002

Bus depot above A10 West, Amsterdam, Study
Infrastructural interventions, overpass, soundscreen, Everdingen-Deil and
Zaltbommel Empel, Design/realization
Theatre, Lelystad, Design/realization
Glanerbrug bridge, Enschede, Competition
Ground Zero, New York, Competition 3rd prize
Blijdesteijn Mode, renovation and extension, Tiel, Design

2003

Portland Aerial Tram, Portland, Competition **(01)**
Mahler 4 Tower, South-axis Amsterdam, Design/realization
'Envisioning Architecture', exhibition design, Schirn Kunsthalle, Frankfurt,
Design/realization **(02)**
Aquaduct N57, Zeeland, Design/realization
European Central Bank, Frankfurt, Competition
'NEO', exhibition design, Centraal Museum, Utrecht, Design/realization **(03)**
Coffee cup, Alessi, Design/realization
Research laboratory University of Groningen, Design/realization **(04)**
Park Amsterdam North, Amsterdam, Competition
Van Hasseltkanaal bridge, Amsterdam, Competition
Schloß Velden apartments, landscape, hotel renovation, Velden, Competition
(05)
Galleria Department Store, façade and interior renovation, Seoul, Design/
realization
Bypass Canale, Candiano, Design
Popular music centre, Almelo, Design/realization
Guandong Museum, Guangzhou, Competition **(07)**
Art Museum, Neuhaus, Competition **(06)**

2004

Urban plan and transfer hall, train station, Vienna, Competition
SUM, table, Gispen, Design/realization
Former postal distribution centres, Sternet, Netherlands Architecture Institute,
  Study/design
Pedestrian bridge, Wembley Stadium, London, Competition **(08)**
Battersea Weave Office Building, London, Design/realization
Patent Office, The Hague, Competition **(09)**
Streetlight design, New York, Competition
Pop podium, Almelo, Design
Tea House, Kantwijk, Competition/design/realization **(12)**
Railway station, Tianjin West Railway, Tianjin, Competition **(10)**
Urban plan Siemens city, Vienna, Competition 1st prize
Central Station, Wien Mitte Urban, Vienna, Competition

2005

Port, Las Palmas, Canary Islands, Competition
Sofa Circle, Zetel, Design/realization
Exhibition design, Institute for Contemporary Art, Philadelphia, Design/
  realization
'Summer of Love', exhibition design, Schirn Kunsthalle, Frankfurt, Design/
  realization
Bongerd tunnel, Amsterdam, Design
Arrecife master plan, Lanzarote, Competition
Umm all Nassan master plan island, Bahrain, Study
Bauhaus Archive, Berlin, Competition **(13)**
Wellington Waterfront, Waitangi Precinct Design Competition, Competition
  1st Prize **(11)**
Congress hall Expo Agua 2008, Zaragoza, Competition **(14)**
Pop podium Tagrijn, Hilversum, Competition
Parking study Q-park, De Pijp, Amsterdam, Study
Redevelopment Leidseplein, Amsterdam, Design
Beijing Fashion Centre, Beijing, Design
Living Tomorrow pavilion, San Jose, Design
Wilo office building, Zaanstad, Design
Office renovation and extension, UN Studio Stadhouderskade, Amsterdam,
  Design

Exhibitions

1988
'Docklands, Van Rooy Gallery', Amsterdam
'Intertwining landscapes', Technical University, Delft

1989
'Docklands and Raaks', Musea d'Art Contemporani de Barcelona,
   Barcelona
'Urban proposal Gare d'Austerlitz, architecture et utopie',
   Gallery Aedes **(05)**

1992
'Ruimte verruimd/Dimensions expanded', Museum Kröller-Müller, Otterlo

1993
'Application & Implication', Centre National d'Arts Contemporain
   de Grenoble **(04)**

1995
'Light Construction', Museum of Modern Art, New York

1996
'Modernisme without dogma', Architecture Biennale, Venice

1997
'Mobile Forces', Artist's Space gallery, New York

1999
'UN Studio – Move', Architektenforum Tirol, Innsbruck
'The un-private house', Museum of Modern Art, New York

2000
'The long view', Museum of Modern Art, New York
'Deep Planning', Architecture Biennale, Venice
'Move', Architekturforum Tirol, Innsbruck

2001
'Architectural freehand drawing', GA Gallery, Tokyo
'Matrixshow UN US', Wadsworth Atheneum, Hartford **(07)**
'Retrospective UN Studio – UN Fold', Netherlands Architecture Institute,
   Rotterdam **(01)**
'Cases IM-PRÒPIES', Musea d'Art Contemporani de Barcelona, Barcelona
'Folds, Blobs + Boxes: Architecture in the Digital Era', The Heinz Architectural
   Center, Carnegie Museum of Art, Pittsburgh

2002
'Urban study Hypercatalunya', Musea d'Art Contemporani de Barcelona,
   Barcelona
'Latent Utopias', Steirisc[:her:]bst, Graz
'UN Studio', Dutch pavilion, Architecture Biennale, Venice
'Modern Trains and Splendid Stations', Art Institute of Chicago, Chicago

2003
'Non-standard Architecture', Centre Pompidou, Paris **(02)**
'Deep Planning', Architektur-Galerie am Weissenhof, Stuttgart

2004
'One day 1:1', Italian pavilion, Architecture Biennale, Venice **(03)**
'UN Studio, Biennale China', Beijing **(06)**

2005
'European Design Show', Design Museum, London
'Dutch Architects in Booming China', Arcam, Amsterdam
'Mercedes-Benz Museum, UN Studio', BDA, Stuttgart

2006
'Holiday Home', Institute for Contemporary Art, Philadelphia

Publications

Ben van Berkel, monograph (Rotterdam, 1992).

Delinquent Visionaries, a collection of essays (Rotterdam, 1993; reprint 1994).

Mobile Forces, monograph (Berlin, 1994).

'Ben van Berkel', monograph issue, *El Croquis* (May 1995).

'Ben van Berkel', monograph issue, *Korean Architects* (November 1996).

'Diagram work', special issue, *ANY* (*Architecture New York*), guest editors
    Caroline Bos and Ben van Berkel (1998).

'UN Studio', monograph issue, *L'Architecture d'aujourd'hui* (March 1999).

'Rem and Ben', monograph issue, *A+U* (March 1999).

Museum Het Valkhof (Amsterdam, 1999).

Move, 3 vol. (Amsterdam, 1999).

UN Studio: Unfold (Rotterdam, 2002).

'Love it, live it: UN Studio', monograph issue, *DD Magazine* (2003).

UN Studio, Space, Seoul, September 2004

Caroline Bos, 'Forget about the architects', *UmBau* (2004).

United Architects

Ground Zero competition, New York, 2002

Five architectural practices and one media practice joined forces to participate in the Ground Zero competition, and, plus or minus a few members, two subsequent competitions.

In New York, the intense weeks of collaboration resulted in a network of interconnected, memorial-related civic and cultural spaces with different spatial characteristics, user profiles, moods, and levels of public and private access.

The group was reluctant to create a dramatic rhetoric, and instead addressed the complex connotations of the encumbered site in an oblique way. The interest in skyscraper typology, therefore, deferred to the need for increased safety; commercial office buildings entwined central cores with elevators and stairs. The future for Ground Zero was envisioned as a proud, forward-looking space, evocative and rich in meaning.

Design: United Architects
Foreign Office Architects, Greg Lynn FORM, Imaginary Forces, Kevin Kennon Architects, RUR Architecture P.C., UN Studio

European Central Bank competition, Frankfurt am Main, 2004

The second United Architects scheme was, if possible, even more exuberant and buoyant about the future of post-metropolitan architecture than the first.

A sphere with a diameter of 120 metres (394 ft), a height of 100 metres (328 ft), and containing 30 office layers, was proposed to enrich the city with the image of a giant glittering orb, like a sun beside the riverfront.

The sphere combines structural logic and typological experimentation with the kind of iconic qualities not seen since Boullée and Ledoux, and thus continues some of the issues that preoccupy members of the UA group. As a result of the concave outline of the building, each floor plan is different; there are circular floor plates, triangular plates, and propeller-shaped plates at the heart of the sphere, where the central void is interrupted and the floor plates interconnect.

Design: United Architects
Greg Lynn FORM, Imaginary Forces, Kevin Kennon Architects, UN Studio

Superliving,
Sternet, 2004

The third, and so far last, UA project was instigated by
the Netherlands Architecture Institute, and addressed
possibilities for the future of a now obsolete rail-linked
network of twelve postal distribution centres.

UA rejected a piecemeal commercial development, and
instead chose to convert the Sternet sites into a network
of highrises that would raise the profile of the Netherlands
and provide each location, from northernmost Groningen to
Roosendaal in the south, with a new skyline.

Each of the Sternet towers is based on the recurring
principle of a rotational transformation of stacked floor
plans, ranging in intricacy from the very simple to the highly
complex. Rotating and shifting the plates results in varying
interstitial spaces that can be programmed for different uses;
those proposed are for residences, businesses, leisure
activities and educational facilities.

Design: United Architects
Greg Lynn FORM, Imaginary Forces, Kevin Kennon Architects,
UN Studio

Curriculum vitae

Ben van Berkel

Prior to becoming an architect, Ben van Berkel worked as a graphic designer, designing posters for the Holland Festival and VPRO TV magazine covers, while at the same time studying architectural design at the Rietveld Academy, in Amsterdam.

In 1982, he enrolled at London's Architectural Association and completed his degree despite a furore over the fact that most of his graduate work had already been sold by an Amsterdam gallery. While still a student, Ben resolved to become the most prolific architect of his generation. His first projects were built almost immediately after founding Van Berkel & Bos Architectuur Bureau, before any of his former teachers in London, the 'paper generation', had realized their own designs. Among the buildings of this first period are Karbouw, the Remu electricity station, and Villa Wilbrink.

Being elected to design the Erasmus bridge, in Rotterdam (completed 1996), profoundly affected his understanding of the role of the architect today and of a collaborative approach to the practice of architecture; an understanding that ultimately led to the foundation of UN Studio in 1999. The interim period resulted in the realization of such projects as the Möbius House (1993–1998), Museum Het Valkhof (1995–1998), NMR Laboratory (1997–2001), and the Prince Claus bridge (1998–2003).

Recent projects that reflect his longstanding interest in the integration of construction and architecture include the Mercedes-Benz Museum (completed 2006), Ponte Parodi (2000–2009), and Arnhem Central (1996–2008).

Ben van Berkel has been guest professor at Princeton University, and has taught at Columbia University, the Berlage Institute and UCLA. He is currently professor and head of architecture at the Staedelschule, in Frankfurt.

Caroline Bos

Caroline Bos was an aspiring writer with four unfinished manuscripts when she and Ben van Berkel began their collaboration by becoming correspondents for *De Volkskrant*, writing long articles (paid by the word) about the art and architecture scene in London.

While working, she completed her studies in the history of art. Her writing became increasingly focused on architecture, and, some years after co-founding Van Berkel & Bos Architectuur Bureau, she stopped working as journalist to devote her time to being the practice's resident critic, writing everything from employment contracts to essays, to descriptions of future projects.

Together with Ben, Caroline co-edited *Forum* (1985–1986) and the ANY publication, *Diagram Works* (1999), as well as co-writing *Ben van Berkel Architect* (1992), *Delinquent Visionaries* (1993), *Mobile Forces* (1994), *Move* (1999), and *Unfold* (2002). She has also taught at Princeton University, the Berlage Institute and UCLA.

UN Studio

In 1999, UN Studio detached itself from Van Berkel & Bos, like an orbiter detaching itself from a space shuttle after a successful launch. The old architectural practice had burnt itself out in helping to get the new one under way; now the United Network for urbanism, infrastructure and architecture was on a mission to explore new territories.

New visions, new styles, new skills and a fresh approach were all needed to realize the new type of project that Van Berkel & Bos was increasingly confronted with. These projects entailed a non-hierarchical, complex, generative and integral design process, and used technologies that allowed for a maximum creative exchange.

New people entered the practice; the craftsmen that had taught us the business of building in the 1990s now found themselves working next to Columbia and Harvard postgrads, and consultants from the UK and Germany were hired alongside local firms. With the internal organization redesigned, UN Studio set out to excel equally at business, art and design. Since 2001, the firm has employed a quality system that adheres to the requirements of ISO 9001.

UN Studio quickly became bigger than Van Berkel & Bos ever was. Two longstanding collaborators became associates, and subsequently partners: Tobias Wallisser as design director, and Harm Wassink as strategic director responsible for the internal organization. A third associate, Gerard Loozekoot, was appointed in 2005.

Awards and competitions

2005 Housing project, Broadway, New York City
2005 Wellington waterfront, Waitangi, New Zealand
2005 Nominee, Architecture Award, Almere 2005
2005 Nominee, Mies van der Rohe Award
2005 Nominee, Schreuders Award
2005 ANWB Award
2005 Lighting Award
2005 Nominee, Rietveld Award
2005 Best of Europe – Colour
2004 Siemens City, 1st prize, Vienna, Austria
2004 Belgian Steel Award
2004 British Steel Award
2003 1822-Kunstpreis 2003
2002 Mercedes-Benz Museum, 1st prize, Stuttgart
2001 Jewish Historical Museum, 1st prize, Amsterdam
2001 Nominee, Mies van der Rohe Award
2000 Ponte Parodi, 1st prize, Genova
1999 Concrete Award
1999 IFCCA, 2nd prize, Ground Zero, New York City
1998 Music Theatre, 1st prize competition, Graz
1997 Member of Honor of the Bond Deutsche Architekten
1997 Substation, 1st prize, Innsbruck
1995 Museum Het Valkhof, 1st prize, Nijmegen
1995 Main Police station, 1st prize, Berlin Köpenick
1991 Charlotte Köhler Award
1990 Antwerp, City on the River, 1st prize
1986 British Council Fellowship
1983 Eileen Gray Award

Bibliography

1987–1988

Hans van Dijk, 'De initiatie tot architect: De studieprojecten van Ben van Berkel', *Archis* (May 1987), pp 32–37.

Hans van Dijk, 'Die jungen Niederlande: Zwischen Idealismus und Pragmatismus', *Bauwelt* (May 8, 1987), pp 644–657.

Hans van Dijk, 'AA diploma honours, 1986–1987 Ben van Berkel', *AA Files* (Summer 1987), pp 98–99.

Hans Ibelings, 'Drie grillige torens voor de Docklands, oogstrelende ontwerpen van Ben van Berkel geëxposeerd in Amsterdam', *NRC Handelsblad* (October 29, 1988).

1989

Willem Ellenbroek, 'Hartstikke tof, ik zal mijn best doen: Het Fonds voor de Kunst geeft als grootste subsidiënt van beeldende kunst in Nederland opening van zaken', *De Volkskrant* (September 1, 1989).

Catherine van Houts, 'Rijp en groen in een wonderlijke mengeling', *Het Parool* (September 8, 1989).

Reneé Steenbergen, 'Individueel gesubsidieerde kunst in de Hal', *NRC Handelsblad* (September 18, 1989).

Liesbeth Melis, 'Ben van Berkel ontwerpt gevangenistuin', *De Architect* (October 1989), pp 119–121.

Hans Ibelings, 'Ben van Berkel', in *Architectuur en Verbeelding* (Zwolle, 1989), pp 306–309.

1990

Ronald Zoetbrood, 'Antwerpen moet weer "rafelige" Schelde-oever krijgen: Ben van Berkel zag ontwerp Stad aan de stroom bekroond', *Utrechts Nieuwsblad* (July 21, 1990).

Hélène Damen, 'Experimenteren als ontwerpopgave: Sloker-opdracht BouwRAI 1990', *De Architect* (July/August 1990).

Paul Vermeulen, 'Sleutelen aan het Antwerpse trauma: Stad aan de Stroom; stedebouwkundige prijsvraag voor Antwerps havengebied', *Archis* (September 1990), pp 46–51.

D'Laine Camp, 'Ontwerpen tussen droom en daad, vier voorstellen voor de boulevard van Domburg', *De Architect* (November 1990).

'De beweging van het lichaam: Gesprek met Ben van Berkel', *Platform* (1990), pp 8–9.

1991

Peter Schat, 'Over bruggen', *NRC Handelsblad* (February 8, 1991).

D'laine Camp, 'Nieuwe maasbrug in Rotterdam', *De Architect* (February 1991), p 19.

Arjen Oosterman, 'De nieuwe stadsbrug in Rotterdam', *Archis* (February 1991), pp 10–11.

Bart Lootsma, 'Eindelijk echt ambidexter: recent werk van Ben van Berkel', *De Architect* (March 1991), pp 36–45.

'Un nouveau pont pour Rotterdam', *AMC Le Moniteur Architecture* (May 1991), p 16.

Tracy Metz, 'Een brug heeft oneindig veel façades', *NRC Handelsblad* (November 15, 1991).

Janny Rodermond, 'Modernisme als smaakmaker: De Nederlands inzending voor de Biënnale', *De Architect* (November 1991), pp 47–51.

Bart Lootsma, 'Erasmusbrug als crossing point', *De Architect* (December 1991), pp 27–37.

Hans Ibelings, 'Ben van Berkel', in *Modernisme zonder Dogma* (Rotterdam, 1991), pp 18–21.

1992

John Welsh, 'Van Berkel & Bos', *Building Design* (April 24, 1992), p 15.

Liesbeth Melis, 'Architectuur in beweging: Ben van Berkel ontwerpt Karbouw', *De Architect* (April 1992), pp 40–53.

Bart Lootsma, 'In Bewegung: Geschaftsgebaude Fa. Karbouw in Amersfoort', *Bauwelt* (May 8, 1992), pp 1017–1025.

Gerrit Confurius, 'Philosophie im Restaurant', *Bauwelt* (July 17, 1992), pp 1584–1589.

Jaap Huisman, 'Villa Härtel: Alleen de tafels staan recht', *De Volkskrant* (July 25, 1992).

'Buffalo Ben', *Blueprint* (September 1992), pp 36–38.

Bart Lootsma, 'Villa Härtel, Amersfoort', *De Architect* (September 1992), pp 49–53.

'New in Pictures', *Building Design* (October 9, 1992), p 8.

Sabine Schneider, 'Gewerbebau in Amersfoort', *Baumeister* (November 1992), pp 30–33.

'Van Berkel & Bos: Uffici e stabilimento a Amersfoort', *Domus* (November 1992), pp 1–3.

'Ben van Berkel: Office buildings, Amersfoort, Holland', *Architectural Design* (November/December 1992), pp 68–69.

Bernard Leupen, 'Het construeren van de gewaarwording: Ben van Berkels idee van de stad', *Archis* (December 1992), pp 24–31.

'Van Berkel & Bos: Karbouw, Amersfoort', *A+U* (1992), pp 58–63.

Egbert Koster, 'De aaibaarheids-factor van architectuur', *Architectuur/Bouwen* (1992), pp 26–27.

G. van Colmjon, 'Ben van Berkel: Een offensief tegen het deconstructivisme', *Items* (1992), pp 54–59.

Bernard Hulsman, 'The taut muscles of the water buffalo', in *Architecture in the Netherlands: Yearbook 1991–1992* (Rotterdam, 1992), pp 154–157.

1993

Michael Mönninger, 'Das Bauwerk im Zeitalter seiner technischen Reproduzierbarkeit', *Frankfurter Allgemeine Zeitung* (July 2, 1993).

Bart Lootsma, 'Application and implication, *De Architect* (July/August 1993), pp 19–24.

'Two Projects', *Archis* (October 1993), pp 68–69.

'Vrijheidscarillon in Den Haag markeert 50 jaar bevrijding', *Trouw* (November 25, 1993).

Max van Rooy, 'De gouden eeuw van het transformatorhuisje', *De Volkskrant* (December 10, 1993).

'Transformer', *Daidalos* (December 1993), pp 134–135.

'Soloist on the River Maas', *A1* (1993), pp 26–29.

'Erasmus bridge a Rotterdam', *L'Arca* (1993), pp 48–53.

'Industrial Building Karbouw: Edificio Industriale', *Quaderns* (1993), pp 4–11.

'ACOM, Amersfoort (van Berkel & Bos)', *Quaderns* (1993), pp 4–9.

1994

Connie van Cleef, 'Dutch dynamic', *Architectural Review* (January 1994), p 60.

Connie van Cleef, 'Electric behemoth', *Architectural Review* (January 1994), pp 64–66.

'Ben van Berkel. Crossing Points', Columbia University, Graduate School of Architecture, Planning and Preservation, *Newsline* (January/February 1994), p 5.

Hans van Dijk, 'Geen plaats voor stedelijk muziekinstrument', *Archis* (March 1994), pp 12–13.

Christian F. Müller, 'Hochspannung in Amersfoort', *Hochparterre* (April 1994), pp 36–37.

'Travelling architects: Van Berkel & Bos', *Architectural Design* (May/June 1994), p 28.

'Ben van Berkel', *AA Files* (Autumn 1994), pp 15–25.

Ed Melet, 'De herdefiniëring van het detail', *De Architect* (November 1994), pp 106–115.

Matino Canonico and Olindo Caso, 'Ben van Berkel. Unternehmens-zentrum Nijkerk', *Arch+* (December 1994), pp 34–37.

Jeremy Meus, 'Il Taglio, la frattura, l'armonia', *L'Area* (1994), pp 14–25.

'L'architteto e la città post-industriale: Wiel Arets, Ben van Berkel, Willem Jan Neutelings', *Controspazio* (1994), pp 63–65.

Ineke Schwartz, 'Ben van Berkel laat iedereen zijn transparante kijkdoos zien', *Streams* (1994), pp 92–95.

Otto Riewoldt, 'Karbouw', in *New Office Design* (London, 1994), pp 128–129.

1995

Ursula Daus, 'Bauwerk in Rotation', *Tagesspiegel* (January 21, 1995).

'Ben van Berkel', *Arquitectos Holandeses* (1995), pp 21–49.

Jeffrey Kipnis, 'Hybridization', *A+U* (May 1995), pp 62–63.

'Villa Wilbrink in Amersfoort', *Bauwelt* (May 5, 1995), pp 962–963.

Greg Lynn, 'Conversation by modem with Ben van Berkel', *El Croquis* (May 1995), pp 6–15.

'Terminal voor de haven van Yokohama', *De Architect* (May 1995), pp 48–49.

Paul Vermeulen, 'Ben van Berkel:

A villa at Amersfoort', *Domus* (June 1995), pp 30–37.

Kong Chul, 'The trajectory of another generation', *Space Arts & Architecture, Environment* (June 1995), pp 64–73.

Clinton Terry, 'City under influence: Erasmus bridge, Rotterdam', *Daidalos* (September 15, 1995), pp 126–131.

Dietmar Danner, 'Die Architektur-galerie Aedes in den Hackeschen Höfen, Berlin', *AIT* (September 1995), pp 54–59.

'Yokohama Terminal', *Arch+* (September 1995), pp 32–33.

'Gallery and café in Berlin', *Detail* (October/November 1995), pp 879–882.

'Van Berkel strikes again', *Items* (1995), p 57.

Terence Riley, 'ACOM office building', in *Light Construction*, exhibition catalogue, Museum of Modern Art (New York, 1995), pp 66–67.

Thies Schröder, 'Das Schloß: Eine Rekonstruktion des Wandels', in *Berlin, Berlin: Architektur für ein neues Jahrhundert* (Berlin, 1995), pp 63–66.

1996

Ares Kalandides, 'Subtiele Wache', *AIT* (January/February 1996), p 18.

'Real Space in Quick Times', *Arch+* (April 1996), pp 42–47.

Janny Rodermond, 'Uitbreiding Rijksmuseum Twente door Ben van Berkel', *De Architect* (July 1996), pp 22–27.

Janny Rodermond, 'Tussen globaal en lokaal: Van Berkel & Bos over veranderende ontwerpcondities', *De Architect* (September 1996), pp 56–61.

Bart Lootsma, 'Van Berkel & Bos', *L'Architecture d'aujourd'hui* (September 1996), pp 58–63.

Hans van Dijk, 'Tektoniek, golven, sediment: Ben van Berkel en Caroline Bos; nieuw werk', *Archis* (October 1996), pp 36–49.

'Bunker Mentality', *Architectural Review* (October 1996), pp 74–78.

'Ben van Berkel: Villa Wilbrink, Amersfoort', *GA Houses* (October 1996), pp 96–103.

Raymond Ryan, 'Objective Rotterdam', *Blueprint* (November 1996), pp 31–36.

'Ben van Berkel`: National Museum Twenthe', *GA Document* (November 1996), pp 36–43.

Bart Lootsma, 'A bridge for Rotterdam', *Domus* (December 1996), pp 26–32.

Maurici Pla, 'Drifts, containers, storms: Architectures without anchor', *Quaderns* (1996), pp 82–83.

'Ben van Berkel', monograph issue, *Korean Architects* (1996).

'Competition for the 6th police headquarters in Berlin', *Compe & Contest* (1996), pp 19–21.

Ole Bouman, *Real Space in Quick Times* (Rotterdam, 1996).

'Ben van Berkel', in *Contemporary European Architects*, vol. 4 (Cologne, 1996), pp 68–75.

'Ben van Berkel', in *Seeing the Future: The Architect as Seismograph*, exhibition catalogue, 6th International Architecture Exhibition, La Biennale di Venezia (1996), pp 232–233.

1997

David Brown, 'Erasmus bridge', *World Architecture* (February 1997), pp 98–99.

Aaron Betsky, 'Van Berkel & Bos: Holland's hypermodernist', *Architecture* (March 1997), pp 76–87.

'Ben van Berkel: Möbius house', *GA Houses* (April 1997), pp 21–23.

Janny Rodermond, 'Gevelarchitectuur in tijden van stijlloosheid', *De Architect* (May 1997), pp 88–93.

Verena M. Schindler, 'Anti-Tradition im Experiment: Die Erasmusbrücke als kristalline Selbstdarstellung der Stadt Rotterdam', *Archithese* (May/June 1997), pp 34–37.

'Ontwerp stationsgebied Arnhem', *De Architect* (July/August 1997), pp 21–23.

'Van Berkel & Bos: the Erasmus bridge', *Architectural Design* (September/October 1997), pp 84–87.

'Acom, Amersfoort', *SD* (October 1997), pp 33–35.

Hubertus Adam, 'Intervention in der Innenstadt: Der Komplex "Der Kolk" in Amsterdam', *Bauwelt* (October 24, 1997), pp 2287–2293.

'An und über den Wassern', *Deutsche Bauzeitung* (1997), pp 40–41.

'The cathedral on the water', *Licht & Architektur* (1997), pp 24–27.

'National Museum Twenthe', *A+U* (1997), pp 108–117.

'Gallery Aedes East', in *Commercial Spaces* (Barcelona, 1997), pp 32–39.

1998

'Dream house, Berlin', *GA Houses* (March 1998), pp 16–17.

'Real space in quick times pavilion', *Architectural Design* (May/June 1998), pp 70–73.

'Op weg naar een inclusieve ontwerpstrategie: In gesprek met Caroline Bos en Ben van Berkel', *De Architect* (June 1998), pp 60–65.

'Hot building: the Möbius House', *Rolling Stone* (August 20, 1998), p 86.

Ludger Fischer, 'Grau und grün in Glas verpackt', *Bauwelt* (November 27, 1998), pp 2528–2531.

'Between ideogram and image-diagram: Like Bijlsma, Wouter Deen en Udo Garritzmann in gesprek met Ben van Berkel en Peter Trümmer', *Oase* (1998), pp 63–71.

'Möbius Haus', *Arch+* (1998), pp 78–81.

Francisco Asensio Cerver, 'Shopping centre in Emmen', in *The Architecture of Glass: Shaping Light*, (New York, 1998), pp 8–19.

'Piet Hein tunnel buildings', in *Architecture in the Netherlands: Yearbook 1997–1998* (Rotterdam, 1998), pp 146–147.

1999

Patrik Schumacher, 'Ben van Berkel moves towards a capacity for endlessness', *AA News* (Winter 1999), p 4.

Ahmed Sarbutu, 'Von der Ekliptik des Lebens', in *Architese* (January/February 1999), pp 40–45.

Patrik Schumacher, 'Master plan: Arnhem Central, 1996–2020; Architects UN Studio Van Berkel & Bos' *AA Files* (Spring 1999), pp 23–36.

Lucy Bullivant, 'A day in the life: Ben van Berkel of UN Studio', *Building Design* (March 5, 1999), pp 14–21.

Connie van Cleef, 'On the bridge', *Architectural Review* (March 1999), pp 30–31.

Joseph Giovannini, 'Infinite Space', *Architecture* (March 1999), pp 96–103.

Hubertus Adam, 'Endloser Weg, nach innen gedreht', *Bauwelt* (March 12, 1999), pp 550–555.

Axel Sowa, 'UN Studio: Ben van Berkel & Caroline Bos', *L'Architecture d'aujourd'hui* (March 1999), pp 43–101.

Franziska Leeb, 'Ein Haus als gebautes Manifest', *Architektur* (March 1999), pp 33–37.

'Die Spirale als Organisations-prinzip', *Architektur & Bau Forum* (March/April 1999), pp 109–114.

Bart Lootsma, 'Möbius one-family house', *Domus* (April 1999), pp 40–49.

Nicolai Ouroussoff, 'Pleasure Principle', *Los Angeles Times Magazine* (May 16, 1999), pp 14–17, 52–57.

Janny Rodermond, 'Learning from Van Berkel & Bos', *De Architect* (June 1999), pp 67–68.

'UN Studio Van Berkel & Bos', *Baumeister* (July 1999), p 40.

Philip Jodidio, 'La maison nouvelle', *Connaissance des Arts* (July/August 1999), pp 106–117.

Neil Spiller, 'Moving with the times or repeating them?', *Building Design* (August 13, 1999), p 25.

Philip Nobel, 'Toward a Future with Flair', *New York Times* (October 28, 1999), p. F1, F8.

Lucy Bullivant, 'Content and Continuity', *Building Design* (November 12, 1999), pp 16–19.

'Museum Het Valkhof', *GA Document* (November 1999), pp 66–75.

Hubertus Adam, 'Vom Dreiklang zur Modulation', *Archithese* (November/December 1999), pp 52–55.

Hubertus Adam, 'Synthetischer Kusbismus: Ben van Berkels programmatische "The Formal Muscle"', *Arquitectura Viva* (1999), pp 64–71.

Bart Lootsma, Diagrams in Costumes', *A+U* (1999), pp 97–151.

'Ben van Berkel', *Quaderns* (1999), pp 74–95.

'UN Studio', in *Archilab 1999*, exhibition catalogue, Orléans (1999).
'Möbius House', *Architecture in the Netherlands: Yearbook 1998–1999* (Rotterdam, 1999), pp 100–103.
Terence Riley, 'Möbius House', *The Un–Private House*, exhibition catalogue, Museum of Modern Art (New York, 1999), pp 128–131.

2000

Ludger Fischer, 'Museum Het Valkhof in Nijmegen', *Bauwelt* (January 14, 2000), pp 12–17.
Janny Rodermond, 'Van shopping center tot convenience city', *De Architect* (February 2000), pp 36–39.
Aaron Betsky, 'A visit to the Ice Palace', *Architecture* (February 2000), pp 86–93.
Axel Sowa, 'Museo Het Valkhof', *Domus* (March 2000), pp 42–49.
Connie van Cleef, 'Light waves', *Architectural Review* (March 2000), pp 54–57.
Franziska Leeb, 'Durchs Museum surfen: Museum Het Valkhof', *Architektur* (April 2000), pp 44–47.
Laura Negrini, 'UN Studio, Ben Van Berkel & Caroline Bos: Una ricerca in evoluzione', monograph issue, *L'Industria delle costruzioni* (May 2000), pp 6–61.
Ali Rahim, 'Deep planning: West Side, New York', *Architectural Design* (June 2000), pp 44–55.
'Another museum piece', *Building Design* (July 7, 2000), pp 20–21.
Franziska Leeb, 'Dichte Packung', *Architektur* (September 2000), pp 45–50.
'La ventana perfectible', *Arquitectura Viva* (November/December 2000), pp 14–15.
Bradford McKee, 'Off the wall', *Harper's Bazaar* (December 2000), pp 231–233, 253.
Christian Tröster, 'Caroline Bos and Ben van Berkel', *Häuser* (2000), pp 156–164.
'Architect Ben van Berkel', *Contemporary Architecture* (2000), pp 13–70.
Sally Godwin, 'The Möbius house', *Architectural Design* (2000), pp 76–78.
'A spatial concept guiding public circulation', *Concept* (2000), pp 50–69.
'UN Studio / Ben van Berkel & Caroline Bos', in *Less Aesthetics, More Ethics*, exhibition catalogue, 7th International Architecture Exhibition, La Biennale di Venezia

(Venice, 2000), pp 382–383.
Jessica Cargill Thompson (ed.), 'UN Studio', in *40 Architects Under 40* (Cologne, 2000), pp 520–533.

2001

'Klappbrücke und Brueckenmeisterhaus in Purmerend', in *Architektur + Wettbewerbe* (March 2001), pp 2–3.
Janny Rodermond, 'Deep Planning in de praktijk', *De Architect* (May 2001), pp 20–35.
Franziska Leeb, 'Dreidimensionale Piazza am Wasser', *Architektur* (June 2001), pp 54–56.
'Ponte Parodi', *Bauwelt* (July 2001), p 8.
Robert Uhde, 'Form follows disposal. Muell-Verladestation in Delft', *Architektur Aktuell* (July/August 2001), pp 88–95.
'Arnhem transfer zone: deep planning at work', *Dialogue* (August 2001), pp 64–69.
Dominique Pieters, 'Een gebouw inwikkelen: Het Nuclear Magnetic Resonance (NMR) laboratorium', *De Architect* (September 2001), pp 86–89.
Dirk Liedtke, 'Computer als Baumeister', *Stern* (October 18, 2001), pp 116–120.
Konstanze Crüwell, 'Was Architekten von Künstlern lernen können', *Frankfurter Allgemeien Zeitung* (December 20, 2001).
'UN Studio: Van Berkel & Bos', *A+U* (2001), pp 38–51.
Frederic Migayrou and Marie–Ange Brayer, ed., 'UN Studio', *Archilab: Radical Experiments in Global Architecture* (London, 2001), pp 458–265.
Laura Negrini, *Ben van Berkel* (Rome, 2001).

2002

Lars Hertelt, 'Einzel- und Reihenhäuser in Almere. UN Studio Van Berkel & Bos', *Baumeister* (January 2002), pp 50–54.
J. Christoph Bürkle, 'Burgkristall im Engadin', *Archithese* (January/February 2002), pp 74–75.
'A material world', *Vivenda* (February 2002), pp 20–21.
Catherine Croft, 'Out of the blue', *Building Design* (February 1, 2002), pp 14 15.
Owen McNally, 'Architecture Comes Alive at Atheneum', *Hartford Courant* (February 18, 2002).
Tracy Metz, 'Ijsselstein city hall',

Architectural Record (March 2000), pp 116–119.
UN Studio, 'Ponte Parodi Genoa', *Materia* (March/August 2002).
Harm Tilman, 'Virtuele en reële complexiteit', *De Architect* (May 2002), pp 22–31.
Jaap Huisman, 'Architectuur and design', *Vrij Nederland* (May 24–30, 2002).
Sophie Treclat, 'Parking et tunnel Arnhem', *L'Architecture d' aujourd'hui* (May/June 2002), pp 106–111.
Bob Witman, 'Wat nou mooi?!', *De Volkskrant* (June 2002).
Laura Negrini, 'Teatro e centro civico a Ijsselstein', *L'Industria delle costruzioni* (July 2002).
'NMR', *A+U* (September 2002).
Niklas Maak, 'The Möbius house: living in looped infinity', *Premium* (2002), pp 60–67.
'Neues Mercedes-Benz Museum', *Architektur Wettbewerbe* (2002), pp 38–39.
Alexander Salangin, 'Imperceptible beauty', in *Four Rooms* (2002), pp 80–87.
'NMR Laboratorium', in *Architecture in the Netherlands: Yearbook 2001–2002* (Rotterdam, 2002), pp 110–111.

2003

Raquel Vassalo, 'Soluciones para La Zona Cero?', *Arquitectura y Critica* (March 2003), pp 5–8.
Ursula Seibold-Bultmann, 'Zwischen Tanz und Taumel', *Neue Zuricher Zeitung* (March 29–30, 2003).
Henrietta Thompson, 'Future Perfect', *Blueprint* (April 2003), p 30.
Mercel Krenz, 'All eyes on Manhattan', *Blueprint* (April 2003), pp 42–48.
Maurizio Vogliazzo, 'Una risposta troppo rapida?', *L'Arca* (April 2003), pp 18–29.
Edmund Summer, 'Future systems', *Icon* (April 2003).
'Laboratory Building in Utrecht', *Detail* (April 2003), p 352.
Harm Tilman and Rene Erven, 'Roep om nieuw engagement in design', *De Architect* (May 2003), pp 50–58.
Giovanni Padula, 'Quel grande business chiamato citta', *Il Sole–24 Ore* (May 1, 2003), p 11.
Toos van der Weit, 'Lelystad krijgt diamantvormig theater', *Cobouw* (May 26, 2003), p 3.
Bart van Oosterhout, 'Bij ons is een gebouw nooit wat het lijkt',

Intermediair (June 2003), pp 30–33.
'UN Studio in Stuttgart, dynamische gevels: Mercedes-Benz Museum en la Defense', *Stedebouw & Architectuur* (July 2003).
Kobi Gantenbein, 'Das Glashaus ohne Aussicht', *Brennpunk* (2003), pp 48–51.
Giovanna Carnevali et al., *Geno(v)a* (Rotterdam, 2003).
Alessandro Mendini, ed., *Tea & Coffee Towers*, exhibition catalogue, Wexner Center Galleries (Columbus, Ohio, 2003).

2004

Hans Ibelings, 'Flow UN Studio's new transit', *New Metropolis* (January 2004), p 70.
Harm Tillman, 'Architectuur van de toekomst', *De Architect* (January 2004), p 26.
Mimari Tasarim, 'Möbius Evi, Het Gooi, Hollanda', *Yapi* (January 2004), p 63.
David Keuning, 'Futuristische vorm met conventionele opbouw', *Detail in Architectuur* (January 2004), p 16.
Stan Allen, 'Stocktaking 2004: Nine questions about the present and future of design', *Harvard Design Magazine* (Spring/Summer 2004), p 5.
'Holland: Experimental field of modern architecture', *Colorfulness* (March 2004), pp 128–130.
John Weich, 'Chasing domestic Utopia', *34 Magazine* (April 2004), p 29.
'Wochenschau: Living Tomorrow', *Bauwelt* (April 2004), p 2.
'Het doemscenario van een fantasieloze toekomst', *Archis* (May 2004), pp 98–101.
Gregory More, 'Message in a bottle', *Monument* (July 2004), p 60.
Domizia Mandolesi, 'Edificio per la sperimentazione sull'abitare ad Amsterdam', *L'Industria delle costruzioni* (August 2004), p 60.
Nanni Baltzer, 'Photographie d'architecture: Saisir l'impalpable', *L'Architecture d'aujourd'hui* (October 2004), p 64.
Kieran Long, 'UN Studio's latest building is, perhaps, typically Dutch', *Icon* (November 2004), p 104.
Jane Szita, 'What's so great about the future', *Dwell* (December 2004), p 148.
Par Karine Dana, 'Un ile de Fun Shopping', *AMC Le Moniteur Architecture* (December 2004), p 13.
Harm Tillman, 'Architectuur van

stations', *De Architect* (2004), p 34.
'Galleria Fashion Store, Seoul, Korea', *Bob* (2004), p 74.

2005
Tracy Metz, 'UN Studio and the amazing technicolor dreamcoat', *i-D Magazine* (December 2004/ January 2005), p 29.
Aaron Betsky, 'With flying colour', *Azure* (January 2005), p 25.
Paul Makovsky, 'The rainbow connection', *Metropolis* (January 2005), p 62.
Harm Tillman, 'UN Studio, kantoorgebouw La Defense, Almere', *De Architect* (February 2005), p 46.
Jeroen Junte, 'Architect ontwerpt bank voor conflictbemiddeling', *De Volkskrant* (February 7, 2005), p 17.
'UN Studio Grandi Magazzini Galleria', *The Plan* (February 2005), p 105.
Ajay Najak, 'The multi-dimensional contemporary', *Indian Architect* (February 2005), p 72.
Kristin Feireiss, 'Form follows fun: Central Station Arnhem' (February 2005), p 237.
Christiane Gabler, 'Kunst und Hamam', *Bauwelt* (March 2005).
John Stones, 'Space race', *Design Week* (March 2005), p 16.
Catherine Croft, 'Möbiushuis', *Concrete Architecture* (March 2005), p 38.
Axel Simon, 'Sinnesrausch im Engadin', *Baumeister* (April 2005), pp 32–38.
Catherine Slessor, 'UN Studio, house upstate New York', *Architectural Review* (April 2005), p 88.
Ursula Baus, 'Speeding up', *A10* (April 2005), p 10.
Tachy Mora, 'UN Studio', *NEO2* (May 2005), p 90.
Shonguis Moreno, 'The hills are alive', *Frame* (May 2005), p 77.
Dietmar Klein, 'Das neue Mercedes-Benz Museum in Stuttgart', *Beton und Stahlbetonbau* (May 2005), pp 325.
Harm Tilman, 'Maatschappelijke betekenis van vormgeving verdiept', *De Architect* (May 2005), p 10.
Ekow Eshun, 'Art & Seoul', *Wallpaper* (June 2005), p 162.
Paul Schilpenoord, 'Barbapapa architectuur', *Bright* (June 2005), p 38.
Catherine Slessor, 'Stuttgart spiral', *Architectural Review* (June 2005), p 74.
J. Christoph Bürkle, 'Interventionen im castell', *Archithese* (June 2005), p 34.
'Work at place', *Pol Oxygen* (June 2005), p 123.
'UN Studio gestaltet Farbestreifen für die neue Ait', *AIT* (July 2005).
'War Silence and other stories', *Frame* (July 2005), p 71.
'Ampliamento dell Hotel Castell a Zuoz', *L'Industria della costruzioni* (August 2005), p 60.
'Hamam del Hotel Castell', *Diseño Interior* (September 2005), p 104.
'Mercedes Benz Museum', *ATD* (September 2005), p 96.
Yves Calmejane, 'Hotel Castell, extension, Zuoz', *L'Architecture d'aujourd'hui* (October 2005), pp 20–28.

Project credits

Rijksmuseum Twenthe, Enschede 1992–1996
Client: Rijksgebouwendienst, The Hague
Programme: museum addition and renovation
Gross floor surface: existing 2,600m² and addition 900 m²
Volume: 2,700 m³

Design
UN Studio: Ben van Berkel with Harrie Pappot, Joost Hovenier, Hugo Beschoor Plug, Pieter Koster, Peter Meier, Martin Visscher, Jan van der Erven, Serge Darding, Arjan van Ruyven

Museum Het Valkhof, Nijmegen 1995–1998
Client: Stichting Museum Het Valkhof, Nijmegen
Programme: museum for contemporary art and archaeology
Gross floor surface: 6,100 m²
Volume: 40,000 m³

Design
UN Studio: Ben van Berkel with Henri Snel, Remco Bruggink and Rob Hootsmans, Hugo Beschoor Plug, Walther Kloet, Marc Dijkman, Jacco van Wengerden, Luc Veeger, Florian Fischer, Carsten Kiselowsky

Landscape architect
Bureau B&B, Stedenbouw en landschapsarchitectuur, Amsterdam

Advisors
Exhibition design: Studio Dumbar, Rotterdam in collaboration with WAACs, Rotterdam
Graphic design: Total Design, Amsterdam
Technical management: ABT, Velp
Technical consultants: Ketel Raadgevende Ingenieurs, Arnhem
Project management: Berns Projekt Management, Nijmegen

NMR Laboratory, Utrecht 1997–2001
Client: University of Utrecht
Programme: laboratory for NMR Spectroscopy
Gross floor surface: 2,050 m²

Volume: 10,000 m³
Site: 21,000 m²

Design
UN Studio: Ben van Berkel with Harm Wassink, Ludo Grooteman, Walter Kloet, Mark Westerhuis, Jacco van Wengerden, Aad Krom, Paul Vriend, Marion Regitko, Jeroen Kreijnen, Henri Snel, Laura Negrini, Remco Bruggink, Marc Prins

Advisors
Engineering: ABT, Amersfoort
Installations: BAM Techniques, Rotterdam

Architecture Faculty, Venice 1998
Client: Istituto Universitario di Architettura di Venezia (IUAV)
Programme: faculty building for the Architecture University, Venice
Gross floor surface: 3,100 m²

Design
UN Studio: Ben van Berkel with Remco Bruggink, Laura Negrini, Hans Sterck, Caroline Bos, Sonja Cabalt, Hanneke Damste, Ludo Grooteman, Alexander Jung, Ksk Tamura, Paul Vriend, Yury Werner, Walther Kloet, Henri Snel, Jacco van Wengerden

Advisors
Engineering: Arup, London

ViILA NM, Upstate New York 2000–2005
Client: Mr and Ms Tsimmer-Lee
Programme: Single-family house
Gross floor surface: 250 m²
Volume: 700 m³
Site: 7,423 m²

Design
UN Studio: Ben van Berkel with Olaf Gipser and Andrew Benn, Colette Parras, Jacco van Wengerden, Maria Eugenia Diaz, Jan Debelius, Martin Kuitert, Pablo Rica, Olga Vazquez-Ruano

Advisors
Project Consultant: Roemer Pierik, Rotterdam, The Netherlands

Construction
Henry & Quick Construction, Inc. Brooklyn, NY

Wadsworth Atheneum, Hartford 2000
Client: Wadsworth Atheneum Museum of Art
Programme: museum addition and renovation
Gross floor surface: 25,000 m²

Design
UN Studio: Ben van Berkel, Caroline Bos, Tobias Wallisser with Arjan Dingsté, Olga Vazquez-Ruano and Colette Parras, Mike Green, Jorge Pereira, Cristina Bollis, Nuno Almeida, Katrin Kloetzer, Kieran O'Brien, Remco Bruggink, Mica Cimola, Igor Kebel, Sophie Valla, Cynthia Morales

Executive architect
Fox & Fowle, New York

Advisors
Structure: Arup, London with DesImone, New York
Energy concept: Transsolar, Stuttgart
Installations: AltieriSieborWeber, Connecticut
Lighting: Richard Renfro, New York

Hotel Castell, Zuoz 2000–2004
Client: Castell Zuoz AG, Herrliberg
Programme: apartment building, hotel renovation and hammam
Gross floor surface: 5,500 m²
Apartment building: 3,000 m²
Parking building: 1,100m²
Hotel kitchen: 400 m²
Hammam: 260 m²
Hotel rooms: 700m²
Volume: 15,000 m³
Site: 2,200 m²

Design
UN Studio: Ben van Berkel with Olaf Gipser and Pablo Rica, Sebastian Schaeffer, Andrew Benn, Dag Thies, Eric den Eerzamen, Hon Hoos, Claudia Dorner, Martin Kuitert , Marco Hemmerling, Sophie Valla, Tina Bayerl, Peter Irmscher

Executive architect
Walter Dietsche AG, Chur

Advisors
Structural engineering: Edy Toscano AG, Pontresina
MEP engineering: Juerg Bulach AG, St Moritz; Kaelin AG, St Moritz; Giston AG, Samedan
Building physics: Kuster + Partner AG, Chur

Mahler 4 Tower, Amsterdam 2003–2006
Client: Mahler 4 VOF – Fortis Vastgoed, G&S Vastgoed, ING Vastgoed
Programme: commercial spaces and offices
Gross floor surface: 27,000 m²
Volume: 105,000 m³

Design
UN Studio: Ben van Berkel with Ger Gijzen, Gerard Loozekoot and Olaf Gipser, Albert Gnodde, Alicia Velazquez, Andrew Benn, Arjan van der Bliek, Barry Munster, Christian Veddeler, Evert Klinkenberg, Fabian Hernandez, Marcus Berger, Pablo Rica, Satoshi Matsuoka, Thomas Bryans, Tina Bayerl

Advisors
Conceptual engineering: Arup, Amsterdam
Technical engineering: Van Rossum, Amsterdam
Climate concept: Transsolar, Stuttgart
Installations: Techniplan, Rotterdam

Sum, Gispen 2004
Client: Gispen, Cullemborg

Design
UN Studio: Ben van Berkel and Caroline Bos with Khoi Tran, Thomas de Vries

Sofa Circle, Knoll 2005
Client design phase: Zetel, Amsterdam
Client execution phase: Walter Knoll, Herrenberg

Design
UN Studio: Ben van Berkel, Caroline Bos with Khoi Tran, Thomas de Vries and Job Mouwen, Marco Hemmerling

Schirn Kunsthalle, Frankfurt 2005
Client: Schirn Kunsthalle, Frankfurt
Programme: exhibition design, 'Summer of Love'
Gross floor surface: 800 m²

Design
UN Studio: Ben van Berkel and Caroline Bos with Job Mouwen, Christian Veddeler and Cristina Bolis, Holger Hoffmann, Kristoph Nowak, Kristin Sandner

Advisors
Production: p & p, Fürth/Odenwald

Construction
H + M Bühnenservice GmbH/Nüssli–Deutschland GmbH, Giessen

Erasmus Bridge, Rotterdam, 1990–1996
Client: Municipality of Rotterdam
Programme: single pylon bridge with integrated parking garage and office building
Span: 284 m
Pylon height: 140 m

Design
UN Studio: Ben van Berkel with Freek Loos, Hans Cromjongh and Ger Gijzen, Willemijn Lofvers, Sibo de Man, Gerard Nijenhuis, Manon Patinama, John Rebel, Ernst van Rijn, Hugo Schuurman, Caspar Smeets, Paul Toornend, Jan Willem Walraad, Dick Wetzels, Karel Vollers

Advisors
Engineering: Ingenieursbureau Gemeentewerken Rotterdam, Rotterdam
Contractor steel works: Grootint, Dordrecht
Contractor concrete works: MBG/CFE, Brussel/Antwerpen

Villa Wilbrink, Amersfoort 1992–1994
Client: Mr and Mrs Wilbrink-van den Berg
Programme: single-family house
Gross floor surface: 190 m²
Volume. 550 m³
Site: 179 m²

Design
UN Studio: Ben van Berkel with Aad Krom and Jan van der Erven, Branimir Medic

Advisors
Engineering: Bureau Bouwpartners, Hilversum

Möbius House, Het Gooi 1993–1998
Client: Anonymous
Programme: single-family house
Gross floor surface: 520 m²
Volume: 2,250 m³
Site: 20,000 m²

Design
UN Studio: Ben van Berkel with Aad Krom, Jen Alkema and Matthias Blass, Remco Bruggink, Marc Dijkman, Casper le Fevre, Rob Hootsmans, Tycho Soffree, Giovanni Tedesco, Harm Wassink

Landscape architect
West 8, Rotterdam

Advisors
Structural engineering: ABT, Velp

Living Tomorrow, Amsterdam 2000–2003
Client: Living Tomorrow, Vilvoorde
Programme: showroom pavilion with House of the Future and Office of the Future
Gross floor surface: 3,500 m²
Volume: 32,000 m³

Design
UN Studio: Ben van Berkel with Igor Kebel, Aad Krom, Martin Kuitert, Markus Berger
Ron Roos, Andreas Bogenschütz

Executive architect
Living Tomorrow, Vilvoorde

Tea & Coffee Towers, Alessi 2001
Client: Alessi, Crusinallo d'Omgena
Programme: tea and coffee pot, sugar jug and milk bowl on tray

Design
UN Studio: Ben van Berkel with Marco Hemmerling, Tiago S Nunes and Aad Krom, Nuno Almeida, Igor Kebel, Cynthia Markhoff

Mercedes–Benz Museum, Stuttgart 2001–2006
Client: DaimlerChrysler Immobilien, Berlin
User: Mercedes–Benz Museums GmbH
Project management: Drees & Sommer, Stuttgart
Gross floor surface: 35,000 m²
Volume: 270,000 m³
Site: 28,5500 m²

Design
UN Studio: Ben van Berkel, Tobias Wallisser, Caroline Bos with Marco Hemmerling, Hannes Pfau
Team: Wouter de Jonge, Arjan Dingsté, Götz Feldmann, Björn Rimner, Sebastian Schaeffer, Andreas Bogenschütz, Uli Horner, Ivonne Schickler, Dennis Ruarus, Erwin Horstmanshof, Derrick Diporedjo, Nanang Santoso, Robert Brixner, Alexander Jung, Matthew Johnston, Rombout Loman, Arjan van der Bliek, Fabian Evers, Nuno Almeida, Ger Gijzen, Tjago Nunes, Boudewijn Rosman, Ergian Alberg, Gregor Kahlau, Mike Herud, Thomas Klein, Simon Streit, Taehoon Oh, Jenny Weiss, Philipp Dury, Carin Lamm, Anna Carlquist, Jan Debelius, Daniel Kalani, Evert Klinkenberg

Realization
UN Studio und Wenzel + Wenzel, Karlsruhe
Matias Wenzel with Markus Schwarz, Nicola Kühnle, Ina Karbon, Clemens Schulte–Mattler, Peter Holzer, Ingolf Gössel, Walter Ulrich, Christoph Krinn, Christoph Friedrich, Stefan Linder, Thomas Koch, Michael Fischinger, Florian Erhard, Christina

Brecher, Stefanie Hertweck, Volker Hilpert, Ulrike Kolb, Bendix Pallesen-Mustaky, Marc Schwesinger

Exhibition concept and design
HG Merz, Stuttgart

Interior restaurant and shop
UN Studio and Concrete Architectural Associates, Amsterdam

Special elements
Inside outside: Petra Blaisse, Amsterdam

Advisors
Structure: Werner Sobek Ingenieure mit Boll&Partner, Stuttgart
Climate engineering: Transsolar Energietechnik, Stuttgart
Costing: Nanna Fütterer, Stuttgart/Berlin
Infrastructure: David Johnston, Arup, London
Geometry: Arnold Walz, Stuttgart

Battersea Weave Office Building, London 2004–2010
Client: Parkview International Ltd, London and Arup AGU, London
Programme: building with showcase spaces and office spaces
Gross floor surface: 51,000 m²

Design
UN Studio: Ben van Berkel, Caroline Bos with Gerard Loozekoot, Astrid Piber and Ger Gijzen, Holger Hoffmann, Colette Parras, Albert Gnodde, Christian Veddeler, Hape Nuenning, Markus Berger, Markus Hudert, Matthew Johnston, Michaela Tomaselli, Elke Uitz, Jeroen Tacx, Louis Gadd, Eric Coppoolse, Jan Schellhoff, Katrin Härtel, Maria Eugenia Diaz, Marie Morin

Advisors
Master plan: Arup AGU
Engineering: Arup, London
Building services: Arup, London
Landscape: West 8, Rotterdam
Lighting: ArupLighting

Electrical Substation, Amersfoort 1989–1994
Client: Regionale Energie Maatschappij Utrecht (REMU)

Programme: 50/10 kV substation
Gross floor surface: 1,520 m²
Volume: 4,500 m³

Design

UN Studio: Ben van Berkel with
Harrie Pappot and Pieter Koster,
Hugo Beschoor Plug, Jaap Punt, Rik
van Dolderen

Advisors

Engineering: Hollandsche Beton
Maatschappij, Rijswijk

Karbouw, Amersfoort
1990–1992

Client: Schipper Bosch
Projectontwikkeling, Amersfoort
Programme: offices
Gross floor surface: 1,155 m²

Design

UN Studio: Ben van Berkel with
Aad Krom Kasper Aussems, Frank
Verhoeven, Stephan de Bever

Advisors

Engineering: Buro Bouwpartners,
Hilversum

Church Hall, Hilversum
1995–2000

Client: Regenboog kerk, Hilversum
Programme: church and social
meeting centre
Gross floor surface: 2,250 m²
Volume: 11,250 m³

Design

UN Studio: Ben van Berkel with
Harm Wassink and Hans Sterck,
Hjalmar Fredriksson, Jacco van
Wengerden

Electrical Substation,
Innsbruck 1996–2000

Client: Innsbrucker
Kommunalbetriebe AG
Programme: 50/10 kV Substation
Gross floor surface: 2,518 m²
Volume: 9,000 m³
Site: 2,510 m²

Design

UN Studio: Ben van Berkel with
Hannes Pfau, Jacco van Wengerden
and Gianni Cito, Ludo Grooteman,
Laura Negrini, Casper le Fèvre, Eli
Aschkenasy, Hjalmar Frederikson,
Hans Sterck, Boudewijn Rosman,
Yuri Werner

Advisors

Engineering: Peter Ladurner–
Rennau, Innsbruck
Building physics: Peter Fiby,
Innsbruck

Prince Claus Bridge, Utrecht
1998–2003

Client: Municipality of Utrecht
Programme: single pylon bridge
Pylon height: 91.4 m

Design

UN Studio: Ben van Berkel with
Freek Loos, Ger Gijzen and Armin
Hess, Suzanne Boyer, Jeroen,
Jacques van Wijk, Ludo Grooteman,
Henk Bultstra, Tobias Wallisser, Ron
Roos

Advisors

Management: DHV, Amersfoort
Engineering concrete foundations:
DHV, Amersfoort
Engineering pylon and deck:
Halcrow UK, London and Swindon

Music Theatre, Graz
1998–2007

Client: Immobilienmanagementgesel
lschaft des Bundes MBH
Landesdirektion Steiermark
Programme: university faculty
building
Gross floor surface: 3,503 m²
Volume: 27,000 m³
Site: 2,745 m²

Design

Ben van Berkel in collaboration with
Cecil Balmond (Arup, London)

Design phase

UN Studio: Ben van Berkel with
Hannes Pfau, Markus Berger and
Peter Trummer, Susanne Boyer, Mike
Green, Monica Pacheco, Wouter
de Jonge, Ger Gijzen, Maarten van
Tuijl, Matthew Johnston, Remco
Bruggink, Pedro Campos Costa,
Ludo Grooteman, Ksk Tamura,
Tobias Wallisser, Karel Deckers, Do
Janne Vermeulen

Advisors

Engineering design development:
Arup, London
Engineering execution: Arge
– Zenker & Handel – Grabner &
Szyszkowitz
Acoustics and building physics:
Gerhard Tomberger, Graz

Light and sound: Reiner Traub, Graz
Electrical engineering: Hermann
Klauss, Graz
Service engineering: TB Pickl &
Partner, Graz
Costing: Housinc Bauconsult, Wien

Theatre, Lelystad
2002–2006

Client: Municipality of Lelystad
Programme: theatre with two
halls and a multifunctional space,
restaurant and bar
Gross floor surface: 7,000 m²
Volume: 30,000 m³
Site: 2,925 m²

Design

UN Studio: Ben van Berkel with
Gerard Loozekoot, Jacques van Wijk
and Job Mouwen, Holger Hoffmann,
Khoi Tran, Christian Veddeler,
Christian Bergmann, Sabine
Habicht, Ramon Hernandez, Ron
Roos, Rene Wysk, Claudia Dorner,
Markus Berger, Markus Jacobi, Ken
Okonkwo, Jorgen Grahl–Madsen

Executive architect

B+M, Den Haag

Advisors

Theatre technique: Prinssen en Bus
Raadgevende Ingenieurs, Uden
Engineering: Pieters Bouwtechniek,
Almere
Acoustics/fire strategy: DGMR,
Arnhem

Arnhem Central, Arnhem
1996–2008

Client: Municipality of Arnhem
Programme: master plan station
area with infrastructure including
two tunnels; transfer hall including
parking, bus terminal, retail and
offices
Gross floor surface:
Transfer hall: 6,000 m²
Underground parking: 44,000 m²
Bus terminal: 7,500 m²
Office towers 22,000 m²
Capacity: 110,000 transfers per day

Design

UN Studio in collaboration with Cecil
Balmond (Arup)
UN Studio: Ben van Berkel with
Tobias Wallisser and Sibo de Man
Master plan study: Freek Loos,
Peter Trummer, Henk Bultstra, Cees
Gajentaan, John Rebel, Andreas

Krause
Master plan: Sibo de Man, Tobias
Wallisser, Henk Bultstra, Edgar
Bosman, Astrid Piber, Oliver
Bormann, Yuko Tokunaga, Ulrike
Bahr, Ivan Hernandez
Transfer Hall: Tobias Wallisser, Sibo
de Man, Nuno Almeida, Matthew
Johnston, Antony Calcott, Ton van
den Berg, Norbert Palz
Bus deck: Sibo de Man, Tobias
Wallisser, Jacco van Wengerden,
Jacques van Wijk, Nuno Almeida,
Paul Vriend, Phillip Koelher, Marco
Hemmerling
Parking: Sibo de Man, Tobias
Wallisser, Jacques van Wijk, Ton van
den Berg, Nuno Almeida, , Jacco
van Wengerden, Mark Westerhuis,
Matthew Johnston, Marc Herschel,
Paul Vriend, Eli Aschkenasy, Remko
van Heumen
Tunnel: Freek Loos, Ger Gijzen,
Jacques van Wijk, John Rebel

Advisors

Engineering: Arup, Amsterdam
Structure: Van der Werf & Lankhort,
Arnhem

Ponte Parodi, Genoa
2000–2009

Client: Porto Antico di Genova Spa
and ALTAREA Italia Progetti S.r.l.
Programme: harbour redevelopment
with mixed-use public building
including cruise terminal, cultural
and commercial programme
Gross floor surface: 76,000m²
Volume: 160,000 m³
Site: 36,000 m²

Design

UN Studio: Ben van Berkel, Caroline
Bos with Astrid Piber, Nuno Almeida
and Cristina Bolis, Paolo Bassetto,
Alice Gramigna, Michaela Tomaselli,
Peter Trummer, Tobias Wallisser,
Olga Vazquez–Ruano, Ergian
Alberg, Stephan Miller, George
Young, Jorge Pereira, Mónica
Pacheco, Tanja Koch, Ton van den
Berg

Advisors

Competition:
Infrastructure and structure: Arup,
London; Arup Project management,
London
Offshore Construction: Grootint bv,
Zwijndrecht
Project:
Project financing: Banca OPI, Rome;

Proger, Rome
Structure: d'Appolonia, Genoa
Building services: Manens, Verona

Wien Mitte Urban Competition, Vienna 2004

Client: City of Vienna
Programme: urban redevelopment with train station and subway node
Gross floor surface: 126,609 m²
Volume: 602,895 m³
Site: 25,000 m²

Design

UN Studio: Ben van Berkel, Caroline Bos, Tobias Wallisser with Markus Hudert, Alicia Velazquez and Michaela Tomaselli, Christina Bolis, Cornelia Faisst, Alice Gramigna, Olaf Gipser, Hannes Pfau, Astrid Piber

Advisors

Infrastructure: David Johnston, Arup, London
Structural engineering: Werner Sobek Ingenieure, Stuttgart
Feasibility: Pablo Vaggione, Madrid

Shopping Centre Renovation, Emmen 1994–1996

Client: Multi Vastgoed, Gouda
Programme: shopping centre with passage and apartments
Gross floor surface: 10,294 m²

Design

UN Studio: Ben van Berkel with René Bouman, Harrie Pappot and Monica Bauer, Henk Smallenburg, Frank van Hierk, Edwin van Namen, Ronald van Nieuwkerk, Sanderijn Amsberg, Hans Kuypers, Hanna Euro, Tycho Soffree, Marc Dijkman, Jan van Erven Dorens, Fenja Riks

Advisors

Engineering: Maat, Rotterdam

Bridge and Bridge Master's House, Purmerend 1995–1998

Client: Municipality of Purmerend
Programme: bascule bridge and bridge master's house
Gross floor surface: 90 m²
Volume: 300 m³

Design

UN Studio: Ben van Berkel with Freek Loos, Ger Gijzen and Sibo

de Man, John Rebel, Stefan Böwer, Stefan Lungmuss

Advisors

Management: IBA, Amsterdam
Engineering: IBA, Amsterdam

IFCCA Competition, New York 1997

Client: Canadian Centre for Architecture, Montreal
Programme: urban plan between 42nd and 23rd Streets, New York

Design

UN Studio: Ben van Berkel, Caroline Bos with Tobias Wallisser, Olaf Gipser and Hans Sterck, Ludo Grooteman, Remco Bruggink, Andreas Bogenschütz, Jasper Jaegers, Philip Koehler, Stephanie Kulmann, Bas Kwaaitaal, Alexander Jung

Advisors

Infrastructure: David Johnston, Arup, London
Construction: Cecil Balmond, Arup, London
Programming: Office 21 Fraunhofer IAO, Stuttgart

Offices La Defense, Almere 1999–2004

Client: Eurocommerce, Deventer
Programme: offices
Gross floor surface: 23,000 m² and 15,000 m² parking
Volume: 82,618 m³
Site: 8,833 m²

Design

UN Studio: Ben van Berkel with Marco Hemmerling, Martin Kuitert and Henri Snel, Gianni Cito, Marco van Helden, Yuri Werner, Tanja Koch, Katrin Meyer, Stella Vesselinova, Igor Kebel, Olaf Gisper, Marc Prins, Aad Krom

Advisors

Engineering: JVZ Raadgevend Ingenieursburo, Deventer
Climate concept: Transsolar, Stuttgart
Façade cladding: 3M, Zoetermeer

Galleria Department Store, Seoul 2003–2004

Client: Hanwha Stores Co., Ltd
Programme: design of façade renovation, refurbishment of interior and furniture design for Galleria department store
Gross floor surface: 21,986 m²
Façade area: 3,279 m²
Volume: 81,250 m³
Site: 9,640 m²

Design

UN Studio: Ben van Berkel, Caroline Bos with Astrid Piber, Ger Gijzen and Cristina Bolis, Markus Hudert, Colette Parras, Arjan van der Bliek, Christian Veddeler, Albert Gnodde, Richard Crofts, Barry Munster, Mafalda Botelho, Elke Uitz, Harm Wassink

Advisors

Structural design: Arup, Amsterdam
Lighting design: ArupLighting, Amsterdam
Way-finding design: Bureau Mijksenaar, Amsterdam

Executive Architects

Façade design: RAC-Rah Architecture Consulting, Seoul
Interior design: Kesson International, Seoul
Lighting design: Eon/St.D, Seoul

Port, Las Palmas 2005

Client: Private-Public Partnership: Cabildo Insular de Gran Canaria, Ayuntamiento de Las Palmas de Gran Canaria
Autoridad Portuaria de Las Palmas
Programme: master plan harbour and redevelopment of the port
Gross floor surface: 500,000 m²

Design

UN Studio: Ben van Berkel, Caroline Bos with Astrid Piber, Alicia Velazquez, Holger Hoffmann, Day Thies, Michaela Tomaselli, Ramon Hernandez, Ali Eray, Joakim Kaminsky, Colette Parras, Elke Uitz, Matthew Johnston, Tobias Wallisser

Local architect

L-P-A, Laboratorio de planeamiento y arquitectura, Las Palmas
Juan Palop, Bonifacio Jiménez, Alejandro Pérez Carmona

Advisors

Engineering: Arup, Madrid
Programme and Feasibility:

Designconvergence, J. M. Iribas
Pablo Vaggione, Jose Miguel Iribas

Photo credits

All photos in this publication are by Christian Richters, except for those on the following pages:

81–83 Michael Moran; 122–125 Gispen; 128–131 Knoll; 143 H. J. Commerell; 146 F. van Hanswijk; 153, 220, 223–224, 225a J. Derwig; 154–155 Ingmar Swalue, with Stef Bakker; 167, 171 Michael van Oosten; 178–181 Carlo Lavatori; 189 Daimler Chrysler; 196–198, 202–203, 285b, 293–294, 302–303, 341–342, 356, 367 UN Studio; 206–209 Brigida Gonzales; 221, 225 H. Binet; 250–252, 343 L. Kramer; 260 RoVorm; 322 IBA; 346–347 Viviane Sassen, with Stef Bakker; 350–351 Aerophoto-Schiphol; 371–379 Ben van Berkel; 390–391 Wolfgang Staiger

All computer generated images in this publication are by UN Studio, except for those on the following pages: 24–25 David Lee; 388–389 United Architects

Every effort has been made to contact all copyright holders. If proper acknowledgment has not been made, we ask copyright holders to contact UN Studio.

Acknowledgments

Our primary thanks go to the following people from UN Studio, who have made valuable contributions to this book: Leon Bloemendaal, who transformed his life for a year and became a fully-fledged member of the team while designing this project; Machteld Kors, who coordinated every aspect of production and, together with Katrien Otten, found long-lost images in our messy archives, kept an eagle eye on the deadlines, and generally kept everyone in order; Holger Hoffmann, who produced the diagrams of the design models on pages 22 and 23; and Colette Parras, who enhanced the project texts.

We are grateful to everyone who has, at any time, and in whatever capacity, worked with UN Studio and Van Berkel & Bos, and has thus contributed to the work featured here. Special thanks to Harm Wassink, Gerard Loozekoot and Tobias Wallisser, who, with Astrid Piber, shared their views on the application of design models in our projects. We furthermore thank the people and institutions who let us experiment with the initial, and somewhat fuzzy, notion of the design model, and thus helped shape the project's concept. Among them are Ralph Lerner, Mario Gandalsonas, Stan Allen, Beatriz Colomina, Christine Boyer, Brendan Hookway, and the students we encountered and worked with over a period of four years at the Princeton University School of Architecture, as well as Alejandro Zaera Polo, Vedran Mimica, and Gabu Heindl from the Berlage Institute, and its fun-loving, creative students. From the Städelschule, we thank Daniel Birnbaum and the many professors from the art department who have shown an interest in the architecture programme, including Isabelle Graw, Wolfgang Tillmans and Tobias Rehberger. We are particularly grateful to Johan Bettum, assistant professor at the architecture department, and the capable and dedicated students of the Städelschule.

Our ultimate thanks go to Lucas Dietrich of Thames & Hudson, the book's editor, for providing guidance and inspiration throughout its gestation.

First published in the United States of America in 2006 by Rizzoli International Publications, Inc.
300 Park Avenue South
New York, NY 10010
www.rizzoliusa.com

Originally published in the United Kingdom in 2006 by Thames & Hudson Ltd
181A High Holborn
London WC1V 7QX

© 2006 UN Studio

ISBN-10: 0-8478-2878-6
ISBN-13: 978-0-8478-2878-4

Library of Congress Control Number 2005938883

2006 2007 2008 2009 / 10 9 8 7 6 5 4 3 2 1

Designed by Bloemendaal & Dekkers, Amsterdam
Printed in China